Values, Trends and Alternatives in Swiss Society

Armin Gretler
Pierre-Emeric Mandl

The Praeger Special Studies program—utilizing the most modern and efficient book production techniques and a selective worldwide distribution network—makes available to the academic, government, and business communities significant, timely research in U.S. and international economic, social, and political development.

Values, Trends and Alternatives in Swiss Society

A Prospective Analysis

PRAEGER SPECIAL STUDIES IN INTERNATIONAL ECONOMICS AND DEVELOPMENT

Praeger Publishers   New York   Washington   London

PRAEGER PUBLISHERS
111 Fourth Avenue, New York, N.Y. 10003, U.S.A.
5, Cromwell Place, London S.W.7, England

Published in the United States of America in 1973
by Praeger Publishers, Inc.

Library of Congress Catalog Card Number: 73-170376

Printed in the United States of America

CONTENTS

Page

LIST OF TABLES   ix

Chapter

1 INTRODUCTION   3

   Objectives   3
   Method   5
   Some Methodological Problems   7

2 THE PARTIES' IDEALS AND CONCEPT OF
   HUMANITY   10

   Ideals   10
   Concept of Humanity   12

3 DEMOGRAPHY   15

   The Swiss Population and Its Age Structure   15
   The Proportion of Pensioners and Dependents   20
   Alternative Population Forecasts   22
   A Brief Explanation of Methods and
       Assumptions   22
       Stochastic Model   22
       Biometric Model   22
       Static Model   24
       Semidynamic Model   24
       Dynamic Model   24
   Average Life Expectancy   25
   Rate and Age of Marriage   26

4 THE LABOR FORCE   27

   Changes in the Structure of the Labor Force,
       1941-60   27
       Structural Changes According to Occupation   35
   Foreign Manpower   38
   The Effects of Rationalization and Automation on
       the Structure of the Labor Force   43

Chapter   Page

    Prospects and Alternatives   45
       Alternatives in Production Potential   45
       Future Development of Labor Potential   46
    The Parties' Attitudes toward the Employer-
      Employee Relationship and the Different
      Forms of Codetermination   49
    Educational Demands Arising out of the
      Development of Society   50
       The Parties' Values and Aims   50
       Educational Demands Resulting from
        Developments in Social Subsectors   53

5   THE CONDITIONS OF WOMEN   57

    The Parties' Values and Aims   57
    The Legal Position of Women   59
    Education of Girls and Women   59
      Differences in the Education of Boys and
       Girls   60
      The Educational Level of Three Generations
       of Men and Women   61
    The Working Woman   63
      Gainful Employment of Mothers   70
      The Shift in Women's Employment   75
      Women's Employment, by Individual
       Occupation   76
      Part-Time Employment of Women   77
      Reintegration of Women in Occupational
       Activity   80
      Differences in Remuneration between Women
       and Men   82
    A Forecast of Trends   83

6   THE FAMILY   86

    The Parties' Values and Aims   86
    The Peasant-Artisan Family   88
    The Functions of the Family   90
    Forecasts on the Functions of Marriage and
      Family   99
      Divorce   99
      Legal and Sociological Aspects of Divorce   101
      The Sexual Revolution   105
    Summary   106

Chapter		Page
7	WORKING TIME, WORK-FREE TIME, AND LEISURE TIME	107
	Working Time	107
	The Duration of Gainful Activity	108
	The Time of Retirement	108
	Reduction of Hours of Work	109
	The Parties' Values and Aims	115
	Free Time	117
	The Distinction between Free Time and Leisure	118
	Some Further Intersectoral Relations	121
8	STANDARD OF LIVING	123
	Per Capita Income and Distribution of Working Population	124
	Ownership of Various Appliances and Machines	126
	Household Accounts	136
	Housing Conditions	137
	Holidays Away From Home	146
	Taxation in the Cantons	147
	Cantonal Differences in Living Standards	150
	Criticism of the Priority Given to Economic Growth	150
9	PROPERTY	153
	The Parties' Values and Aims	153
	Ownership of Agricultural Land	156
	Ownership of Houses and Apartments	156
	Ownership of Nonagricultural Means of Production and Control of Industrial Enterprises	166
	Alternatives to the Present Structure of Industrial Control	172
10	URBANIZATION	177
	Demographic Growth of Swiss Cities	177
	Factors Causing or Affecting Urbanization	184
	The Parties' Positions on the Interplay of Concentration and Depopulation	188
	Alternative Possibilities for Development	190
	Assistance for Mountain Farmers	192

Chapter   Page

        Promotion of Local Education Facilities
           in Depopulated Areas   192
        Establishment of Enterprises in De-
           populated Areas   193
        Settlement of Pensioners in Climatically
           Suitable Depopulated Areas   193
        The Parties' Statements on National City and
           Country Planning   194
        The Referendum of July 2, 1967, on the Socialist
           Initiative against Land Speculation   196

11   TYPES OF HOUSING AND SOCIAL RELATIONS   199

        The Irreversible Trend Toward Urbanization   199
        The Problems of Cities   200
        The Effect of the Urban Way of Life on Rural
           Areas   201
        The Neighborhood Community: A Myth of the
           Urbanists?   201
        Other Planning Alternatives   203
        Some Fundamental Concepts   204

12   CANTONAL PARTY SYSTEMS, POLITICAL PAR-
     TICIPATION, AND STRENGTH OF PARTIES   207

        The Parties' Statements on the Question of
           Federalism   212

13   EXTERNAL INFLUENCES ON THE DEVELOPMENT
     OF SWITZERLAND   214

        The Parties' Views on Worldwide Interdependence,
           the UN, and the EEC   218

NOTES   222

ABOUT THE AUTHORS   241

LIST OF TABLES

Table   Page

1   Distribution of Seats in National Council, 1967-71
Legislative Period and after 1971 Elections   8

2   Population, by Age, 1860-2040   16

3   Population, by Age, 1860-2040   17

4   Population and Population Surplus Trends until
1961 and Semidynamic Assumptions from 1962   18

5   Pensioner and Dependency Proportions, 1860-2040   21

6   Hypotheses of Possible Population Trends   23

7   Proportion of Self-Employed Persons in Labor
Force, 1941-60   28

8   Proportions of Various Categories of Salaried
Employees in Labor Force, 1941-60   31

9   Proportion of Various Categories of Production
Workers in Labor Force, 1941-60   33

10   Proportion of Apprentices in Labor Force,
1941-60   34

11   Proportion of Foreigners in Population, 1888-1967   39

12   Total Labor Force and Proportion Foreign, 1930-60   40

13   Distribution of Swiss and Foreigners, by Occupation,
1960, and Changes as Compared with 1930   41

14   Increases of Swiss and Foreigners in Labor Force,
by Occupation, 1930-60   42

15   Quantitative Education Survey, by Qualification Grades,
for the Year 2000   48

16   Differences in Primary School Curricula for Boys
and Girls   60

Table   Page

17   Persons No Longer Attending School, by Three
      Selected Age Groups, Sex, and Last School
      Attended, 1960   64

18   Rates of Female Employment and Proportion of
      Women in Labor Force, 1888-1960   66

19   Gainfully Employed Women, by Age Group, 1930,
      1950, and 1960   67

20   Female Employment Rates, by Marital Status,
      1930-60   68

21   Number of Women Employed and Employment
      Rates by Degree of Qualification, 1960   69

22   Proportion of Women in Labor Force of Cities
      over 30,000, 1960   70

23   Distribution of Working Women among Three
      Economic Sectors, 1900-60   75

24   Leading Female Occupations, 1960   76

25   Trends in Selected Female Occupations, 1941-60   78

26   Principal Female Occupation, Part-Time Work,
      and Household Duties, 1960   80

27   Part-Time Female Workers, by Occupational
      Group, 1960   81

28   Average Hourly Earnings of Industrial Employees,
      1939-70   83

29   Number of Family Collaborators in Proportion to
      Total Active Population, 1941-60   90

30   Number of Households and Average Number of
      Persons per Household, 1850-1970   92

31   Number of Households and Average Number of Per-
      sons per Household, by Canton, 1970   93

Table		Page
32	Private Households in Cantons and Cities, by Number of Members, 1960	94
33	Persons in Private Households, by Status, 1960	95
34	Marriages and Divorces, 1906-69	100
35	Marriages and Divorces in Selected Cities, 1965	101
36	Divorces, by Years of Marriage, 1969	104
37	Average Number of Weekly Working Hours in Industry, 1850-1965	110
38	Changes in Productivity in Three Economic Sectors, United States, 1870-1937	112
39	Alternative Possibilities for Yearly Working Hours and Distribution per Week and Day, Assuming Continued Long-Term Reduction of Working Hours	113
40	Distribution of Gainfully Employed Population, by Income Class, 1960, and Forecast for 2000	125
41	Ownership of Various Appliances and Machines as Indicator of Standard of Living, among subscribers to the Schweizerischer Beobachter, 1950-65	128
42	Household Accounts: Families by Number of Children, Income Grades, Composition of Income, and Composition of Expenditure, 1969	130
43	Household Accounts in Wage-Earners' and Salaried Employees' Families, 1920-69	132
44	Consumer Expenditure of Private Households, 1966, and Forecasts for 2000	134
45	Inhabited Buildings, Households, and Households and Persons per Inhabited Building, 1850-1960	137

Table   Page

46   Inhabited Buildings, Households, and Households
      and Persons Per Inhabited Building, by Canton,
      1960   139

47   Dwellings, by Period of Construction, Ownership,
      and Population Density, by Size of Community,
      1960   141

48   Dwelling, by Social Position, Population Density,
      and Rent, 1960   142

49   Private Households According to Equipment and
      Number of Persons and Rooms, 1960   143

50   Some Indicators of Living Conditions among
      Schweizerischer Beobachter Subscribers,
      1950-65   144

51   Households with Own Country House, by Area of
      Residence and PPC among Schweizerischer
      Beobachter Subscribers, 1965   146

52   Sweizerischer Beobachter Subscribers with Vaca-
      tions, 1950-65   147

53   Weight of Income and Property Taxation, by Canton   149

54   Selected, Partially Estimated Indicators of Standard
      of Living, by Canton, 1966   151

55   Per Thousand Distribution of Farmlands, by Owned
      Land, and Land Used by Arrangement, 1955 and
      1965   157

56   Dwelling, by Owner and Size of Community, 1960   159

57   Dwelling, by Owner and Size of Community, 1960   160

58   New Dwellings, Classified by Proprietors, 1948-70   161

59   Dwelling, by Status of Occupancy and Size of Com-
      munity, 1960   162

Table   Page

60   Families Living in Own Homes, by Residence,
      Occupation and PPC, among Schweizerischer
      Beobachter Subscribers, 1950, 1960, and 1965   165

61   Refrigerators among Schweizerischer Beobachter
      Subscribers, by Category of Owner, 1965   166

62   Washing Machines among Schweizerischer
      Beobachter Subscribers, by Category of
      Owner, 1965   167

63   Registered Firms, by Legal Status, since 1951   169

64   Number and Capital of Holding Companies, since
      1954   170

65   Important Directors of Boards, according to the
      Number of Seats Occupied by Them, 1960   171

66   Distribution of Gainfully Active Population by In-
      come Class and by Social Stratum, 1957-58   172

67   Demographic Growth of Selected Cities under
      Ancien Régime, at Beginning of Industrial
      Revolution, and in 1850-1960   178

68   Changes in Number of Cities, by Size, 1850-1960   179

69   Distribution of Cities, by Size, 1960, and Growth
      Rate between 1850 and 1960   180

70   Distribution of Cities, by Size, 1960, and Growth
      Rate between 1950 and 1960   181

71   Distribution of Cities, by Geopolitical Situation,
      and Growth Rate between 1950 and 1960   182

72   Distribution of Population, by Size of Community,
      1850-1960   183

73   Evolution of Urbanization, by Size of Community,
      1850-1960   185

Table		Page
74	Degree of Urbanization, by Canton, 1960	186
75	Total Vote and Votes in Favor, Referendum of July 2, 1967, on Land Speculation by Canton	197
76	Degree of Urbanization, Proportion Voting in Referenda and Elections, and Party Systems, by Canton	208
77	Distribution of Voters, by Party and Size of Community, Federal Elections, 1959	210
78	Number of Persons in Various Sizes of Communities Voting for Three Major National Parties, 1959	211

Values, Trends and Alternatives in Swiss Society

OBJECTIVES

Under Ordinance I dated February 22, 1966, implementing the Federal Law of 1965 relating to measures designed to encourage the building of dwellings, the Institut für Orts-, Regional- und Landes-planung (Town and Country Planning Institute, or ORL) of the Federal Polytechnical College of Zurich was given the assignment to work out "guiding images"* for town and country planning in Switzerland. In a sentence that has the merit of demonstrating the all-embracing, complex, and interdisciplinary nature of the task and the demerit of being couched in rather vague terms, the Institute defines its assignment as follows:

> The result of this work, the guiding image proper of town and country planning in Switzerland, will be related to ethical, cultural, social, political, administrative, economic, aesthetic, and other factors. The prerequisite for a valid overall conception is therefore the identification and comprehension of all these factors.

---

*Leitbild in German. This term, which is frequently used without being explicitly defined, has no exact equivalent in French or English. Conception pilote or idée directrice in French and "guiding image" in English are possible translations. In French the first term, although not entirely satisfactory, has been chosen as the best solution. The term Leitbild is also related to the concepts of "alternative futures" (Kahn) and of futuribles (de Jouvenel), with emphasis on the normative element.

In order to establish the foundations of the overall guiding image of town and country planning, the Institute has decided to work out sectoral guiding images (Teilleitbilder) in the following sectors:

political institutions
Swiss society
the national economy
urban structures and human habitat
education
public health
industry and the arts and crafts
transport
communications
energy or power problems
water supply and its problems
agriculture
tourism and recreational activities
forestry
preservation of nature and of the national heritage
national defense.

Each sectoral guiding image comprises two phases. In the first phase the objectives and principles of organization are determined, a kind of ideal image of the sector being presented. The second phase takes into consideration the technical, social, financial, and legal aspects involved in the attainment of the objectives. Between these two phases will be an initial confrontation between the sectoral objectives (with the aid of a comparative matrix). Schematically, three types of relations can be distinguished between the objectives of the various sectors: agreement, indifference, and contradiction.

The 16 sectors listed above are divided into two groups: the guiding images of the first three sectors are of primary importance, the other 13 are of secondary importance. The first three provide in a sense the frame of reference for the other 13, and these others provide essentially the concrete foundations for the overall spatial conception. The details with regard to the process of working out the final conception or image will not be gone into here. Suffice it to say that the end result of this work, which is still in progress, will be the overall guiding image of town and country planning in Switzerland in several variants. These will then be submitted to the political authorities.

Thus far a general description of the Institute's actual assignment and of its method of approaching it has been presented. What follows is a description of a specific task in the context of this assignment, the methods employed, and some specific problems. The task to be dealt with is the working out of the guiding image in the sector Swiss society.

The objective of this sectoral guiding image was to outline the possible, desirable, and irreversible developments of Swiss society in the last decades of this century. This objective was to be reached by taking stock, analyzing (describing the present state of Swiss society), and forecasting factors influencing social evolution (actual facts and values and their prospective interactions). This procedure was chosen in order to permit identification of the salient evolutionary trends and their interdependence, recognition of existing conflicts and possible future ones, and indications of the action that might be taken with a view to influencing evolutionary trends in the desired direction.

METHOD

For structural purposes the whole subject area of society was divided into the following subsectors:

demography
the labor force
the conditions of women
the family
working time, work-free time, and leisure time
standards of living
property ownership
urbanization
types of housing and social relations
cantonal party systems, political participation, and strength
    of parties
external influences on the development of Switzerland,
    worldwide interdependence

In principle, the following methodological scheme was applied to each of these subsectors (with modifications, however, where required by the peculiarities of a particular subsector): (a) quantitative and qualitative description of the evolution in the past; (b) identification of factors influencing the general evolution and evaluation of their future significance; (c) confrontation of evolutionary trends and of values and objectives prevailing in the subsector; and (d) forecasting of future evolution in several variants, with particular attention to interdependencies between the various subsectors of society as well as between society and the other sectors in which guiding images are being established.

In a scheme of confrontation between evolutionary trends and values, albeit still extremely rudimentary, the following may be distinguished.[1] Considered from the point of view of action, two trends are observable: (a) evolutionary trends that cannot be influenced, that is, that are irreversible, and (b) evolutionary trends that can be influenced. Considered from the point of view of values, two trends are as follows: (a) a multiplicity of values present in a subsector (the relation between the different values ranging from more or less compatible to contradictory) and (b) the presence in a subsector of an individual value unanimously or virtually unanimously recognized. This scheme comprises four fundamental types of relations between evolutionary trends and values, each type comprising in its turn two possibilities. These types are as follows:

1. Irreversible trend—multiplicity of values: (a) The trend toward one of the values or a group of values that are more or less compatible is desirable for certain groups and undesirable for others. The values held by the groups of the second category will have to adapt. Failing this, a partial conflict will arise. Any action taken must be in line with the evolutionary trend. (b) The trend toward none of the values present is unanimously regarded as undesirable but is overriding. All the values will have to disappear or to adapt. Failing this, the result will be total conflict. Any action taken will have to be in line with the evolutionary trend.

2. Irreversible trend—value unanimously or virtually unanimously recognized: (a) The trend toward the value unanimously or virtually unanimously recognized is unanimously regarded as desirable. Action might be taken to accelerate the trend. Any action taken must be in line with the evolutionary trend. (b) The trend not toward the value unanimously or virtually unanimously recognized is unanimously regarded as undesirable but is overriding. The value will have to disappear or to adapt. Otherwise, total conflict will result. Any action taken must be in line with the evolutionary trend.

3. Trend that can be influenced—multiplicity of values: (a) The trend toward one of the values or a group of values that are more or less compatible is desirable for certain groups and undesirable for others. Political struggle results between the various groups to influence the evolution in the direction of their respective values. (b) The trend not toward any values present is unanimously regarded as undesirable. Action is to be taken to influence the evolution in the direction desired.

4. Trend that can be influenced—value unanimously or virtually unanimously recognized: (a) The trend toward a value unanimously or virtually unanimously recognized is unanimously regarded as desirable. Action might be taken to accelerate the trend. Action

contrary to the trend should be prevented. (b) The trend not toward a value unanimously or virtually unanimously recognized is unanimously regarded as undesirable. Action is to be taken to influence the trend in the desired direction.

SOME METHODOLOGICAL PROBLEMS

Here, two major problems that have arisen during the working-out of the guiding image in the Swiss society sector will be touched on briefly. These two problems have, however, a much more general purport.

The first problem is that, since this is a somewhat novel assignment in this form and since science offers no complete method for tackling it, one is constantly obliged to resort not only to scientific but also to nonscientific methods, notably to intuition and common sense. There is, for example, no problem in the scientific identification of evolutionary trends (provided, of course, that statistical data are available).* On the other hand, the determination of sectors and the subdivision of a sector into subsectors are effected on a more or less intuitive basis. (How can one guarantee that the essential evolutionary trends are covered by any particular system of sectors or subsectors?) Equally intuitive is the distinction between trends that can be influenced and irreversible trends. (On what criteria can one determine the qualitative threshhold between the one type of trend and the other?) The second problem is that of identifying values and of determining the relations between them.

The solution adopted as an initial approach during the working-out of the guiding image of Swiss society was to analyze the programs of all the political parties represented in the two houses of the federal parliament (account was also taken of the values of certain extra-parliamentary groups). This procedure relies on the unproved hypothesis that the different political parties express in an appropriate manner the values to which Swiss society subscribes. In a second approach the inventory of values might be completed by an analysis of various legal and ecclesiastical texts, of texts of various types of associations, of publicity, and of other sources from which values might be identified. Table 1 shows the distribution of seats in the

---

*The most recent comprehensive data is used here throughout. Except in cases in which yearly statistics are available these are mainly based on the 1960 federal census. The detailed 1970 census results will not be available, with some exceptions that have been taken into account, for some years yet.

TABLE 1

Distribution of Seats in National Council, 1967-71
Legislative Period and after 1971 Elections

| | Number of Seats | |
Party	1967	1971
Conservative Christian Social People's Party (KCVP)[a]	45	44
Free Democratic Party	50	49
Social Democratic Party (SPS)	51	46
Peasants', Traders', and Citizens' Party (BGB)	23	23
National Independent Association (LdU)	16	13
Liberal Democratic Citizens' Party	6	6
Evangelical People's Party	3	3
Labor Party (PdA)	5	5
Republicans and National Action Movement[b]	1	11
Total	200	200

[a]Since renamed the Christian Democrat Party.
[b]First participated in national elections in 1971; the only representative elected for the 1967-71 period sat as a nonparty member.
The programs of these two parties were not available at the time
this study was made.

National Council (the major chamber of the federal parliament) during
the 1967-71 legislature and after the elections of 1971. All political
parties represented in the two houses of the federal parliament were
asked (at the end of 1968) to send in their programs and other relevant
material. All policy statements listed in the present research are
direct quotations from this material.

The field of values, which is of crucial importance to any prospective study and to any planning scheme, has hitherto been inadequately explored and often gives the impression of being badly organized
or even positively chaotic. An attempt should be made at extending
the field of science, if this is possible, to a science of values. The
realm of such a science would comprise at least two major domains:
identification of the values held by a society and its different subgroups
and what might be called the systematization of values, a field in which
almost everything remains to be done.

A description is given in this book, relating to the various sub-sectors, of the changes brought about in Swiss society by the process of evolution, starting at the industrial stage and proceeding toward the tertiary (services) stage. Underlying the guiding image is the idea that the transformation is to be accepted and that, where irre-versible evolutionary trends are confronted with historico-institutional expressions of certain values, the latter should adapt themselves to the change. A particular effort has been made to forecast future values so as to be able to use these as criteria for decisions to be taken here and now.

Certain evolutionary trends are identified as being most likely irreversible, as follows: further urbanization (not to be confused with the process of agglomeration), further reduction of working time, increasing importance of leisure time, further emancipation of women, acceleration of technological change, increasing complexity in many fields (concerning, among other things, political structures in regions where they still are relatively simple), increasing external influences on Swiss society, and, therefore, increasing universal interdependence. Most of these trends are not typically Swiss but hold for any highly developed Western society. It might therefore be said that the problems analyzed in this book are relevant not only to the Swiss case but to any highly developed Western, and particularly European, society.

2

THE PARTIES' IDEALS
AND CONCEPT OF HUMANITY

Still by way of introduction this chapter presents a selection of straight quotations from the political parties' programs and other declarations designed to show how the ideological and intellectual background to their concepts has been formed, what values they cherish most, and what concept of humanity they cultivate.

IDEALS

KCVP:
"The Conservative Christian Social People's Party of Switzerland [KCVP] unites Swiss citizens of all faiths who acknowledge the common aim of a Christian, democratic, federalistic, and social Confederation and recognize the Christian ethic as the essential foundation of both private and public life."

"The KCVP is determined to mold public life according to Christian values. Its aim is to achieve a just and freedom-loving existence in society and nation for the well-being of all."

"The KCVP charts the course of historical development and is guided by the following universal principles: first, the social principle of individuality, which teaches that the immortal personality is the concern of Creation; second, the principle of mutual support, which teaches that each person has his place in society, depends upon society and attains his purposes and goals through society; and third, the principle of subsidiarity and federalism, which proclaims that there is a right to independence and freedom within the individual sphere and that every group within society and the nation is autonomous in that sphere and may legitimately pursue its collective well-being."

Free Democratic Party:
        "The guiding factor is and remains freedom, which constitutes
not just one of the various political values but the truly fundamental
value."
        "The Free Democratic Party of Switzerland seeks to bring
together freedom-loving fellow citizens of all occupations, classes,
and faiths, of all ages, and of both sexes to form a major people's
party on the basis of its program. . . . as the only universal
national party committed to the ideals of liberalism."
        "The Free Democratic Party of Switzerland seeks the further-
ance of national well-being on the basis of freedom, equality, and
national sovereignty. It places the well-being of the community above
the particular interests of any section of the population, economic
group, or faith."

SPS:
        "The Social Democrats [Social Democratic Party of Switzerland,
or SPS] strive to attain a social order that will free human beings
from economic exploitation. Irrespective of origin or property each
person should be able freely to develop his character and abilities.
People must not suffer from any prerogatives or be exploited by any
economic forces. Mutual support and social justice must form the
pillars of the human community. Only then will our social order be
so constituted as to free the members of society from economic
hazards and hardship, guarantee their rights, and give them access
to the beauties of life."

BGB:
        "The Swiss Peasants', Traders' and Citizens' Party [BGB] is
an association of federal-minded Swiss citizens . . . It supports all
efforts directed toward preserving and strengthening our country's
political autonomy and our people's spiritual independence . . . It
proclaims its belief in the ideals of the middle class . . . It rejects
any internationalism that is directed against the national community."

LdU:
        "In accomplishing this mighty task [opportunities for develop-
ment on an unprecedented scale] we are assisted by the Christian
ideals, which must continue to form the foundation of Swiss policy."

Liberal Democratic Citizens' Party:
        "The three principles of political freedom, democratic rules
of action, and sense of civic responsibility determine the everyday
policy of the Liberal Democratic Citizens' Party [Basel Town] at
cantonal and federal levels."

"Our party is called Liberal because it demands order within freedom . . . The freedom for which it pleads means that it acknowledges the essential values of Christian culture without sectarian ties . . . It is called Democratic because it takes as its watchword: 'With the people—for the people' . . . It is called a party of citizens because it proclaims the conviction that, at a time when humans are everywhere threatened by the mass, the influence of the citizen who thinks and acts as an individual must be strengthened."

Evangelical People's Party:

"God's universal domination of us humans demands that all areas of life should be subordinated to His will. He calls us to a sense of responsibility toward our neighbors. It is on this domination that we base our political action as evangelical [protestant] citizens of the Swiss Confederation."

"The Party is aiming at the development of the national community as an expression of justice, peace and mutual support."

PdA:

"The theoretical basis of scientific socialism [for the Labor Party, or PdA] consists of dialectic materialism. As the science of the general laws governing the evolution of human society and thought, dialectic materialism teaches that the world is a single entity, that it is material in its essence, and that it is engaged in constant movement and evolution in accordance with laws that may be known."

CONCEPT OF HUMANITY

KCVP:

"It is the party's aim to consolidate the dignity of human personality in all social areas—in the family, at work, and in public life."

"The situation is even more difficult in a society such as ours, with its highly developed but ailing machinery of civilization, its spiritual demands that escape easy ideological labeling, its apparently uncreative system of team work that no longer understands the personality in any but functional terms, and its brutal materialism that seeks and values only economic success, as so prophetically demonstrated by the example of the United States."

Free Democratic Party:

"It remains constantly necessary to uphold a sense of the supreme national aim in the public awareness. In a liberal democracy this aim is not one of national domination but rather the human dignity and freedom that must be held aloft through this system of self-government of the people. According to the liberal conviction it is vital to recognize that this freedom is indivisible by nature."

"By furthering effort in these three areas [hierarchic relationship of State and Church; problems of school education, research and doctrine; general cultural activity] the State supports the individual in his quest for self-fulfilment and contributes at the same time to that free dialogue that develops the spiritual and moral standards vital for any society concerned for human dignity."

"The party recognizes the promotion of the individual's capacity for free and harmonious development of his personality as the best means of raising the level of national well-being; state intervention should be limited to instances in which self-help fails."

"The success of the liberal concept of the State is due primarily to the fact that the goal and the political method of liberalism are not conceived in utopian terms but allow for all the imperfections of human reality."

SPS:
      "Man with his needs, his rights, and his dignity is central to Social Democratic economic policy. Economic democracy and human values must be placed above technology and profit."

"Efforts to seek justice in material matters become truly meaningful and purposeful only if they promote the mental liberation of the individual. It is the socialist belief that everyone can share in cultural values and that the development of mentally independent and creative human beings should be pursued by every means."

BGB:
      "The party's economic policy is derived from the citizen's fundamental duty to ensure his livelihood through conscientious and energetic effort and the fullest development of his individual potential. The party opposes all forms of exploitation and parasitism and all machinations that are harmful to production or promote class warfare. From the State it demands an economic policy that will safeguard human honor and dignity in economic life and secure a proper reward for all forms of honest work in the form of appropriate prices and wages."

LdU:
      "The greater the technological potential, the more necessary it becomes to have human beings of stable character who can make proper use of the world and its potential."

Evangelical People's Party:
      "Efforts to renew national life and the spiritual environment of the national community must start with each individual . . . The

solution of social problems and the establishment of a social order
worthy of mankind lies in the spiritual renovation of human beings.
Injustice, inhumanity, and deceit come from the individual and not
just from external conditions and circumstances. Our fundamental
concepts of social policy are: 1. A social order that permits human
beings to fulfil their God-given destinies and to develop their person-
alities freely within that meaning."

PdA:
        "Only by planning the economy and further social develop-
ment . . . can man become the master of his destiny . . . Only socialist
solutions can permit human development within a just and prosperous
society."

THE SWISS POPULATION AND ITS AGE STRUCTURE

Using statistical data for the past and an average forecast for the future, the rough pattern of trends in the Swiss population and its broad age breakdown is obtained for the period 1860-2040 in Table 2. In per-thousand figures the same data appear in Table 3.

Without analyzing the factors affecting past trends, the following assumptions used in the forecast may be mentioned.* The calculation of the birth rate is based on the figure of 100,000 births in 1965 (in actual fact there were already over that number of births in 1962). The trend in the birth rate after 1962 is determined by combining the static alternative (constant figure of 95,000 births per year) with the dynamic one (which assumes a 1 percent increase each year, with 156,000 births in 50 years' time) in the proportion of 2:1. This produces a final figure of 118,000 births for 2025. The Swiss mortality figures show a constant decline in the death rate. Mortality tables were prepared in connection with the sixth revision of the old-age and survivors' insurance system (AHV) on the assumption that this trend would continue. They were produced from the national mortality table 1948-53 in accordance with P. Nolfi's theory of extrapolation which will not be discussed here. The semidynamic version** of interest

---

*The details are borrowed from Fricker's article, which describes a static, a semidynamic and a dynamic model. The semidynamic model is the one used here.

**Of the three models—static, semidynamic, and dynamic—the semidynamic model is of interest. It is the medium one (static-minimum, dynamic, and maximum).

here was based on table AHV III (for the period 1963-92) and on table
AHV III second version (for the period from 1993). These tables have
been prepared by the experts of the old-age and survivors' "scheme"
and are quoted by Fricker.

Reference is made here only to migration to or from Switzerland
but not within the country. The semidynamic model under consideration takes an annual migration surplus declining from 60,000 to 0 for
the 20-year period 1965-85; from 1985 onward the foreign manpower
level of about 900,000 persons is assumed as remaining stationary,
according to this hypothesis. These assumptions are consolidated in
Table 4.

TABLE 2

Population, by Age, 1860-2040

| Year | Age Group | | | Total |
	19 and under	20-64	65 and over	
1860	984,555	1,394,413	127,817	2,510,494*
1880	1,178,020	1,510,676	157,406	2,846,102
1900	1,343,950	1,778,227	193,266	3,315,443
1910	1,529,760	2,005,755	217,778	3,753,293
1920	1,470,195	2,183,163	226,962	3,880,320
1930	1,361,513	2,425,082	279,805	4,066,400
1941	1,284,133	2,616,533	365,037	4,265,703
1950	1,438,540	2,823,226	453,226	4,714,992
1960	1,702,067	3,172,754	554,240	5,429,061
1965	1,697,335	3,624,399	649,049	5,970,783
1970	1,747,659	3,916,268	731,415	6,395,342
1975	1,833,341	4,064,393	814,287	6,712,021
1985	1,930,740	4,339,437	868,358	7,138,535
2000	2,037,155	4,554,150	1,054,270	7,645,575
2020	2,181,818	4,355,674	1,546,265	8,083,757
2040	2,220,906	4,654,535	1,379,248	8,254,689

*This figure includes 3,709 persons of unknown age.

Sources: To 1960: Statistisches Jahrbuch der Schweiz 1967,
p. 22. After 1960: Kurt Fricker, "Basis of Calculation for the Old-
Age and Survivors' Scheme, a Semidynamic Model: Mean Forecast,"
Schweizerische Zeitschrift für Volkswirtschaft und Statistik (Bern),
CI, 2 (June 1965), 126.

TABLE 3

Population, by Age, 1860-2040
(per thousand)

| Year | Age Group | | |
	0-19	20-64	65 and over
1860	392	557	51
1880	414	531	55
1900	405	537	58
1910	408	534	58
1920	380	562	58
1930	335	597	68
1941	302	613	85
1950	305	599	96
1960	314	584	102
1965	284	607	109
1970	273	612	115
1975	273	606	121
1985	270	608	122
2000	266	596	138
2020	270	539	191
2040	269	564	167

Sources: To 1960: Statistisches Jahrbuch der Schweiz 1967, p. 22. After 1960: Kurt Fricker, "Basis of Calculation for the Old-Age and Survivors' Scheme, a Semidynamic Model: Mean Forecast," Schweizersche Zeitschrift für Volkswirtschaft und Statistik (Bern), CI, 2 (June 1965), 126.

To supplement these figures some of the most important assumptions used by the Working Group on Long-Range Projections are briefly set out below,* but without going into any divergence or convergence between these and the other assumptions dealt with here. The assumptions (A) applied by the Working Group for its population forecasts include the following:[1]

---

*Arbeitsgruppe Perspektivstudien, headed by Professor F. Kneschaurek, Hochschule für Wirtschafts und Sozialwissenschaften St. Gallen (St. Gall Business School).

A1: "The birth rate of the Swiss resident population will continue to decline, from 1.53 percent in 1967 to 1.37 percent in 2000."

A2: "In the age-specific birth rate there will be a continuation of the clear trend in recent decades whereby the rate increases in the age groups up to 25, but decreases thereafter."

A5: "Up to 2000 the Swiss resident population is reckoned as increasing by about 4,560 persons per year as a result of naturalization, surplus from migration and gains through marriage. We expect that naturalization and the migration balance will roughly equal out, although differences in the age structure of these two components should be

TABLE 4

Population and Population Surplus Trends until 1961 and
Semidynamic Assumptions from 1962

Calendar Year	Population at End of Period or Year	Actual Annual Average		Percent Increase as Annual Average
		Live Births	Migration Surplus	
1871/80	2,831,787	84,674	- 2,316	0.65
1881/88	2,917,754	81,956	-10,895	0.37
1889/00	3,315,443	86,518	6,177	1.07
1901/10	3,753,293	95,087	7,924	1.25
1911/20	3,880,320	80,893	-11,752	0.33
1921/30	4,066,400	72,938	- 5,904	0.47
1931/41	4,265,703	66,243	481	0.44
1942/50	4,714,992	85,577	13,852	1.12
1951/60	5,429,061	87,444	34,022	1.42
1960	5,429,061	94,372	98,000	2.23
1961	5,560,000	99,238	80,117	2.41
1965	5,970,783	100,000	60,000	1.89
1970	6,395,342	101,678	30,000	1.12
1975	6,712,021	103,384	20,000	0.97
1985	7,138,535	106,882	0	0.51
2000	7,645,575	112,353	0	0.48
2020	8,083,757	118,103	0	0.20
2040	8,254,689	118,103	0	0.10

Source: Kurt Fricker, "Basis of Calculation for the Old-Age and Survivors' 'Scheme,' a Semidynamic Model: Mean Forecast," Schweizerische Zeitschrift für Volkswirtschaft und Statistik, CI, 2 (Bern, June 1965), 125, 126.

taken into consideration. We believe that the decisive factor will come from trends in the population increase due to gains through marriage and the relevant age structure, with the female element naturally predominating."

Regarding trends in the foreign population of Switzerland various hypotheses have been advanced but they will not be examined in detail here. They may be summarized by means of the following two alternatives: with a total projected population of about 7.5 million in 2000 the first assumes a foreign contingent of about 1.4 million (i.e., roughly 18.5 percent of the total population), whereas the second, based on a different naturalization policy, reckons that there will be slightly over 1 million foreigners (or 14.2 percent of the total). In 1965 the proportion amounted to 15.3 percent.[2]

As Tables 2 and 3 show, the total population of Switzerland has been steadily rising from about 2.5 million in 1860 and will amount to some 8.25 million in 2040. This means it will have slightly more than tripled in the space of 180 years.

The age structure will have undergone a radical change in this period. Toward the end of the last century Switzerland was still like a present-day developing country in this respect, with a high proportion of people under 20 and a small proportion over 65; a decline in the proportion of the population under 20 had already begun in 1880, although it revived to a limited extent in 1910, 1950, and 1960. The decrease in the proportion of young people from 414 per thousand in 1880 to 284 per thousand in 1965 will continue, although to a lesser extent, reaching its lowest point of 266 around 2000. After that the proportion will rise slightly to 270 in 2020 and 269 in 2040.

The actual numbers of people under 20 increased from 1860 to 1910 and then fell slightly but steadily until 1941. Since then the numbers have been rising again, although there was a slight decline in the mid-1960s. The rising trend will continue in the future, so that in 2000 there will be 2 million persons under 20 and in 2040 slightly over 2.2 million.

In 1860 the proportion of people over 65 amounted to 51 per thousand and rose to 109 per thousand in 1965, with a stationary period between 1900 and 1920. This trend will continue uninterrupted, resulting in a proportion of 138 per thousand in 2000 and 191 in 2020, but the figure will drop to 167 per thousand by 2040. This means that, where 1 in 20 inhabitants in 1860 was over 65, in 1960 it was 1 in 10 and in 2020 it will be nearly 1 in 5. The extent to which this trend can be successfully met will depend on timely action. In absolute terms the steady increase in the number over 65 between 1860 and 2020 is from 127,817 to slightly more than 1.5 million, but between 1960 and 2020 the figure will almost triple. Between 2020 and 2040 the number will fall to a little below 1.4 million.

The changing proportions of the elderly and the young mean a corresponding fluctuation in the proportion of people between 20 and 64, although the figures for the beginning and the end of the period are very close (557 and 564 per thousand, respectively). The lowest figures are 531 in 1880 (coupled with the peak proportion of young persons at 414) and 539 in 2020 (coupled with the peak proportion of the elderly at 191); the highest points are 613 per thousand in 1941 and 612 in 1970.

In absolute terms the number of persons between 20 and 64 rises steadily from 1,394,413 in 1860 to 3,624,399 in 1965 and then to around 4,550,000 in 2000, declining slightly after that until 2020 but then starting to rise again and arriving at 4,650,000 by 2040.

THE PROPORTION OF PENSIONERS AND DEPENDENTS

Using the figures in Tables 2 and 3 it is possible to calculate two interesting quotients, in the form of the proportion of pensioners and the proportion of dependants. The proportion of pensioners means the quotient obtained by dividing the number over 65 by the number between 20 and 64. If this proportion is calculated back to 1860, it must not be forgotten that the institution that gave them their name— that is, the payment of a pension after a certain age—was practically nonexistent at the time. Time comparison is worthwhile and inter- esting, however, because the situation of fact it describes—crudely expressed, the number of old people requiring economic support in relation to the number of able-bodied persons supporting them—has remained by and large the same.

Whereas the proportion of pensioners considers only the elderly and the able-bodied, the dependency proportion represents the quotient of the number over 65 plus the number between 0 and 19 divided by the number between 20 and 64, in other words, the ratio of those not normally in gainful activity to those normally capable of gainful activity. The dividing line is often drawn at age 15 rather than 20, which was certainly correct when the period of education used to be shorter than is common nowadays. The present stage is one of transition, but the longer average periods of education to be expected in the future will make the 20-year dividing line more realistic. If the dependency proportion is calculated on a uniform basis for the whole period of nearly 200 years, it must be borne in mind that the resulting figures will be nearer to the truth for the future than for the past, in view of the shift in the average age of entry into occupational life.

Table 5 shows changes in the two quotients during the period under consideration. As the table shows, the proportion of pensioners has been steadily rising, from 92 in 1860, expect for a slight dip

TABLE 5

Pensioner and Dependency Proportions, 1860-2040

Year	Proportion of Pensioners	Dependency Proportion
1860	92	795
1880	104	883
1900	108	862
1910	109	873
1920	103	779
1930	114	675
1941	139	631
1950	160	669
1960	175	712
1965	179	647
1970	187	634
1975	200	650
1985	200	645
2000	231	678
2020	355	855
2040	296	773

Source: Calculated from the figures in Tables 2 and 3.

around 1920, to 179 in 1965. It will then continue to rise to its peak of 355 in 2020, after which it will drop back to 296 in 2040. The dependency proportion oscillates between a peak of 883 in 1880 and a low of 631 in 1941; other peaks are 873 in 1910, 712 in 1960, and 855 in 2020, with another low at 634 in 1970.

To summarize, it may be said that, if the semidynamic hypothesis turns out to be fairly accurate, the period around 2020 will be a critical one from the point of view of demography: the number of people aged over 65 will reach a peak in both absolute and relative terms, whereas the able-bodied population will be moving toward a relative low and will even be slightly declining for the first time in actual numbers, which might result in an acute labor shortage depending on the economic situation. This critical phase will be reflected in an absolute maximum in the proportion of pensioners by far in excess of any previous values, and the dependency proportion will be at a maximum equaled only by the figures around the end of the nineteenth and the beginning of the twentieth centuries, which were due to the high proportion of people under age 20.

ALTERNATIVE POPULATION FORECASTS

The forecasts described thus far have been based exclusively on the semidynamic variant constructed in connection with the old-age and survivors' insurance system.* This was used to calculate the sixth revision of the system and was held by the experts as most likely to correspond to the real situation, at least in the immediate future. In a medium-range forecast the results vary between two extremes (see Table 6) and the figures lie closer to the maximum alternative at the start, moving toward the minimum one as time goes on.[3] Table 6 presents a synoptic view of various population forecasts, representing the different hypotheses of possible population trends. It takes only the overall figures at various points in time; the methods and the relevant assumptions are only briefly touched upon.

A BRIEF EXPLANATION OF METHODS AND ASSUMPTIONS

Stochastic Model

"Estimates based on a simple stochastic model extrapolate only the total resident population without considering the age and sex composition."[4] Everything depends on the base period selected for extrapolation. In this connection Wilhelm Bickel believes that

we are in danger of committing the same mistakes as in the past. The rapid increase in the Swiss resident population in the 50s tempts one into overestimating the future growth rate. In order to arrive at a balanced judgment I believe it is vital first to consider the long-range trend in the population of Switzerland.[5]

Biometric Model

The biometric model is based on an initial situation (first generation) determined by age x of men and age y of

---

*Old-age and survivors' insurance system (scheme), periodically revised. This is the sixth revision.

TABLE 6

Hypotheses of Possible Population Trends

Author of Forecast	Method of Calculation	Total Resident Population (millions)							
		1980	1985	1993	2000	2013	2020	2033	2040
Federal Statistical Office and Commission of the Association of Swiss Statistical Offices	Stochastic model								
	1st Variant (basis 1850-1960)				6.860		7.930		
	2nd Variant (basis 1880-1960)				7.050				
	3rd Variant (basis 1900-60)	6.023			6.993				
	4th Variant (basis -930-60)	6.247			7.418				
	5th Variant (basis -950-60)	7.197			9.542				
	Biometric method								
	Swiss and permanently resident foreigners, plus foreigners subject to surveillance, not including migrants	6.399	6.682						
Wilhelm Bickel	Personal assessment on basis of official forecasts				6.900-7.000		8.000		
	Personal assessment on basis of official forecasts and assuming a relatively high number of foreign workers and progressive integration of Switzerland in a comprehensive European economic zone								
Old-age and Survivors' Insurance System (AHV)	Static model				7.200		8.300		
	Semidynamic model		7.139	6.366	7.646	6.632	8.084	6.757	8.255
	Dynamic model			8.409		9.672			10.369
Working Group on Long-Range Projections F. Kneschaurek, chairman	See the relevant assumptions on page 18				7.544				
Swiss Institute for Foreign Economic and Market Research, University of St. Gallen					7.500				

women. The first stage is to calculate how many persons
in this first generation will survive for a specified time t,
such as 5, 10, 15 . . . years. For this purpose it is necessary to know the likelihood of surviving t years, i.e., the
likelihood that a man aged x (or a woman aged y) will live
for the next t years. . . . The second stage consists of
calculating the number of births in the next t years. The
usual practice is to determine the number of live births
from the number of women. Empirical means are used to
ascertain the average yearly number of live births for y-
aged mothers, related to a woman of the relevant age,
which gives a picture of the age-specific birth rate. . . .
The final situation at time t is then obtained from the
number of survivors of the first generation and the number of survivors born in the intervening years.[6]

Thanks to its analytic system the biometric method produces more
precise forecasts than is possible by means of stochastic models.
This is particularly true of relatively short-range forecasts (up to 20
years), but in the longer range it is difficult to estimate changes in
the determining factors.

Static Model

The AHV static model is based on the assumption of a constant
level of 95,000 births per year from 1962 and on mortality table AHV
III.* The number of foreign workers for 1965 was assumed to amount
to 600,000; the static model makes no allowance for any migration
surplus, so this figure of 600,000 is taken as constant. In this minimum
forecast the age structure is characterized by a relatively fast rise
in the proportion of pensioners to about 25 percent toward the turn of
the century.[7]

Semidynamic Model

The assumptions underlying this hypothesis have already been
discussed.

_____

*AHV is the acronym for Alters und Hinterbleibenen Versicherung
(Old-Age and Survivors' Scheme). AHV is an internal document
referred to by Fricker in his article.

Dynamic Model

Starting with the figures of 95,000 births in 1962, this model estimates an average increase in the birth rate of 1 percent each year for 50 years; for the period 1963-92 it uses mortality table AHV IV, and from 1993 table AHV III second version. Regarding migration, it is assumed that the surplus of 71,156 persons in 1962 will gradually decline to 0 by the turn of the century. Under this maximum forecast, therefore, there would still be a substantial increase in the number of foreign workers, who would have to become more assimilated than hitherto and might consequently contribute to the assumed increase in the birth rate. Under this hypothesis the proportion of pensioners remains practically constant for an additional 30 years, only rising after the turn of the century, but then climbing sharply to 30 percent or more.

The choice of the AHV semidynamic model as seeming the most likely hypothesis among the long-range forecasts on present evidence is not of course claimed as final or irreversible. The data will have to be regularly examined to find out which model approximates best to the actual trends.

Summarizing the overall situation and considering the various methods proposed, the commission established by the Association of Swiss Statistical Offices under the chairmanship of Otto Messmer concluded in 1963 that the population in 2000 would amount to 7-8 million, depending on the numbers of foreigners, so that the 10-million level is not to be expected until later than is frequently mooted at present.[8]

A figure of 7.5 million for the year 2000 is also offered by the later estimates produced by the Swiss Institute for Foreign Economic and Market Research of the University of St. Gallen and the Working Group on Long-Range Projections. A general consensus appears to be gradually forming about this order of magnitude.

AVERAGE LIFE EXPECTANCY

In 1881-1888 the average life expectancy at birth was 43.3 years for men; since then it has risen continuously, reaching 68.72 years for the period 1958-63. For women life expectancy rose from 45.7 to 74.13 years. Since the first year of life is one of particular exposure, the corresponding rates at the age of 1 have always been accordingly higher: in 1881-88 they were 51.8 and 52.8 years for men and women, respectively, and in 1958-63 they were 69.43 and 74.53, respectively.[9]

It is to be expected that there will be a further rise in average
life expectancy, and this is allowed for to varying degrees in the
population forecasts already described. (The Working Group on Long-
Range Projections reckons that the average life expectancy in 2000
will be 74.5 for men and 80.3 for women.) The pattern will be influenced
primarily by absolute progress in medical science, extension of its
application, the development of preventive medicine, extra leisure,
the higher level of education, the rising per capita income, improved
housing conditions, and changes in the social and occupational structure.

RATE AND AGE OF MARRIAGE

[Since 1900,] leaving aside 1920, the proportion of single
Swiss men and women has declined from one census to the
next as a result of the increasing rate of marriage, while
the proportion of married people has accordingly risen.
In 1900 the proportion of married people in the nubile
population (i.e. women from the age of 18 and men from
the age of 20) amounted to 54%, while in 1960 it was 66%.
In the foreign resident population the trend was in the
opposite direction owing to the heavier influx of young,
single workers, and the proportion of married people
declined in the same 60-year period from 50 to 46%.[10]

Assuming that the major trend is related to economic development, in other words, that economic obstacles to marriage have
disappeared with rising prosperity, it seems likely that the rate of
marriage will remain at least at its present level. Regarding foreigners, the assumption of an intensified policy of assimilation in the
future points to the likelihood of a higher marriage rate.
The age of first marriage has fallen in the past 25 years. The
average proportion of people marrying at the age of 24 or under over
the period 1941-50 was 245 per thousand for men and 495 per thousand
for women, as compared with 379 and 613 in 1960 and 455 and 693 in
1966.[11] Forecasts concerning the age of marriage and, in addition
to what has been said above, the rate of marriage will be discussed
in connection with the longer average duration of education, the
employment of women, and the evolution of the family.

4

THE LABOR FORCE

This chapter is made up of six sections. The first four sections deal with changes in the structure of the labor force according to occupational position and job, matters concerning foreign manpower, the results of research into the effects of automation on the structure of the labor force, and forecasts of possible courses of development. The last two sections cover the parties' attitudes on labor-management relations, with particular reference to codetermination, and the needs in education and training arising out of social evolution, together with the parties' views on the subject.

CHANGES IN THE STRUCTURE OF THE LABOR FORCE, 1941-60

Although the absence of comprehensive production and productivity statistics in Switzerland places a severe handicap on research relating to manpower forecasts, the labor force statistics for Switzerland offer a rich source of material for determining long-range trends in past periods. In regard to occupational position Swiss statistics distinguish between the following categories:

self-employed persons
family collaborators
directors
senior technical personnel
other senior personnel
subordinate technical personnel
other subordinate personnel
home workers
skilled production workers

      semiskilled production workers
      unskilled production workers
      production apprentices
      commercial apprentices

Changes in the distribution of the labor force according to occupational position, economic sector, and branch will be discussed. Only the national economic figures will be presented in tabular form; although reasons of space prevent the inclusion of the corresponding tables for individual sectors and earning categories, the relevant results are considered in the commentary.

      The proportion of self-employed persons in the total labor force fell by 66 per thousand during the period 1941-60 (see Table 7). This breaks down into 53 per thousand for the secondary sector and 41 per thousand for the tertiary sector, but in the primary sector there was an increase amounting to 43 per thousand. This relative upswing is due wholly to agriculture, including animal husbandry, because the same decline as elsewhere took place in the remaining branches of the primary sector. All branches in the secondary sector show the same declining trend in the rate of self-employment except for the minor group made up of mining and quarrying (up 14 per thousand). Similarly, the only exception in the tertiary sector consisted of "other services" (up 26 per thousand.

      During the period 1960-64 the proportion of self-employed persons declined further from 145 to 129 per thousand. The postwar trend followed the same lines in other comparable countries such as the United States, the Netherlands, and Sweden, where the average decline was from slightly over 20 to about 13 percent. Only in Belgium and the United Kingdom did the proportion fall even more sharply.[1]

TABLE 7

Proportion of Self-Employed Persons in
Labor Force, 1941-60

Year	Total Labor Force	Self-Employed Persons	
		Absolute	Per Thousand
1941	1,992,487	420,910	211
1950	2,155,656	408,889	190
1960	2,512,411	365,501	145

      Source: Federal Statistical Office, Federal Census: 1941, Vol. 21, Table 44; 1950, Vol. 25, Table 10; 1960, Vol. 28, Table 13.

The absolute and relative decline in the rate of self-employment is contrary to the aims of some of the parties, as demonstrated in the following survey. One party recognized the trend early and called for appropriate values to be followed. The parties have made the following statements on the subject:

KCVP:
"The party and its parliamentary fraction support self-help action by industry and call for measures to facilitate self-employment."

BGB:
"The BGB demands the development of economic legislation and the implementation of an economic policy aimed at preserving the greatest possible number of independent operators in all branches of the economy, in the political, economic, and cultural interests of the country."

"The BGB is in favor of free occupational activity and supports efforts toward self-employment."

"For national considerations the BGB advocates the preservation of the greatest possible number of independent operators. It accordingly supports small farmers and mountain farmers by stressing the particular values so abundantly inherent in their existence. Large families, diligence, and thrift are their characteristics, and they deserve public acknowledgement and encouragement on both educational and social grounds."

LdU:
"Production workers and salaried employees must be able to feel that they are essential members of their firms and must be respected as such by their employers. This ethical element must be injected into economic life. Work well done and conscientious endeavor have an uplifting effect and leave no room for any form of discriminatory social evaluation as between employees and self-employed persons."

The proportion of salaried employees in the labor force increased over the period by 77 per thousand (see Table 8). This is both the most important trend in numerical terms and the most generally valid one as well. To a greater or lesser extent it is common to all three sectors and to 34 of the 39 economic groups.* The four groups in

---

*These groups are: Landwirtschaft, Tierzucht (agriculture); Gartenbau (gardening); Forstwirtschaft, Holzhauerei (forestry, felling);

which the opposite trend is observed are the numerically insignificant branch of private care (the total employed in this branch amounted to only 3,235 persons in 1960), the operational staff of hospitals (down 11 per thousand), banks (down 3 per thousand), and the group consisting of public administration, the law, and national defense (down 15 per thousand). In the last two groups the decline in the proportion of salaried employees is offset or even exceeded by the increase in the proportion of commercial trainees.

The increase in the proportion of salaried employees is common to both senior and subordinate categories in all three sectors and in 33 and 32, respectively, of the economic groups. In the primary sector, where the proportion of salaried employees rose from 6 to 11 per thousand, they still account for a very small number only. With the exception of directors and other senior personnel in the primary sector all categories of salaried employees grew in proportion in all three sectors. The number of economic groups affected by this trend fluctuates between 26 and 36 of the various categories. In some economic groups the proportion for subordinate categories declines or remains stationary, whereas the figure for senior categories rises. This is the case of the beverages industry, banks, insurance, general

---

Fischerei, Fischzucht, Jagd (fisheries, pisciculture, hunting); Bergbau, Steinbrüche, Gruben (mining and quarrying); Wahrungsmittel (foodstuffs); Spirituosen, Getränke (beverages); Tabak (tobacco); Textilien (textiles); Kleider, Wäsche, Schuhe (clothing and footwear); Holz, Kork (wood, cork); Papier (paper); Graphisches Gewerbe (printing trades); Leder, ohne Schuhe (leather); Kautschuk, ohne Kleider (rubber); Chemie (chemical industry); Steine, Erden (stone, earthenware); Metalle (metal trades); Maschinen, Apparate (machinery, instrument-manufacturing); Uhren, Bijouterie (clocks, watches, jewelry); Anderere Industrien und Handwerke (other industries and handicrafts); Baugewerbe (building); Elektrizität, Gas, Wasser (electricity, gas, water); Handel (commerce); Banken (banking); Versicherungen (insurance); Vermittlung, Interessenvertretung (mediation, representation of interests); Verkehr (transport); Gastgewerbe (hotels and restaurants); Öffentliche Verwaltung, Rechtspflege, Landetverteidigung (public administration, the law, national defense); Gesundheit, Hygiene (health, hygiene); Unterricht, Wissenschaft (education, science); Seelsorge, Kirchendienst (religious institutions); Private Wohlfahrtipflege (private care); Kunst, Unterhaltung, Sport (art, entertainment, sport); Hauswirtschaft (domestic service); Andere Dienstleistungen (other services); Anstalten (homes, hospitals, and similar institutions); Arbeitslose (unemployed).

TABLE 8

Proportions of Various Categories of Salaried
Employees in Labor Force, 1941-60

	1941		1950		1960	
Category	Absolute	Per Thou-sand*	Absolute	Per Thou-sand*	Absolute	Per Thou-sand*
Directors	7,067	4	10,256	5	17,035	7
Senior technical personnel	8,678	4	12,448	6	19,953	8
Other technical Personnel	34,432	17	48,685	22	58,726	23
Total technical personnel	50,177	25	71,389	33	95,714	38
Subordinate technical personnel	50,385	25	71,539	33	119,281	47
Other subordinate personnel	247,624	125	315,815	147	418,475	167
Total subordinate personnel	298,009	150	387,354	180	537,756	214
Total salaried employees	348,186	175	458,743	213	633,470	252

*Proportion per thousand of the entire labor force.

Source: Federal Statistical Office, Federal Census: 1941, Vol.
21, Table 44; 1950, Vol. 25, Table 10; 1960, Vol. 28, Table 13.

public administration, and private care. The opposite trend, consisting
of a decline in the proportion of senior categories accompanied by an
increase in subordinate categories, is seen in fisheries and hunting;
in the printing trades; in religious institutions; and in art, entertainment, and sports.
     In some economic groups a decrease in the proportion of other
categories is accompanied by an increase in the proportion of technical
personnel. At the senior level this applies to forestry and lumbering;
the printing trades; electricity, gas, and water; general public

administration, law, and national defense; education and science; art, entertainment, and sports; and the operational staff of hospitals. At the subordinate level this applies to the beverages industry; banks; insurance; communications and representation of interests;* transport; general public administration, law, and national defense; and private care. But the opposite phenomenon—a declining or stagnating proportion of technical personnel accompanied by an increase in other personnel—is seen in the case of senior employees in mining and quarrying; in the beverages industry; textiles; rubber; insurance; transport; and health and hygiene. The last of these groups is the only one in which the same trend is observed in the case of subordinate employees as well.

In contrast to the relative increase in the number of salaried employees of all categories, affecting all three sectors and the vast majority of economic groups in a fairly uniform manner, most of the exceptions having been noted in the preceding paragraphs, there is far more variation among production workers. Over the whole economy the proportion of production workers rose very slightly (up 3 per thousand), yet this was accompanied by a decline in all three sectors (primary sector down 35, secondary sector down 9, and tertiary sector down 52 per thousand). The complete lack of uniformity is apparent in regard to economic groups: in 17 there was an increase (2 in the primary, 7 in the secondary, and 8 in the tertiary sectors), whereas there was a decrease in 21 (2 in the primary, 12 in the secondary, and 7 in the tertiary sectors). Thus the variation cuts right across the sectors.

Taking the individual categories of production workers (Table 9), it is seen that the proportion of skilled workers increased both in the whole economy (up 11 per thousand) and in two of the three sectors (primary up 4 and tertiary up 17 per thousand), whereas it fell by 20 per thousand in the secondary sector. In the overall economy the increase was restricted to the period 1941-50 since the figure remained stationary at 160 per thousand after that. The proportion fell in 10 out of the 19 groups in the secondary sector (with an increase in the other 9); in the tertiary sector there was a rise in 13 groups and a fall in 2 only.

The proportion of semiskilled manpower declined both in general and in each of the three sectors. In 18 economic groups (3 in the primary, 8 in the secondary, and 7 in the tertiary sectors) there was

---

*"Representation of interests" (Interessenvertretung) covers lawyers and similar professionals who represent the interests of others.

TABLE 9

Proportion of Various Categories of Production
Workers in Labor Force, 1941-60

Category	1941		1950		1960	
	Absolute	Per Thou- sand*	Absolute	Per Thou- sand*	Absolute	Per Thou- sand*
Home workers	12,154	6	12,229	6	11,620	4
Skilled workers	295,978	149	345,240	160	401,327	160
Semiskilled workers	524,876	263	566,584	263	612,643	244
Unskilled workers	168,980	85	144,761	67	246,383	98
Total	1,001,988	503	1,068,814	496	1,271,973	506

*Proportion per thousand of the entire labor force.

Source: Federal Statistical Office, Federal Census: 1941, Vol.
21, Table 44; 1950, Vol. 25, Table 10; 1960, Vol. 28, Table 13.

an increase, while 21 showed a decrease (1 in the primary, 11 in the
secondary, and 9 in the tertiary sectors).

In regard to occupational groups the same trend is to be observed
among unskilled workers: 18 with an increase and 21 with a decrease.
In contrast to the semiskilled workers, however, the trends at the
sectoral level were reasonably clear: there was a decline in the
primary sector both as a whole (down 26 per thousand) and in 3 of
the 4 economic groups; the only exception was gardening (up 58 per
thousand). In the secondary sector (up 39 per thousand) the proportion
of unskilled labor increased in 15 economic groups; there was a
decrease in only 4 groups (mining and quarrying; machinery and
instrument manufacturing; building; and electricity, gas, and water).
What is particularly striking about the trend in this sector is that in
all 15 of the groups showing an increase the proportion of unskilled
labor declined between 1941 and a time between 1950 and 1960, after
which the trend was reversed. Although this might be attributed to
the effects of technological change, it was more probably due to the
short supply of skilled manpower. In the tertiary sector the proportion
of unskilled workers fell by 17 per thousand, the same pattern occurred
in 11 of the occupational groups, whereas in 5 there was an increase
in the unskilled rate.

Taking semiskilled and unskilled workers together and contrasting them with skilled workers, it is seen that partial or full replacement occurred in both directions. In four groups in the secondary sector (foodstuffs; clothing and footwear; leather; and other industries and handicrafts) and in gardening skilled labor was replaced. The opposite trend, whereby skilled workers either partly or entirely took the place of semiskilled or unskilled workers, occurred in the primary and tertiary sectors as a whole; in electricity, gas, and water; and in three tertiary groups (transport; general public administration, law, and national defense; and insurance).

At both national and sectoral levels the proportion of apprentices followed a uniform pattern (see Table 10). The rates of both industrial and commercial apprenticeship rose in all cases (although commercial training in the primary sector is of negligible importance). The sharpest relative increase was in the tertiary sector (up 17 per thousand). In regard to occupational groups the same uniform pattern is found in the proportion of commercial trainees, with an increase in 33 of the 36 groups concerned, the figure remaining stationary in the other 3. Things are different for industrial training, however, with an increase in 23 economic groups and a decrease in 11. Of the 11, 8 are in the secondary sector (foodstuffs; tobacco; clothing and footwear; wood and cork; leather; stone and earthenware; clocks and watches and jewelry; and other industries and handicrafts); the other 3 are gardening, private care (private social work), and gainfully employed inmates of homes, hospitals, and similar institutions.

TABLE 10

Proportion of Apprentices in Labor Force, 1941-60

Category	1941		1950		1960	
	Absolute	Per Thou- sand*	Absolute	Per Thou- sand*	Absolute	Per Thou- sand*
Industrial apprentices	53,969	27	65,973	31	87,510	35
Commercial apprentices	16,629	8	22,261	10	36,753	15
Total	70,598	35	88,234	41	124,263	50

*Proportion per thousand of the entire labor force.

Source: Federal Statistical Office, Federal Census: 1941, Vol. 21, Table 44; 1950, Vol. 25, Table 10; 1960, Vol. 28, Table 13.

Considering the whole situation, one observes, first, that the proportion of salaried employees of all grades, both technical and other, increased during the period. This structural change may be seen as a consequence of technological and organizational modifications within economic branches and in the branch structure as well. In addition, the number of unskilled workers rose in both absolute and relative terms, owing primarily to the massive influx of usually unskilled foreign workers. It is only natural to deduce that technological renewal of the production apparatus was partly neglected because foreign manpower offered the means for purely expansive growth. These points will be returned to in connection with foreign labor and the effects of automation.

Structural Changes According to Occupation

At the time of the 1960 census the statistical authorities distinguished between 13 classes of occupations, breaking them down into 51 groups and 479 subgroups.[2] These were used in classifying the over 11,000 job titles given by people answering the question on personal occupation. For reasons of space tabular presentation will not be used in this connection. The trends will not be described entirely in accordance with this system of classification but also by taking a small number of occupational groups regarded as strategically important in a research hypothesis established for the secondary sector. This hypothesis is that, as a result of technological and organizational trends, the proportion of production personnel is declining in favor of maintenance staff and of administrative and planning personnel. The occupational groups regarded as strategically important are the "basic group," the commercial and administrative occupations, the technical occupations, and those in mechanical and electrical engineering. Except for the "basic group," all of these correspond to the definitions used in official statistics. The newly coined term "basic group" is used in each case to cover the group or groups of occupations intrinsically belonging to the industry or branch under consideration, and this is normally clear immediately from its name. As a rule people coming within the particular industry or branch mainly belong to the appropriate occupational group or groups, and the converse also applies. The hypothesis further suggests that most of the basic groups are shrinking in importance as the economy develops, so that the description of the concept as given above is becoming less and less applicable. To test the validity of the hypothesis the basic group is identified with the nucleus of production personnel in each branch; jobs in the mechanical and electrical engineering industries and in some cases technicians' posts are identified with maintenance and

the commercial and administrative jobs as well as technical posts
are identified with administrative and planning responsibilities. Although this is an overly simple approach, it is not inappropriate in
the macroeconomic context.

The proportion represented by the basic groups in the two
occupational branches in the primary sector is exceedingly high, at
995 and 948 per thousand, respectively, but in the secondary sector
it varies between 136 (beverages) and 704 (wood and cork). The two
at the bottom of the scale (beverages and textiles) have high rates
(391 and 398) under the category of "miscellaneous," in which many
unskilled workers are included. In the tertiary sector the proportion
of the basic groups varies between 655 per thousand (art, entertainment, and sports) and 953 (insurance), if one leaves out the untypical,
extreme case of private care (337). Except for the beverages industry
(up 4), there was a downward trend in the proportion represented by
the basic groups in all branches of the primary and secondary sectors
for which reliable data exist. Even in the beverages industry the trend
was irregular, because an 8 per thousand increase in 1941-50 was
followed by a 4 per thousand decline in 1950-60. The extent of the
fall in the secondary sector ranged from 13 per thousand (wood and
cork) to 155 (clocks and watches and jewelry). In the tertiary sector
the basic group increased in proportion in all five of the branches for
which reliable figures are available.

While the proportion of commercial and administrative posts
remained quite negligible in the primary sector, it ranged between
30 per thousand (building) and 243 (chemical industry) in the secondary
sector in 1960. In the tertiary sector a distinction has to be made
between two types of economic branch: those in which commercial
and administrative occupations form the basic group or one of them
and those in which this is not the case. Among the former the proportion varied between 617 per thousand (general public administration,
law, and national defense) and 953 (insurance), whereas among the
latter the range was between 12 per thousand (hotels and restaurants)
and 364 (private care). Details regarding changes in the proportions
represented by commercial and administrative occupations must be
treated with a certain amount of caution because the 1960 census
obviously included under this heading some occupations that had
previously been grouped under "miscellaneous." This does not in
any way invalidate the resulting trend as such, which is perfectly
clear, since all economic groups show increasing proportions in the
commercial and administrative occupations, apart from a few exceptions without any significance. The situation is clearest of all in the
secondary sector, the solitary exception being the beverages industry
(down 3 per thousand). The increases in the sector range from 5 per
thousand (printing trades and stone and earthenware) to 78 (foodstuffs).

Technical jobs are also seen to play a growing role in most of the occupational groups. Their proportion grows in 21 out of the 27 groups for which reliable data exist, while there is a very slight decline in 4 of the groups, and even there in technical auxiliary trades only (beverages; clothing and footwear; hotels and restaurants; and domestic service). Increases in the secondary sector range between 2 per thousand (mining and quarrying; wood and cork; and printing) and 67 per thousand (chemicals). The chemical industry also comes near the top in the absolute proportion of technical posts (135 per thousand), being second only to the electricity, gas, and water group (262 per thousand). High rates are also found in mechanical and electrical engineering (98), building (90), and the metal trades (52); technical jobs are still of little or no significance in other secondary groups.

Clear trends may also be seen through changes in the proportion of occupations in the metal trades and mechanical and electrical engineering among the total work force in the various groups. While the proportion of such jobs in the primary sector continues to be negligible, the rate shows an increase in 13 of the secondary groups; in 2 of them (beverages and rubber) there is a decline amounting to 5 per thousand, in the chemical industry the proportion remains stationary, and for the group "other industries and handicrafts" no reliable data are available. A special situation is noted in the metal trades industry and in machinery and instrument manufacturing, in which this occupational group (metal trades, mechanical and electrical engineering) is also the basic one; in consistency with the trend of a relative decline in secondary basic groups the proportion of jobs in these two occupational groups in the metal trades industry falls by 80 per thousand and in machinery and instrument manufacturing by 75 per thousand. In the tertiary economic groups, in which these occupations are of no significance at all, the proportion is also marked by a universal rise (trade up 13 per thousand; transport up 49 per thousand; general public administration, law, and national defense up 21 per thousand; and education and science up 6 per thousand). The absolute level of jobs relating to the metal trades and to mechanical and electrical engineering in secondary economic groups, leaving aside the two industries in which they are the basic occupational groups, ranges between 4 per thousand (clothing and footwear) and 400 per thousand (electricity, gas, and water); others with high rates and watchmaking and jewelry (83) and chemicals (61). In the tertiary sector this occupational group represents a fair-sized proportion in transport (81 per thousand); general public administration, law, and national defense (49); and trade (25).

To summarize, it may be said that the hypothesis advanced in regard to the pattern of individual occupations with special reference to the secondary sector is corroborated by empirical investigation:

the proportion of production jobs is declining in favor of maintenance
and administrative and planning posts.

FOREIGN MANPOWER

Among the numerous publications on the subject of foreign
manpower,[3] a specifically sociological survey will be considered
first. A brief summary of the hypothesis it advances and of its empirical examination will be attempted on the basis of a secondary statistical analysis, the material in question coming from official statistical
sources.[4]

From the theory underlying this survey, which cannot be considered here in any further detail, the hypothesis is drawn that in the
case of Switzerland immigration·must lead to stratification of the
receiving system. "Stratification means that foreigners mostly enter
the lowest positions on the social ladder (and form a new infrastratum
beneath the infrastratum of the national population) . . . "[5] The principal consequences of immigration may be described as follows:
changes in the social structure, social prejudice on the part of the
national population, discrimination against immigrants, and problems
of assimilations. Tension is to be expected among the immigrants in
the infrastratum, among the infrastratum of the national population,
and in the lower to middle midstratum, whereas the upper midstratum
and the superstratum are least affected. This stratification provides
greater opportunities for upward mobility to the national population.
The above hypotheses will be examined in the light of a secondary
statistical analysis of Swiss census data for the period 1930-60. As
a preliminary to this, it is useful to review the changes in the foreign
resident population of Switzerland between 1888 and 1967 in Table 11.

The first point revealed by the table is that the foreign population
peak in the mid-1960s is not unique, because a similar peak was
reached before World War I, although the composition differed in
nationality and social strata. The publication in 1909 of a book entitled
A Genevese Problem: The Assimilation of Foreigners shows that
certain matters of present-day concern were just as topical at that
time, too.[6] Table 12 shows how the proportion of foreigners in the
total labor force varied between 1930 and 1960. The table reflects
the sharp increase in the proportion of foreign labor since 1941; after
1960 the increase continued, leading to the introduction of measures
in the mid-1960s to restrain the foreign influx.

Hans-Joachim Hoffmann-Novotny and Jean-Pierre Hoby engage
in a detailed examination of the foreign labor force in terms of the
occupational positions described at the beginning of this chapter.
Here, only two comprehensive tables will be reproduced and the

TABLE 11

Proportion of Foreigners in Population, 1888-1967

| | Foreign Population | |
Year	Absolute (thousands)	Proportion of Total Population (per thousand)
1888	230	79
1900	383	116
1910	552	147
1920	402	104
1930	356	87
1941	224	53
1950	285	61
1960	585	108
1966	860	144
1967	890	148

Source: Das Problem der ausländischen Arbeitskräfte (Bern, 1964), p. 12; and reports of the Federal Justice and Police Department, as quoted in Hans-Joachim Hoffmann-Novotny and Jean-Pierre Hoby, "Structural Consequences of Immigration into Switzerland," paper presented at annual meeting of Swiss Sociological Society (Zurich, November 1968), p. 2. (Mimeo.)

most important findings and conclusions quoted. Tables 13 and 14 immediately confirm the hypothesis of stratification: the proportion of foreigners among unskilled workers was 390 per thousand in 1060, and their proportion among the skilled and semiskilled was 253; both of these figures had risen sharply as compared with 1930. This meant that Swiss people, the actual number and the proportion of whom declined in these categories, were able to fill the jobs created largely as a result of expansion and of structural changes in technology and organization in the category of subordinate employees (see also the first section of this chapter). The actual increase in the number of Swiss in these categories amounted to 257,263 over the whole period, as against a fall of 62,854 in the number of Swiss production workers. Although the stratification theory is wholly borne out by these figures, there is also a striking proportion of foreigners in senior technical posts. This point will be returned to later.

As substantiation for these points, observe the following quote from Hoffmann-Novotny and Hoby:

Although the Swiss in the labor force increased by about
358,000 between 1930 and 1960 the number of Swiss in the
production worker category fell by some 63,000. Even
among the unskilled the number of Swiss fell by about
24,000. In contrast to the category of semiskilled and
skilled workers, where the decline in the number of Swiss
became even more marked between 1950 and 1960, the
proportion of Swiss among unskilled workers continued
to decline even though the actual number rose by about
20,000. This suggests that a minority remained unaf-
fected by the mobility of Swiss manpower resulting from
immigration. But if the increase in the numbers of unskilled Swiss workers is taken separately for men and
for women it is seen that women account for 75 percent.
The obvious conclusion is that from the sociological point
of view immigrants are not the only ones suffering from
discrimination. Stratification of the existing system thus
concerns immigrant labor to by far the largest extent,
Swiss women coming next but in much smaller numbers,
and then Swiss men to a minimal extent.[7]

The stratification theory is further borne out by the following figures:

The foreign manpower increase between 1950 and 1960
took place in the production worker category to the extent
of 91.2 percent, and medium-level or higher posts accounted for only 8.8 percent. This compares with an

TABLE 12

Total Labor Force and Proportion Foreign, 1930-60

Year	Total Labor Force	Swiss Proportion		Foreign Proportion	
		Absolute	Per Thousand	Absolute	Per Thousand
1930	1,942,626	1,732,436	892	210,190	108
1941	1,992,487	1,878,591	943	113,896	57
1950	2,155,656	1,980,265	919	175,391	81
1960	2,512,411	2,090,828	832	421,583	168

Source: Hans-Joachim Hoffmann-Novotny and Jean-Pierre Hoby,
"Structural Consequences of Immigration into Switzerland," paper
presented at annual meeting of Swiss Sociological Society, November
1968 (mimeo.), p. 13.

TABLE 13

Distribution of Swiss and Foreigners, by Occupation,
1960, and Changes as Compared with 1930
(per thousand)

Occupation	Swiss Proportion	Change from 1930 to 1960	Foreign Proportion	Change from 1930 to 1960
Director	901	− 15	99	+ 15
Other senior personnel	923	+ 26	77	− 26
Senior technical personnel	792	− 101	208	+ 101
Other subordinate personnel	932	+ 18	68	− 18
Subordinate technical personnel	907	+ 6	93	− 6
Skilled and semiskilled production worker	747	− 121	253	+ 121
Unskilled production worker	610	− 268	390	+ 268

Source: Hans-Joachim Hoffmann-Novotny and Jean-Pierre
Hoby, "Structural Consequences of Immigration into Switzerland,"
paper presented at annual meeting of Swiss Sociological Society,
November 1968 (mimeo.), p. 29.

increase of 131,084 in the number of Swiss in medium-
level and higher posts between 1950 and 1960, when the
total number of Swiss in the labor force rose by 110,563.[8]

The situation in regard to technical staff in particular suggests that
"the Swiss educational system may not be able to cope with the expansion of the intermediate structure demanded by the spread of the
lower structure" and that "the Swiss potential may no longer be enough
to cover the expansion of higher posts if greater demands are placed
on the instrumental requirements for promotion."[9] These observations
are here considered to be somewhat one-sided because they should be
related to the number of foreign students educated in Switzerland as
well as to the "brain drain." Unfortunately, it would take too long to
examine this point in the present context.

A final quotation, taken this time from the report of the committee of experts appointed by the Federal Council, confirms a supposition

put forward in the first section of this chapter on the basis of this body's investigations:

> The employment of foreign manpower has implanted a
> number of specific characteristics in the Swiss economy's
> production machinery. There are reasons to believe that
> in the long run most of these characteristics will not work
> out to the advantage of our economy's competitive capacity.
> In Switzerland many of the changes in industrial and com-
> mercial structure that are normal for a highly industrialized
> economy have taken place with considerable delay, if at all.
>   Had there not been the foreign manpower available,
> there would probably have been a greater degree of con-
> centration and selection by efficiency among firms in
> industries hampered by structural shortcomings. This
> has meant that firms have been able to keep going despite
> low levels of profitability. For financial reasons many
> such firms have been unable to rationalize their operations
> to an adequate extent, so that their productivity is insuffi-
> cient by present standards. In economic terms this means
> that the labor input needed to produce a given quantity of
> goods is greater than it should be.
>   Thanks to their foreign manpower many firms that
> would otherwise have been edged out owing to lack of
> rationalization potential or capital have been able to re-
> main in production. Productivity has suffered, and eco-
> nomically desirable structural changes have been delayed
> or ruled out altogether.

TABLE 14

Increases of Swiss and Foreigners in Labor Force,
by Occupation, 1930-60

| | Absolute increase from 1930 to 1960 | | |
Occupation	Total	Swiss	Foreign
Director and senior personnel	+ 50,812	+ 45,025	+ 5,787
Subordinate personnel	+273,415	+257,263	+ 16,152
Production worker	+145,202	- 62,854	+ 208,056

Source: Hans-Joachim Hoffmann-Novotny and Jean-Pierre Hoby, "Structural Consequences of Immigration into Switzerland," paper presented at annual meeting of Swiss Sociological Society, November 1968 (mimeo.), p. 30.

Everything indicates that our economy has failed to introduce labor-saving methods to the extent it would have done in the absence of foreign labor.[10]

THE EFFECTS OF RATIONALIZATION* AND AUTOMATION ON THE STRUCTURE OF THE LABOR FORCE

The changes in the Swiss labor force examined in the first section of this chapter are partly attributable to rationalization and even to automation. But as shown in the second section the mass influx of foreign workers, largely in the unskilled categories, has also tended to retard rationalization and automation. Before going on to forecast what may follow, in this section the focus will be on what has emerged from investigations into the effects of rationalization and automation on the labor force structure. It is virtually impossible to encompass all of the literature on the subject, and here mention is made of only a small selection of important and representative titles that could be repeated many times over.[11] Further observations are based extensively on a summary of results so far forthcoming from research on the subject, produced by a Swiss scholar Urs Jaeggi, who has himself worked in this field.[12]

Jaeggi defines automation in the following terms:

In production it means processes guided and controlled by electronic means; in offices it means processes of calculation and evaluation conducted by electronic equipment and mainly covering the operations that frequently occur on a large scale. The final target is integral data processing covering the whole enterprise, transcending and dismantling the barriers between planning, production, and administration.[13]

He describes the effects of the first phases of automation on manpower in the various categories as follows:[14]

1. Unskilled workers: In the vast majority of rationalized work places the proportion of unskilled, i.e., auxiliary, workers in the work force has clearly declined. This is most marked when the

---

*In a narrow sense, rationalization comprises all measures aiming at better organization of work except automation. In its broad sense, it also includes automation.

introduction of multifunctional machines is accompanied by rationalization in the firm's organization.

2. Semiskilled workers: In contrast to the unskilled, the proportion of semiskilled grades has increased in practically all of the examples considered.[15] The heaviest increase occurred where manual operations were almost completely eliminated and major sections of the manufacturing process were made self-operating. The same is true of offices.

3. Skilled workers: The proportion of specialized workers shows a decline everywhere in regard to the direct production sphere. The decline is sharpest where automation of the production process and the relegation of manual jobs to a marginal position are accompanied by the introduction of an electronically guided plant; but the proportion also falls considerably where the changeover to multifunctional machines is connected with only partial automation of the production process. The distinction between qualifications based on apprenticeship and experience, respectively, is often discarded. The main direction in which skilled workers have held their own is in providing a reserve of qualified people for training as foremen and medium-level supervisors. In actual production there is only one group for which occupational requirements have increased—maintenance and repair specialists. The more highly differentiated their work, the greater the need for specialized high-level skills.

4. Administration and salaried employees: Here new jobs are developing as a result of automation (particularly systems analyst, programmer, tabulator, operator, and computer card puncher). To do these jobs a considerable amount of abstract thinking, imagination, and creative spirit is required. There has been a change in structure in that medium-level salaried employees in particular have become less important: their work has been simplified to such an extent that it has been taken over by semiskilled staff without any difficulty. This trend seems likely to continue; two groups will emerge—the highly skilled and those with medium-level skills—and sooner or later it will become necessary to differentiate in their training.

Demands in the sphere of production have developed along the following broad lines. Observation, which replaces active intervention, generally entails greater nervous strain but demands less occupational ability. What counts most is rapid reaction. Generally speaking there is less call for physical and muscular effort. This means that mental and nervous tension increases because (a) the working tempo becomes more rapid; (b) continuous production processes generally demand greater vigilance and concentration; (c) responsibility may be greater, owing to the high cost of the modern plant and the consequences that a breakdown at any point would have for the successive work processes; and (d) in modern processes the uniform pattern of working may produce greater nervous strain. The effects that the changes described here will have no training are discussed in the section on educational demands consequent to social development.

PROSPECTS AND ALTERNATIVES

Alternatives in Production Potential

What has been said in the three preceding sections points to three basic alternative courses of development in the future, of which one already seems largely a foregone conclusion.

The first alternative would consist of further mainly expansive economic growth (whereas plenty of examples of intensive growth exist today), with technological innovation substantially neglected and productivity therefore stagnant. It would involve a continued heavy influx of foreign labor.

The second alternative, which is still a theoretical possibility, would consist of a combination of a voluntary or involuntary decline in the influx of foreign manpower with failure to keep up with technological innovation. It would result in economic contraction or stagnation.

The third alternative would consist of a changeover from expansive to intensive growth, with rising productivity. It would imply accelerated technological innovation and an increase in the labor force's fund of knowledge and skill and would make it possible to manage without any increase in the volume of foreign manpower.

The following comments show that the choice is to a large extent already decided in favor of the third of these alternatives, which is clearly the most desirable one. The first one is out of the question as far as the immediate future is concerned, in view of the political decisions that have already been taken with the aim of stabilizing the volume of foreign manpower. Even assuming one were to consider such a likelihood desirable, the possibility of drawing the necessary numbers of workers from the previous sources of supply seems highly doubtful in view of the economic development of Italy, which supplies the bulk of Switzerland's foreign manpower, as well as trends within the rest of the European Economic Community (EEC). Even if they were successful, attempts to recruit labor from more distant countries would probably exacerbate the tension between the Swiss and the foreign population because of the greater cultural gap that would then have to be overcome. The second alternative, involving economic stagnation,

is ruled out as a deliberate policy because economic growth is one of
the declared aims of Swiss economic policy.*

The third alternative appears to be the most desirable one both
in view of the decisions already taken in regard to the stabilization of
foreign manpower and in view of the partial introduction or completion
of technological innovation (although it cannot remain complete for
long, with the shortening of intervals between successive rounds of
innovation or even the advent of a continous process in which it is
barely possible to distinguish separate phases). If this path is followed
deliberately its implications must be recognized. Requirements in the
field of education will be briefly discussed later, but it may already
be said here that such signs as the promotion of universities, the
increase in the numbers of technical schools, and the move for reform
regarding apprenticeable trades mean that the third alternative has
really been chosen already. Apart from its implications for education
the second corollary of choosing the third alternative is the need to
revise attitudes to foreign workers. This would involve abolishing
any discrimination and permitting the assimilation of those so desiring.[16]
Unless attitudes are thus changed greater tension is to be expected.

Future Development of Labor Potential

The Working Group on Long-Range Projections headed by F.
Kneschaurek, which was commissioned by the Federal Council in
1968 to produce a study on Switzerland with projections up to the year
2000 covering all major aspects of economic life, predicts that the
manpower shortage will continue for the rest of this century and will
probably grow more acute. This will be due essentially to the interplay
of the following three factors: the growth rate of foreign manpower
will fall to 0, perhaps even taking a negative turn; assuming the same
employment rates as hitherto, the growth rate of Swiss manpower will
tend to decline in the coming decades; and, as thus far is evident, the
conditions of demand will not alter to any radical extent by the end of
the century.[17] According to this trend in supply and demand it is only
natural to expect a continued surplus demand for manpower, resulting
in a general shortage of labor.

In considering the problems relating to the future skill structure
of the labor force two separate surveys arrive at different results.

---

*It is nevertheless clear from the relative success in the early
1970s of the new political groups, the National Action and the Republican
Movement, that large numbers of people are beginning to regard the
rate of economic growth as a menace.

Are imbalances to be expected in regard to the skill structure between labor supply and demand? In particular, is overqualification a problem that calls for serious attention? After thoroughly examining the need for trained staff and the demand for education, the Working Group on Long-Range Projections established the outline of a quantitative education survey for the year 2000 reproduced in Table 15. The Working Group comments on this education survey as follows:

> Except for the primary and secondary schools, where com-
> pulsory schooling regulations mean that the need for trained
> persons is identical to the demand for education, the growth
> rate of the need for trained persons is considerably higher
> at all levels of education than that of demand for education.
> The actual figures are less important than the general
> tendency they reflect, which is for the shortage of skills
> to become increasingly pronounced. There can be no
> question whatsoever of any danger of a surplus in the next
> few decades. This is equally true of persons completing
> an apprenticeship and of graduates, whether in medicine,
> arts or the natural and technical sciences.[18]

This utter rejection of any possibility that a surplus of graduates or qualified technicians might occur does not agree with the findings of the Basel Working Group on Educational and Manpower Research, whose structural survey of the total forecast labor force in 1980 is summarized here. The supply of persons with no more than primary schooling will correspond fairly closely to requirements. There will be a shortfall at the secondary school level (13.8 percent below demand) and at the intermediate school level (11.2 percent below demand). But a surplus may be expected among those completing studies at a higher technical college, amounting to 48.2 percent over demand. There will be a similar surplus (46.2 percent) among university graduates.[19]

The model study by the Basel Working Group had a pretty unfavorable reception; the fact that it was a model (which the authors themselves emphasized) was used as an argument to deny any validity to the figures it presented. This is not the place for a critical appraisal of the methods of quantitative educational planning; it is reasonable to wonder, however, to what extent the first of these investigations was favored and the other prejudiced by considerations alien to strictly scientific evaluation, such as current preferences and politicians' justified feelings that nothing must be allowed to hold back the expansion of universities, while failing to allow for all of the relevant factors, including those outside the realm of economics and therefore beyond the scope of either of the investigations. It is equally natural to wonder whether the whole approach to educational planning in terms of

TABLE 15

Quantitative Education Survey, by Qualification Grades, for the Year 2000

School	Number Studying, According to Demand for Education			Number Studying, According to Demand for Trained Staff		
	1970	2000	Percent Increase 1970–2000	1970	2000	Percent Increase 1970–2000
Primary schools, including higher primary schools[a]	625,000	720,000	15	625,000	720,000	15
Secondary and lower intermediate schools, including terminal classes, but without higher primary schools[a]	160,000	230,000	44	160,000	230,000	44
Vocational training	129,000	150,000	16	129,000	190,000	47
Teacher training colleges	11,000	13,500	22	11,000	19,000	65
Higher intermediate schools	66,000	86,000	30	66,000	130,000	100
Technical colleges	8,000	11,000[c]	38	8,000	20,000	150[d]
Higher business and administration colleges	(500)	8,500[c]	–	(500)	10,000[b]	–
Universities	41,800	75,500	80	41,800	85,000	103[d]

[a]This comes within the compulsory nine-year schooling, hence no divergence between pupil supply and demand.

[b]No growth rate is calculated, since this type of school was in its initial stages in 1970.

[c]Average of the two hypotheses established.

[d]Assumes that the development of technical colleges and higher business and administration colleges can be accelerated. Otherwise universities would have to fill the gap and would have to be expanded more rapidly.

Source: F. Kneschaurek, "Problems of Occupational Entry in Switzerland—Some Results of Education Projections until the Year 2000," Mitteilungsblatt des schweizerischer Wissenschaftsrates, V, 3 (Bern, 1971), 19.

manpower demand is not misconceived and whether it would not be more appropriate to examine the possible effects of a higher average level of education, which is desirable for noneconomic reasons, on the organization of employment. (Economic grounds can then reinforce the noneconomic ones, or even at a certain point, vice versa.)

It is to be hoped that these forecasts will give rise to considerable public debate. The structural imbalances predicted by the Basel Working Group would only become a serious matter if substitution between manpower of different levels of education were impossible and the economy were incapable of adjusting to some extent to the manpower supply.

These problems cannot be explored further here, but with regard to prospective social analysis one important point must be underscored. If the existing system is continued unchanged (i.e., assuming that levels of qualification and diplomas, degrees, and so on are not altered, which is true for the traditional forecasts of manpower requirements) and if purely economic needs are taken into consideration to the exclusion of all others, the possibility of overqualification does not seem to be entirely ruled out in the relatively near future. It may thus be necessary to anticipate a surplus of highly qualified people. There will no longer be any guarantee for the right (moral, not legal) to a job corresponding to level of education. This right will come in conflict with the right to education (meaning the right to an education corresponding as closely as possible to the individual's abilities). This problem calls for very special attention. Changes at the work place that are liable to result from codetermination in relations between management and labor (a general rise in educational levels for all the workers) as well as the transformation of the present school and education system into a system of lifelong education might perhaps help to solve this problem.

THE PARTIES' ATTITUDES TOWARD THE EMPLOYER-EMPLOYEE RELATIONSHIP AND THE DIFFERENT FORMS OF CODETERMINATION

The parties have expressed the following attitudes to the relationship between employer and employee and to the various forms of codetermination.*

---

*The initiative on codetermination introduced by three trade unions in August 1971 is described in the Chapter 9.

KCVP:
    "The legal status of employees in undertakings and firms also
needs to be extended. Factory councils and workers' committees
should play a more significant role; the right of participation within
the enterprise should be laid down by means of comprehensive provisions in general collective agreements and so shaped as to become a
new and essential component of Swiss labor law."

Free Democratic Party:
    "The party seeks industrial peace and endorses efforts to extend
and consolidate contractual establishment of employment conditions
based on negotiating equality, subject to the maintenance of freedom
of association."

SPS:
    "The immediate social aims of the Social Democratic Party of
Switzerland are . . . to safeguard human dignity within the economy
. . . to protect the working man through the extension of labor law . . .
To attain these goals the following lines of action are of primary
importance: . . .
        Extension of the workers' right of dialogue and codetermina-
        tion should reshape the relationship between employees and
        employers by guaranteeing equality of rights. Equality of
        opportunity must be sought for all in regard to development
        and promotion . . . "

Evangelical People's Party:
    "Collaboration should be sought between employees and employers.
General collective agreements and their universal application should
be promoted."

PdA:
    "The Labor Party demands the right of codetermination for
wage earners and salaried employees in undertakings, both public and
private."

EDUCATIONAL DEMANDS ARISING OUT OF
THE DEVELOPMENT OF SOCIETY

The Parties' Values and Aims

The parties have made the following statements on education.

KCVP:
"Scientific, research, and educational policy in keeping with the
times is now an urgent necessity; the promotion of new talent among
production workers, handicraft workers, farm workers, salesmen,
technicians, artists, and scientists is of primary concern."

"Greater attention must be devoted to the coordination of educational
facilities at all levels, to adult education, and to the education of girls."

"It is vital that radio and television should be more fully directed
toward the further cultural education of young people."

Free Democratic Party
"Free-minded Swiss people have therefore always striven
energetically to secure the consistent promotion of vocational training
at all levels and the provision of equal educational opportunity for all
talented persons."

"The party's demands: Promotion of general education and of
scientific and technological research. Easier access to technical
colleges and universities for talented young persons, with expanded
scholarship facilities. Providing the Swiss economy and the teaching
faculties of our universities with new generations of scientists. Support
for efforts to provide further training for school dropouts. Promotion
of vocational guidance and training. Provision of thoroughly trained
and competent new employees for the Swiss economy . . . "

"As a democratic entity our State is founded on the conviction
that its destiny depends to a considerable extent on the standard of
education of its citizens. Provision of equal educational opportunities
for all talented persons, irrespective of their financial situation, has
always been one of the principal concerns of the liberal federal state."

SPS:
"The principle that every young person should be enabled to
obtain the training corresponding to his abilities should be incorporated
into the Constitution."

"The SPS proposes . . . the creation of public educational facilities for adults . . . Such facilities should permit primarily:
completion of secondary studies
extensive promotion of nonvocational further education
vocational further education
reintegration in occupational life for all persons obliged
to change occupations and for persons obliged to give
up occupational activity for a certain time, and in
particular women."

BGB:
"The Party demands that schools of all grades and levels should
provide education in the spirit of patriotism and supply sound and

specific knowledge, but also awaken appreciation of work, inculcate
a serious-minded attitude to duty, and cultivate an understanding of
service to one's fellows. . . . It recognizes the principle that access
to higher vocational training and academic study should be determined
exclusively by objective ability and personal suitability. For this
purpose it supports the generous encouragement of talented young
persons by means of scholarships."

"The 'right to education' must be open to all sectors of the
population not only in theory but in practice as well. The encouragement of talent must therefore also cover the more remote parts of
our country in particular."

"One of the first tasks is to increase measures to promote
initial and advanced vocational training, and the lines of action laid
down in the new Vocational Training Act should be fully implemented.
Particular attention should be devoted to interoccupational manager
training. The BGB demands that public promotional action should not
place vocational and technical training at any disadvantage as compared
with academic education."

LdU:

"Education must determine the individual's abilities and fully
develop them; its purpose is not simply to supply skill and knowledge.
The family must bear a greater responsibility in education and vocational training. Valuable private efforts in the field of education and
advanced training should be supported by the State."

"The development of science, technology, and the economy
obliges humans to engage in lifelong education . . . Continuous education is in the interests of the individual and of national self-assertion
. . . Every Swiss citizen is entitled to an education corresponding to
his abilities . . . The federal and cantonal authorities should collabo-
rate closely in encouraging talent and ensure that our Swiss reserve
of talent is used to the full . . . The schools should provide education
and sound knowledge and shape the characters of young persons . . .
Facilities should be provided for the second path of education leading
to readiness for university study. Adult education should be strongly
encouraged through collaboration between the State and private
organizations."

Liberal Democratic Citizens' Party:

"The problem of training the elite is of immediate significance.
No one denies the absolute need to train new managers. It is of vital
importance for the future of our economy."

Evangelical People's Party:

"The Party puts emphasis on the task of upbringing and character
formation by the school . . . and on promotion of adult education . . . "

PdA:
    "Young people are entitled to complete education and thorough
vocational training, the importance of which is constantly growing
with the rapid progress of technology. It is essential first of all for
secondary and advanced education to be democratized, that is to say,
made accessible to all. Knowledge, ability, and diligence must be the
only criteria for admission."

Educational Demands Resulting from Developments in Social Subsectors

    The following observations might equally well be applicable to
the chapters on free time, on political participation, or on the family
or to the codetermination variant in the chapter on property and ownership of industry. Their purpose is to collect under one heading and in
their broad outlines the educational demands that result from developments in the various social subsectors. The intention is to show how
important education is (the parties' statements and recent, although
still largely embryonic, trends in Switzerland reveal that a large part
of public opinion has become aware of this necessity) and that one-
sided conceptions of the function of education do not come to grips
with the complexity of the situation.
    The educational demands arising from the following sources
are briefly described below: technological changes and the consequent
transformation of economic requirements, political participation and
the functioning of democracy, use of leisure time, the preparation of
parents for their educational function, possible rights of codetermination for the workers, and the demand for equality of opportunity.
    It has already been seen in the first part of this chapter how
technological innovation during the period 1941-60 actually affected
the skills and occupational structure of the labor force. One of the
main demands for the future arising out of the acceleration of technological change may be formulated as follows: The function of basic
training lies less in conveying specialized knowledge supposed to be
valid for all time than in developing the ability to adapt oneself and
to assimilate new knowledge. Jean Fourastié writes in this connection:

    The school children of today will be in the prime of life in
    1995. It is out of the question to try teaching them today
    what they will need to know in 1995; it is impossible because
    we do not know ourselves what they will need to know.
    What must be done is to give the people who will be living
    and working in 1995 the ability to do so, by providing them
    with the means of learning whatever they need in a process

of permanent further education. We must give them a
general technical and vocational education that can serve
as the basis for regular further learning.

This means that what is needed in the first place is not so much
special vocational training as broad, all-around vocational training.[20]
(Regarding Switzerland, it is stated in international comparisons that
in view of the relatively small number of apprenticeable trades this
demand is at least partly satisfied in certain occupations.) The graduated training plans are also aimed at achieving greater elasticity in
vocational training. Apprenticeship under the graduated training
system no longer leads to a uniform final examination and can be
concluded at different levels without any need for deciding on the
final level at the outset.

In regard to Switzerland, P. Steinmann stresses the importance
of a broad basic training and general education for apprentices and
comes to the conclusion that "it should be possible to arrive at a
combined approach: basic theoretical and practical training given in
the first instance in a full-time vocational school, followed by special-
ization in industry or crafts, with a session at a full-time school each
year."[21]

But the need for constant adjustment to technological innovation
does not place demands on basic training alone. The future importance
of lifelong further occupational training and retraining can scarcely be
overestimated. An expert report prepared on behalf of the German
Economic Rationalization Institute concluded that as a result of technological evolution one in four employees would have to change his place
of work (not to be confused with his position) or his occupation by 1970.
This lends urgency to the need for the appropriate retraining facilities.

Whereas retraining will continue to predominate in the first
phase, it will come to be superseded more and more by permanent
further training. Here again the necessary facilities will have to be
made available. (Evening courses do not always provide the answer
because they tend to cause excessive fatigue and dropout rates are
often very high.) One possibility that has considerable prospects
consists of paid or unpaid educational leave.[22]

Educational demands arise not only in respect to the economic
sphere but also in connection with political participation, or in other
words the functioning of democracy. In various parts of this book it
is shown that the political activity of the population is declining, and
in some cases the reasons for this are mentioned. One cause, even
if probably not the most important, consists of the growing complexity
of circumstances, which means that the citizen has to determine his
attitude to increasingly difficult factual matters. Greater knowledge
and education will contribute to a better understanding of these matters.

This means that the educational solution to the problem of declining popular participation in democratic life cannot be sought merely in a greater degree of civic instruction, important as this is. What is needed is to enable the citizen by means of his initial and lifelong education (which calls for the appropriate institutions) to visualize and understand complex social and economic processes.

Chapter 7 refers to the change in the significance of labor in human existence as a result of industrial division of labor. It is pointed out that this has caused most production workers' and white-collar workers' center of interest to shift to areas outside their employment. Free time must offer more relaxation and leisure. If free time is not to become a matter of largely passive consumption with the danger of new problems, people must also be prepared for creative use of their leisure and be supported in such efforts. The schools can contribute to this aim by increasing their promotion of creative abilities and cultural interests.

Yet another area involving educational demands relates to the upbringing of children. Without suggesting that the best approach is for the child's mother or father to hold a manual of psychology in their left hand and a diaper in their right, there can be no doubting that greater knowledge of children's development can be useful. As will be pointed out in Chapter 6, the upbringing of children has gone far beyond its natural bounds as a result of the dissolution of the extended family, the need to prepare children for their adaptation to a still unknown world and the fact that mothers are frequently gainfully occupied. This means that parents are in greater need of being specially prepared for their educational function themselves.

In Chapter 9 greater opportunities for workers' participation are mentioned as one of the possible lines of future development. It is obvious that codetermination is possible only when one knows something about the subject to be decided. Educational requirements in this connection jibe largely with those advanced in regard to concern for the functioning of democracy. From the point of view of social development the demand for equality of educational opportunity must be supported as well.[23] This demand is also advanced by all of the political parties' programs.

Chapter 6 refers to the importance of institutions for preschool children, one of the aims being to reduce cultural inequalities before schooling begins. The main differences existing at present in regard to educational opportunity are by region, by social class, and by sex.

Thus the requirements that emerge for a future educational system from the evolution of society and its values, as investigated in the various chapters of this study, are as follows:[24]

greater flexibility in the educational system (also seen in connection with manpower requirements);

an all-around basic training that can permit continuous
     adjustment and the acquisition of new knowledge, in
     view of the rapid advance of technology;
permanent education and training, in view of the rapid
     advance of technology;
a school system built on the principles of democracy and
     participation;
extended preparation for the function of parenthood;
lifelong education to help to give meaning and content to
     the longer duration of old age;
the dual necessity of preschool education, first, as, a
     means of creating equality of opportunity upon school
     entrance and of ensuring the best possible development
     of children (with the possibility of partial integration of
     different forms of parent training), and, second, as a
     means of fulfilling the needs of working mothers;
the educational system should contribute to attainment of
     new freedom for the individual through a choice of
     alternatives enabling the individual to develop his whole
     range of talents;
adaption of the educational system to the fact that the
     traditional life stages of training, occupational activity,
     and retirement are more and more interwoven.
education and training should contribute to leisure activi-
     ties through both method and content;
an educational system not restricted by geographic
     circumstances;
a general rise in the average standard of education—
     especially economic and social knowledge—in the event
     of the codetermination variant and in regard to the
     working of democracy;
eradication of discriminatory differences between boys
     and girls that are still incorporated in numerous school
     programs;
assimilation of cantonal school systems;
fullfilment of the growing social demand for education to
     be anticipated as a result of higher per capita incomes
     and the changing situation of the child within the family;
a way of fulfilling the legitimate social demand for educa-
     tion while avoiding the danger of overqualification (as
     measured in terms of the present system);
an increase in the number and forms of occupational
     reintegration courses for women;
the technical possibility of decentralizing the process of
     learning while centralizing the process of teaching; and
adjustment of living accommodations to the possibilities
     of decentralized study.

5

THE PARTIES' VALUES AND AIMS

KCVP:

"The legal situation of women should be redefined, in regard both to public and to private law."

"Female suffrage should be introduced through cantonal effort as a demand of the times".

Free Democratic Party:

"The party demands: greater participation by women in shaping public life."

"We call for the introduction of general female suffrage in municipal, cantonal, and federal matters and the promotion of equality of rights for women."

SPS:

"Equal wages should be paid for equal performance by men and women."

"But our democracy is incomplete without legal equality between the sexes. Political rights must not continue to be withheld from women. Truly equal rights still need to be established in the other fields of life. The work of housewives and mothers should be valued just as highly as men's occupational activities."

"Since the beginning of the twentieth century the role of women in social life has altered radically. Discrimination of all kinds must be eliminated, whether in the family, in education, or in economic and cultural life."

"The SPS demands:

1. the general introduction of female suffrage at federal, cantonal, and municipal levels;

    2. the revision of family law so as to provide for complete
       equality before the law between men and women;

    3. promotion of study by girls with the appropriate
       abilities;

    4. equal wages for equal performance (starting with the
       public administration);

    5. equal opportunities for promotion;

    6. protection of women part-time workers and home-
       workers against certain crass forms of exploitation."

BGB:
    "The party favors increased participation by women in public
affairs, especially in the church, the schools, and social welfare."

LdU:
    "Swiss men appreciate the advice of their womenfolk, whose
feelings often enable them to judge more accurately than men. Women
are a balancing factor in political and economic affairs and should
therefore be encouraged to play a fuller role in public life than
hitherto."

    "Women must be given the right to vote on municipal, cantonal,
and federal questions as soon as possible, since this is a fundamental
human right. It is equally important to improve women's education,
economic situation, and legal protection and to alleviate mothers'
duties."

PdA:
    "The party calls on all women to fight to win their rights, for
all women, whatever their social origin, their cultural background, or
their political beliefs, suffer from their present condition. It is
enough to think of family law, based on the dependence and inferiority
of women, and education and vocational training, which are still marked
by inequality of treatment between the sexes, to realize that a major
struggle is needed in order to secure for women the same living
conditions and the same opportunities for development as are enjoyed
by men."

    This survey of the parties' aims shows that all without exception
regard the present-day social situation of women as unsatisfactory
and therefore propose a certain number of changes. These proposals
all run in the same direction, namely toward increased participation
by women in matters outside the home. But then the various parties'
proposals stop short at certain points on the way toward the final goal
of complete legal and practical equality for women in all spheres.
Some press for fuller participation by women "especially in the church,

the schools, and public affairs," while others stress—and here again
to differing degrees—political equality for women without expressly
calling for a change in the economic situation of women. There are
also some parties that specifically demand total equality of rights and
situation for women in all spheres.

Changes in the social role of women will also be examined from
a number of angles in Chapter 6 (on the family). The present chapter
will concentrate on the legal situation of women (i.e., suffrage), the
education of women, and girls and female labor.

THE LEGAL POSITION OF WOMEN

Equality of rights between the sexes is specified as a fundamental
provision in international human rights conventions, but federal suffrage
was not extended to women in Switzerland until 1971. The introduction
of female suffrage was the subject of a federal referendum on February
1, 1959, in which the voter turnout was 66.7 percent (the highest figure
for a considerable time). The initiative was rejected by 654,939 to
323,727 votes, a ratio of two to one.[1] Three French-speaking cantons,
Geneva, Neuchâtel, and Vaud, had a majority in favor, and women's
suffrage was subsequently introduced in those cantons. The first
German-speaking canton to follow was Basel. Since then the cantons
have dealt with the subject in various ways, and the proportion of
votes against to votes in favor has been steadily shifting toward the
latter. Finally, and much sooner than many observers had expected,
women were granted political rights in federal matters. In the referendum of February 7, 1971, female suffrage was accepted by 621,403 to
323,596, with a voter turnout of 57%. This meant a complete change
of attitude on the question in a lapse of 12 years: the two-thirds
majority against was replaced by a two-thirds majority in favor. By
canton, $15\frac{1}{2}$ approved the initiative and $6\frac{1}{2}$ rejected it. In descending
order of the proportion of negative votes the rejecting cantons were
Appenzell IR, Uri, Appenzell OR, Glarus, Schwyz, Thurgau, St. Gallen,
Obwalden. The highest proportion of votes against was recorded in
Appenzell IR (71.19 percent), and the highest proportion in favor in
Geneva (91.07 percent).

EDUCATION OF GIRLS AND WOMEN

This section uses a comparison between cantons to show differences in education based on primary school curricula and a comparison in time to show that, although the general level of education
of both sexes is steadily rising, there remain substantial differences
between men's and women's attainments.

Differences in the Education of
Boys and Girls

In view of the frequently inadequate vocational training of girls
and the relatively small number of female university students, the Federation of Swiss Women's Associations carried out an inquiry to find out
whether this situation was not at least partly due to differences in the
education of boys and girls that are already present at primary school
level.[2] The inquiry related to the primary school curricula in force
in all cantons in 1965. The most important results may be summarized
as follows. In 22 cantons the duration of compulsory school attendance
is the same for boys and girls (seven years in 5 cantons, eight years
in 12, and nine years in 5). In the remaining 3 cantons it is one year
more for boys (eight years for boys and seven for girls in 2 cantons,
and nine and eight in 1). Although the compulsory school period is
generally the same for boys and girls, there are some quite considerable differences in curricula, as illustrated by Table 16.

In roughly two-thirds of the cantons there are differences and
sometimes quite considerable ones in the number of class hours for
boys and girls in such basic subjects as native language, mathematics,
and science. These differences are of course partly offset through
hours for girls in specifically "female subjects." A glance at two
more subjects shows that technical draftsmanship is taught to boys (80
to 160 hours) in eight cantons but is not compulsory for girls in a

TABLE 16

Differences in Primary School Curricula
for Boys and Girls

Subject	Class Hours for Boys and Girls		Range of Difference in Hours to Disadvantage of Girls (throughout Schooling)
	Number of Cantons in Which Same	Number of Cantons in Which Different	
Mathematics	7	14	20 to 480
Science	7	15	20 to 180
Native language	5	16	40 to 660

Source: Federation of Swiss Women's Associations, Foundation
for Research into Women's Employment, Erhebung über die Lehrpläne
in den Volksschulen (mimeo.: Zurich, 1967).

single canton and that geometry is taught to boys in nine cantons but
to girls in only one. In that one canton the hours for boys number
140 and for girls 120. In secondary school programs (or, using
internationally standardized terminology to avoid differences arising
through variation in cantonal practices, in the first cycle of the
secondary school degree*) hours of tuition for boys and girls in
chemistry are the same in only eight cantons and in physics in only
five.

These differences obviously result in inequality with regard to
admission to places of advanced education. They also show that schools
still conceive the training of boys and girls to be to a large extent for
quite different roles. The report by the Federation of Swiss Women's
Associations draws the conclusion that for the sake of equality and
justice, and also in order to provide the necessary trained manpower,
the cantonal school authorities should overhaul their curricula.

Marion Janjic refers to another possible institutional reason for
differences in the education and careers of boys and girls.[3] Vocational
guidance services are cantonal, and in many of the cantons they have
separate branches for boys and girls. It would be interesting to find
out how far this institutionalized separation of vocational guidance for
boys and girls tends to preserve stereotyped views regarding what
are held to be typical boys' or girls' jobs.

The Educational Level of
Three Generations of Men and Women

The 1960 census was the first to ascertain the last school
attended, and the answers permit interesting comparisons concerning
the educational levels of different generations living in 1960. Three
generations were selected—those 25-29, 45-49, and 65 and over in
1960. These generations were born, respectively, in 1931-35, in 1911-15,
and before 1895; their school years therefore came in the 1940s, 1920s,
or around 1900. The Federal Statistical Office used the following
categories in classifying answers to the question concerning the last
full-time school attended: primary school, lower intermediate school,
upper intermediate school, technical school, and university. In addition, there were the categories "others, level unknown," "no school,"
and "no indication." It must be emphasized that the question related
to the last full-time school attended and not the most recent finishing

---

*The Federal Statistical Office uses the term "lower intermediate
school."

certificate obtained. This means that those who did and those who
did not obtain a finishing certificate at any particular level of schooling
are lumped together.

Table 17 calls for a further brief explanation. In principle, it
relates to people who are no longer attending a school, and this led to
some complication for those between 25 and 29 in comparing the figures
for the different groups because this category contains a fair number
of people who are still at university and a certain number still attending a technical college. Therefore, the 25-29 age group was counted
twice over: the first time only those no longer attending any educational
establishment were counted; the second time university and technical
college students were added. In this second accounting it was not
possible to distinguish between men and women, however. The table
points to differences in the educational and training levels of men and
women as they have evolved over a period of time. But it also reveals
the rise in the general level of education of the Swiss population in the
course of the century.

The table shows that the proportion who went only to primary
school fell from 646 per thousand in the older generation to 568
in the middle generation, and 481 (or 476) in the younger generation.
The rates for all other degrees rose; they were, respectively, 169,
232, and 265 (or 263) for those ending at the lower intermediate level;
41, 51, and 68 (or 67) for those ending at the upper intermediate level;
6, 9, and 13 (or 14) for those who attended technical college; and 19,
26, and 24 (or 32) for those with university education. There is thus
a general steady rise in the proportion going to higher levels and a
consequent rise in the general standard of education. Nonetheless,
over half of the younger generation had an education that did not go
beyond the primary level. This clearly proves the trend toward
higher education; at various places in this study it will be shown why
this trend will continue in the future.

Turning now to consider the differences in schooling between
males and females over this period of time, it can be seen that at the
primary level the proportion of males is regularly below average and
that of females above; for all other levels except upper intermediate
the proportion is reversed. For those finishing with primary school
the difference between males and females in the older generation is
still 56 per thousand; it falls to 42 in the middle generation and down
to 19 in the younger generation. This means that in this respect the
differences between males and females are becoming less; and the
proportion of those attending only primary school is falling faster
among females. For the lower intermediate level the relationship
remains fairly stable: the proportions of males and females rise by
roughly the same extent, so that the difference also stays about the
same (rising from 30 to 33 and 34). There has been an interesting

shift at the upper intermediate level: whereas there was still a difference of 3 per thousand in the older generation for males, this is turned into a 7 per thousand difference for females in the middle generation, which grows to 15 per thousand in the younger generation. In other words, the proportion of females who go to an upper intermediate school but no further is growing more rapidly than the proportion of males.

Girls who carry on beyond primary school therefore go to an increasing extent to one of the types of school at the upper intermediate level. For technical schools the situation is quite simple: the proportion of girls has always been negligible (far less than 1 per thousand in each of the generations). One is reminded of primary school curricula, although this is only one of many factors, and it is clear that this situation need not necessarily exist. At the university level the vital figures for the younger generation are lacking; from the older to the middle generation the difference rose from 36 to 37 per thousand, although the intake of females doubled. It remains to be examined whether the proportions of men and women among university students have grown at roughly the same rates in recent times or whether there has been a change in the difference to one side or the other. In absolute figures, in the winter semester 1970-71 there were only 6,740 female Swiss university students as compared to 25,969 males.[4]

To summarize the situation, it may be said that, with a general rise in the level of education, differences in schooling nevertheless remain between males and females. Except in the case of those who do not get beyond primary school, these differences are tending to diminish. Regarding education for females after the minimum school dropout age, the various types of upper intermediate school are becoming increasingly important, whereas the technical schools remain virtually closed to girls and the great majority at universities are still male. Some comments on the way in which these trends may continue in the future are made at the end of this chapter.

THE WORKING WOMAN

This section deals with the trends to be noted in the various forms of gainful activity performed by women, drawing largely on the statistics prepared by Käthe Biske on the basis of census returns.[5] The following section will then attempt to summarize the various factors at play, to appraise their future weight, and to advance some forecasts.

Table 18 shows the trends in rates of female employment and the proportion of women in the labor force over the period from 1888 to 1960.

TABLE 17

Persons No Longer Attending School, by Three Selected Age Groups,
Sex, and Last School Attended, 1960

Age	Number of Persons			Last Full-Time School Attended											
				Primary			Lower Intermediate			Upper Intermediate			Technical		
	Total	M	F	Total	M	F	Total	M	F	Total	M	F	Total	M	F
Total Number															
25-29	303,975	144,099	159,876	146,188	67,827	78,361	80,578	40,786	39,792	20,688	8,706	11,982	3,819	3,745	74
25-29*	307,100			146,188	–	–	80,578	–	–	20,688	–	–	4,222	–	62
45-49	318,890	153,543	165,347	181,121	83,881	97,240	73,891	38,166	35,725	16,261	7,270	8,991	2,742	2,680	62
65 and over	523,374	218,719	304,655	337,920	134,089	203,831	88,252	40,745	47,507	21,457	9,315	12,142	2,970	2,939	31
Per Thousand															
25-29				481	471	490	265	283	249	68	60	75	13	26	<1
25-29*				476	–	–	263	–	–	67	–	–	14	–	–
45-49				568	546	588	232	249	216	51	47	54	9	17	<1
65 and over				646	613	669	169	186	156	41	43	40	6	13	<1

Last Full-Time School Attended

Age	University			Others, Level Unknown			No School			No Indication		
	Total	M	F	Total	M	F	Total	M	F	Total	M	F
	Total Number											
25-29	7,126	5,707	1,419	36,920	13,528	23,392	361	194	167	8,295	3,606	4,689
25-29*	9,848	–	–	36,920	–	–	361	–	–	8,295	–	–
45-49	8,223	6,837	1,386	23,437	8,883	14,554	347	183	164	12,868	5,643	7,225
65 and over	9,976	8,793	1,183	23,981	8,512	15,469	834	348	486	37,984	13,978	24,006
	Per Thousand											
25-29	24	40	9	121	94	146	1	1	1	27	25	29
25-29*	32	–	–	120	–	–	1	–	–	27	–	–
45-49	26	45	8	73	58	88	1	1	1	40	37	44
65 and over	19	40	4	46	39	51	1	2	1	72	64	79

*Persons no longer attending school plus present technical school and university students of this age group.

Source: Federal Statistical Office, Eidgenössische Volkszählung December 1, 1960, Vol. 27, "Switzerland," Pt. I, pp. 186-87 and pp. 180-81.

TABLE 18

Rates of Female Employment and Proportion
of Women in Labor Force, 1888-1960

Year	Gainfully employed women in the age group 15-64 (per thousand)	Number of Women per Thousand Gainfully Employed Persons
1888	427*	333
1900	427*	320
1910	469	339
1920	446	339
1930	401	315
1941	355	286
1950	371	297
1960	396	301

*15-69 years.

Source: Käthe Biske, "Women's Work in Occupation and Household," Zürcher Statistische Nachrichten (Zurich), XLIV, 3 (1968), 128.

The table shows that the rate of female employment rose at the end of the last century and reached its peak in 1910, with 469 per thousand. It then began to decline, slowly at first and then faster, reaching the lowest point of 355 per thousand in 1941. The decline since 1910 is probably due to the combination of greater frequency of marriage (see Chapter 3), with increased opportunity for wives to remain at home because of higher per capita incomes, and to an even greater extent the falling demand for unskilled labor as a result of economic crisis and the subsequent mechanization, especially in the textile industry and later in the clothing industry as well. An additional factor consisted of

> the age shift in the population, with a lower proportion of the younger ones who normally account for the heaviest rates of employment and a lower proportion of the older ones, who do not normally account for such a volume of employment . . . The decline in the number of home-workers, who were still very numerous at the beginning of the century, also tended in the same direction.[6]

The fact that the employment rate rose again after 1941 is put down to increased labor demand and, from 1950, to some extent to the employment of immigrant labor. The proportion of foreigners in the female labor force in Switzerland stood at 161 per thousand in 1910, a time when a particularly large number of foreign women were employed—145 in 1950 and 200 in 1960. Since then the proportion has risen further.

The proportion of women in the total labor force followed a parallel development to the female employment rate, with its peak in 1910 and its lowest point in 1941, since which time it has risen slightly. Roughly speaking, women account for just about one-third of the Swiss labor force.

Table 19 shows the distribution of working women by age group in the period from 1930 to 1960. The table shows that the peak of the female employment rate lies in the age group 20-24. It then drops sharply in the 25-29 group (clearly in connection with marriage) and declines more slowly after that; in 1960 it rose again in the 50-59 group and dropped after that. "The assumption that married women are resuming employment in larger numbers once they have completed their family obligations is not confirmed at the national level, at least as far as 1960 is concerned."[7] It will be pointed out later on, however, that married women are more frequently taking on part-time employment in middle age. In time comparison the striking features are the

TABLE 19

Gainfully Employed Women,
by Age Group, 1930, 1950, and 1960
(per thousand)

Age Group	1930	1950	1960
Under 15	5	2	17
15 to 19	630	640	632
20 to 24	675	676	699
25 to 29	451	408	432
30 to 39	314	278	311
40 to 49	281	283	300
50 to 59	261	278	307
60 to 64	236	238	254
65 to 69	207	173	173
70 and over	132	86	74
Total	290	262	274

Source: Käthe Biske, "Women's Work in Occupation and Household," Zürcher Statistische Nachrichten, XLIV, 3 (Zurich, 1968), 139.

rise in the employment rate in the 50-59 age group (from 261 per thousand in 1930 to 307 per thousand in 1960) and to a lesser extent in the 60-64 group. Among the 65-69 group, and even more among those 70 or over, the decline is certainly due to the old-age and survivors' insurance system.

Table 20 shows changes in women's employment rates by marital status for the period from 1930 to 1960. The table shows that single and divorced women have high employment rates, whereas married and widowed women have low rates. Since 1941 the female employment rate has increased in all of these categories except for widowed. The decline in the rate for widows since 1950 is certainly due to the institution of survivors' insurance. The increase in the rate for married women from 88 per thousand in 1941 to 160 in 1960 is very striking.

Table 21 is compiled from Biske's material to show female employment rates by qualification. Since the overall employment rate for the 15-64 age group was found to be 39.6 percent in 1960, the table shows that the rate for women with occupational qualifications is above the average. Within this category of women the rate of employment rises with the level of qualification. This appears to be a generally valid trend (the same was found in the United States).[8] This relationship will be returned to later on. Concerning the proportion of those with qualifications who are actually using them, Biske notes that, of the 164,800 women with acquired skills and gainfully employed (that is to say, not counting the women with university degrees

TABLE 20

Female Employment Rates, by Marital Status, 1930-60
(per thousand)

| Year | Gainfully Employed Women as Proportion of Female Population Age 15 and over | | | |
	Single	Married	Widowed	Divorced
1930	698	116	295	616
1941	666	88	246	615
1950	721	103	247	672
1960	726	160	222	688

Source: Käthe Biske, "Women's Work in Occupation and Household," Zürcher Statistische Nachrichten, XLIV, 3 (Zurich 1968), 139.

TABLE 21

Number of Women Employed and Employment Rates,
by Degree of Qualification, 1960

Degree of Qualification	Total	Number of Women Gainfully Employed Persons	
		Absolute	Percent
University degree	10,800	5,700	53
Technical or intermediate level diploma	59,600	29,900	50
Other acquired qualifications	375,400	164,800	44
Total of women with acquired qualifications	445,800	200,400	45

Note: Column 1 (Total) shows total number of women with given qualifications. Column 2 (Gainfully Employed; absolute Numbers) shows absolute number of women employed with given qualifications. Column 3 (Gainfully Employed Percentage) shows percentage of women employed with given qualifications (Column 2 as a percentage of Column 1).

Source: Käthe Biske, "Women's Work in Occupation and House-hold," Zürcher Statistische Nachrichten, XLIV (Zurich 1968), 205.

and technical or intermediate-level diplomas), a good two-thirds (112,200 or 68 percent) are employed in the jobs they have learned, whereas less than one-third (52,700 or 32 percent) are performing some other work.[9]

Table 22 gives the proportion of women in the total labor force in cities with over 30,000 inhabitants. The table shows that, with one exception, the proportion of women in the total labor force lies above the Swiss average in all of the cities considered, and sometimes well above. The solitary exception is Winterthur, and this is probably due to the city's particular economic structure. The generally greater importance of female employment in the cities is due, among other things, to the fact that certain tertiary branches (especially commerce, banking, and insurance) are concentrated mainly in the cities.

By including only women working at least half-time, the table fails to do justice to farmers' wives in some ways, because for statistical purposes they are normally counted as family members working part-time. Later, the importance of women's part-time work in agriculture will be mentioned. Looking into the future one must

TABLE 22

Proportion of Women in Labor Force of Cities
over 30,000, 1960

City	Population	Proportion of Women per Thousand Employed Persons*
Zurich	440,170	367
Basel	206,746	355
Geneva	176,183	393
Bern	163,172	364
Lausanne	126,328	367
Winterthur	80,352	286
St. Gallen	76,279	391
Lucerne	67,433	359
Biel	59,216	340
La Chaux-de- Fonds	38,906	364
Neuchâtel	33,430	370
Fribourg	32,583	370
Schaffhausen	30,904	315
Total for Switzerland	5,429,061	301

*Persons in half- or full-time employment (20 or more hours
per week).

Source: Käthe Biske, "Women's Work in Occupation and Household," Zürcher Statistische Nachrichten, XLIV (Zurich 1968), 138.

expect the importance of agriculture and consequently the role of
farmers' wives working on a part-time basis to continue to decline
as a whole. It must again be pointed out that the assistance provided
by farmers' wives and the full-time employment of women outside the
home have a completely different sociological significance.

Gainful Employment of Mothers

In 1960 there were some 345,100 families in Switzerland in
which there were children under age 7. In these families 26,400 or
8 percent of the mothers were gainfully employed.[10] According to
a survey held in Geneva, 11.5 percent of the children under school

age (0-6 years) had employed mothers, whereas there were places in
nurseries for only one-sixth of these children.[11] Thus, five out of
six working mothers with children under school age had to find some
other arrangement for looking after them.

Biske made the following observations:

> The younger the wife and the smaller the number of
> children in their care the larger was the proportion of
> working mothers. In one-child families the proportion of
> working mothers under age 20 was over 17 percent, for
> those between 20 and 24 it was 15%, and between 25 and 29
> it was 13%. One in ten mothers with a child under age 7
> was employed. In the case of mothers with two children
> it was one in twenty, and for three children one in thirty.
> The proportion of working women with no children was 17%,
> and nearly one in two married women up to age 29 and with-
> out children were employed.[12]

Extending consideration beyond mothers with children of preschool
age, the following factors emerge:

> Out of the 191,700 married women who were employed in
> 1960—including 16,500 separated from their husbands—
> 84,200, or 44%, had no children. Some 77,500, or 41%, had
> one or two children, and 28,600, or 15%, had three or more
> children. These figures relate only to live births from the
> present marriage, but include grown-up or dead children.
> The statistics do not give the precise ages of children, but
> this can be partly deduced from the length of marriage.
> For example, 52,000 mothers, with 85,300 children, had
> been married for less than 15 years. These were there-
> fore children of preschool or school age. But there were
> certainly school children or younger children among the
> 36,200 children of the 15,600 wives who had been married
> between 15 and 19 years. Altogether, the 106,100 working
> mothers had 219,700 children.[13]

Comparing the situation between 1950 and 1960 it is seen that
the number of mothers in half- or full-time employment more than
doubled over that period. "Thus the employment of mothers increased
more rapidly than the overall employment of married women, which
rose by 84%."[14] Adding to the figure of 130,000 mothers in half- or
full-time employment for 1960 (including 21,000 unmarried mothers,
10,000 widows, and 20,000 divorcees), "the estimated figure of 87,000
married women living in the same household as the husband, having

children under age 18 and performing part-time work, as well as
approximately 1,000 widows with children of these ages, the resulting
figure for 1960 is about 218,000 mothers in part-, half-, or full-time
employment."[15] In appraising the sociological aspects of the employment of mothers, the actual figures are obviously not all that matters:

> It makes a great deal of difference if the mother working on
> the family farm can easily keep an eye on her children, if
> she has her own business or studio, or works in her
> husband's shop, or may keep the books for her husband's
> business at home [activities bound to become less common],
> or if on the other hand she works away from home in an
> office, a shop, or a factory . . . Depending on the mother's
> organizing ability as a housewife, her liking and enthusiasm
> for her work, her energy, and the possibility of bringing up
> her children satisfactorily, and even more depending on
> her husband's attitude, her occupational activity will have
> a more or less favorable effect both for herself and for
> the rest of her family.[16]

As will be seen later, the general rate of female employment
may be expected to increase. In regard to the social consequences
a clear distinction should be made between the employment of mothers
with preschool children, of those with school children, and of other
women. If the employment rate of mothers with small children should
increase, adequate provision would have to be made for the necessary
collective facilities in the form of nurseries, kindergartens, midday
meals, and so on. At present, Swiss society is in a transitional stage
in this connection, and, although the model is gradually losing ground,
it is still largely one of the woman and mother whose place is in the
home.* But this model is not in keeping with present trends, so that
the situation is in many respects unsatisfactory.

An international comparative study on the image of women in
society came to the conclusion that three main "models" could be
distinguished: the single woman should work; the married woman
without children or with grown-up children may work; and the married
woman with small children should not work.[17] This pattern is not

_____

*More recently, since about 1970, publicity campaigns by private
employment bureaus have been helping to change this image in view of
the continuing labor shortage. They show young and elegant mothers
who manage to keep their homes impeccable and yet still find time to
increase their families' earnings through part-time work.

easy to bring into harmony with the demand for complete equality in
employment because the duties inherent in motherhood are an obstacle
to normal occupational advancement.

In a study conducted in Vienna in 1955, Leopold Rosenmayr
showed that the economic need to work grows with the number of
children and therefore also with the need for the mother's presence
within the family.[18] The resulting conflict calls for no further
elaboration. (This result does not jibe with Biske's findings for
Switzerland in the 1960s. The difference may be due to the variation
in standards of living.) Also regarding Switzerland, a survey by
Maria-Immita Cornaz has shown that married women's employment
is motivated chiefly by financial reasons (it will be shown how the
motives for married women to seek employment will probably shift
to an increasing extent in the future).[19]

The direct relationship between the husband's income and the
wife's employment is also demonstrated in a recent publication by
the People's Family Movement.[20] The percentage of women who
work varies in accordance with the husband's occupational situation
as follows: wives of wage earners, 34 percent; wives of subordinate
salaried employees, 29 percent; wives of civil servants, 23 percent;
and wives of senior salaried employees, 20 percent. After comparing
the results of inquiries into the living and working conditions of women
in most of the industrialized countries and analyzing the results of
the international time-budget survey (see Chapter 7), France Govaerts
notes that the choice "to work or not to work" really does not exist
for many women and for industrial society as a whole. She writes,

> Rather than consider problems from the opposing points
> of view of home and work, should we not turn toward
> solutions that aim for integration? The basic question is
> this: since women are obliged to assume multiple re-
> sponsibilities as a result of economic and social forces,
> the adaptation of the releveant structures should be tackled
> in such a way as to reconcile the multiple votes of women
> in the most satisfactory manner.[21]

Research since the last war has shown that the lack of maternal
care and presence has a harmful effect on the physical, mental, and
emotional development of infants.[22] Later comparative studies covering various types of nurseries and children's homes as well as the
normal family have confirmed and elaborated upon the pioneer work
done by R. Spitz. The conclusion has been reached that what counts
is not so much the mother's physical presence as the quality of care
and especially of the emotional relationship.[23] Owing to shortage of
staff and cash these conditions are rarely satisfied in an ideal manner

in present-day child-care institutions. The most enlightened solution
at present applied to the problem of the working mother with small
children consists of granting the woman who has been employed for
a minimum qualifying period before having a child compensation for
loss of earnings that will enable her to look after the child herself
for the first $2\frac{1}{2}$ years if she so desires. Systems of this kind exist in
several of the Eastern European countries.[24] In the Western European
countries it appears vital in the present situation to increase the
number of day-care centers, but this must also be combined with
strict public control. In any event, an approach with a broad social
basis is to be preferred to a collection of individual makeshift
arrangements.[25]

But the employment of mothers also raises problems for children
of school age, and no general or systematic solution has yet been
found.[26] Two of these problems relate, respectively, to institutions
for the care of "latchkey children" and to solutions in cases where
the child is slightly ill. Special day-time hospitals for children have
been created for this purpose in England; another method, also applied
in England, consists of having special auxiliaries to look after children
who are slightly ill, at home and by the hour or by the day. The
International Federation of Women in Legal Careers also called for
the creation of these and similar facilities at its annual assembly in
1967. Since then, the same has been urged by the women's liberation
movement in many countries.[27]

A further organizational problem in connection with working
women that has a direct bearing on local and regional planning relates
to the location of shops and their hours of opening. The OECD has
considered the subject important enough to carry out an inquiry in
all of its 21 member states and to issue recommendations.[28]

In contemporary circumstances the working woman's household
jobs are often added to a normal working day. It is interesting to
observe how the new values of partnership and shared leisure (see
chapters 6 and 7) cause an increasing number of husbands to share
in household chores.[29]

The above comments show how much social organization is
designed to fit the image of the man at work and the woman in the
kitchen and how urgently necessary it is to take into account the
conditions of women's employment and the trend toward the nuclear
family in the context of city and country planning. Since women are
directly affected, they should participate in the decision-making
process: "Among the conditions for the adaption of social structures
to development, the participation of women in the decisions that will
guide the actual adaption is of vital importance, because better everyday living standards coincide in many sectors with improvements in
family well-being."[30]

The Shift in Women's Employment

Table 23 shows changes in the distribution of working women among the three economic sectors for the period 1900-60. The table shows that the proportion of women employed in the primary sector has steadily fallen since 1900, while the proportion in the tertiary sector has steadily risen. In the secondary sector there was a decrease in the proportion over the period 1900-41, since which time there has been a slight increase. Except for the fall in the primary sector, which is clearly connected with the absolute and relative decline in agriculture, these figures cover important shifts within the secondary and tertiary sectors between different industries.

In 1900 nearly half of the women employed in the secondary sector (207 out of 432 per thousand) were in the textile industry. Since then the proportion has dropped to 59. In the clothing industry the proportion fell from 148 to 85 per thousand during the same period. But in all other industries more women were employed in 1960 in relation to the total number of women workers than in 1900. The proportion of foreigners among women industrial employees was particularly high, amounting to nearly one-fourth in 1960.[31] As will be seen in connection with the shifts in female employment according to occupation (Table 25), the women who work in the secondary sector (and particularly Swiss women) are more often employed in offices than in factories, as a result of the growing importance of administration.

Within the tertiary sector the most **important** changes consist of the decline in the number of women engaged in domestic service and "other services" from 226 per thousand in 1900 to 138 per thousand

TABLE 23

Distribution of Working Women among
Three Economic Sectors, 1900-60
(per thousand)

Year	Primary	Secondary	Tertiary
1900	162	432	406
1930	84	353	563
1941	53	351	589
1950	47	355	594
1960	30	370	597

Source: Käthe Biske, "Women's Work in Occupation and Household," Zürcher Statistische Nachrichten, XLIV (Zurich 1968), 219.

in 1960 and the increase in the number of women employed in commerce, banking, and insurance from 51 to 197 per thousand. By and large the housemaid has already been replaced by the typist, and the trend will continue to increase. Another substantial increase has taken place in employment in hospitals—from 12 per thousand in 1900 to 72 per thousand in 1960. Small increases are to be observed in all other tertiary branches.

Women's Employment, by Individual Occupation

Table 24 shows the occupations in which women were most heavily represented in 1960. The table indicates that there is considerable concentration in a small number of occupations because eight occupations together account for over half of female employment. (Incidentally, the same sort of concentration is also to be observed among men.[32]) The greatest number are to be found in office jobs, accounting for 156 per thousand, whereas domestic servants still come second despite the long-term decrease in their total number.

Table 25 shows the trends in female occupations. The occupations expanding most rapidly are in the tertiary sector or in departments

TABLE 24

Leading Female Occupations, 1960

Occupation	Number of Women Employed	
	Absolute	Per Thousand
Office employee	118,021	156
Domestic servant	84,791	112
Sales assistant	74,887	99
Seamstress	24,734	33
Waitress	24,670	33
Nurse	22,190	29
Farmer	18,979	25
Teacher	18,523	25
Subtotal	386,795	512
Other occupation	369,623	488
Total Female workers	756,418	1,000

Source: Käthe Biske, "Women's Work in Occupation and Household," Zürcher Statistische Nachrichten, XLIV, 4 (Zurich 1968), 195.

of firms coming under the secondary sector that are not directly
engaged in production. These occupations also often call for a
technical or scientific bent (draftswoman, laboratory assistant,
dispenser) or artistic leanings (designer, window dresser, florist).
Moreover, the seven most popular occupations all involve skilled
training.

There are also some academic occupations among those that
are expanding to a fair extent. The ones losing most ground are the
textile and clothing industries, domestic service (although maids are
among those with the greatest stability of employment), and agriculture.
These are generally unskilled occupations or at best jobs that can be
learned by means of experience. Occupations with a normal to stagnant
growth rate include kindergarten teachers, nurses, bookkeepers,
packers, ironers, and waitresses.

Part-Time Employment of Women

With regard to full-time and part-time employment Biske
distinguishes between the following three categories: employed full-
time in principal occupation, 30 or more hours per week; employed
part-time in principal occupation, 20-29 hours per week; and employed
part-time in subsidiary occupation, less than 20 hours per week. The
significance of part-time employment in absolute terms is shown by
the following figures: in 1960 there were about 188,200 women in
part-time employment, 722,500 women were employed in a principal
occupation full-time, and 929,000 women devoted their time exclusively to their households. It must be assumed, however, that
part-time employment of women is incompletely covered by statistics.
The largest group among the total of 188,200 part-time women workers
consists of the 144,800 housewives with a subsidiary occupation
amounting to less than 20 hours per week. The next largest group
is made up of the 33,900 women in a principal occupation but not
working full-time: these are mainly sales assistants and office staff
working half-days amounting to 20-29 hours per week.[33]
The breakdown of occupations by marital status is presented
in Table 26. The Table shows the following: (a) the vast majority
of unmarried and divorced women are fully employed in a principal
occupation; (b) part-time work is of importance mainly for widows
and married women; (c) about three-fourths of married women are
engaged exclusively in their own households; and (d) one women in
ten pursues part-time employment, and a good half of all women are
housewives only. Among the housewives in part-time jobs the greatest
number is in the 40-49 age group. Although the rates of activity are
lower in the 50-59 and the 30-39 age groups, part-time employment
is still widespread among them.[34]

TABLE 25

Trends in Selected Female Occupations, 1941-60

Occupation	Index Figures	
	1950 (1941=100)	1960 (1950=100)
Draughtswoman, designer	165	300
Window dresser	257	264
Laboratory assistant	181	235
Florist	120	211
Dispenser	154	203
Hairdresser	94	176
Gardener	162	175
Landlady	92	170
Storekeeper	140	167
Office employee	150	161
Hotel or restaurant keeper	100	160
Upholsteress	222	159
Lawyer	138	159
Telephone operator	122	154
Barmaid	149	150
Photographer	123	149
Secondary school teacher	108	147
Pharmacist	158	147
Dentist	113	144
Sales assistant	139	142
Garment adjuster	148	140
Electric coil winder	225	138
Primary teacher	104	134
Cashier	128	133
Physician	138	133
Welfare officer	172	132
Vocational instructor	105	130
Nurse	109	127
Kindergaten teacher	116	127
Bookkeeper	146	124

Occupation	Index Figures	
	1950 (1941=100)	1960 (1950=100)
Packer	116	120
Ironer	114	115
Waitress	107	109
Dental technician	91	102
Traveling saleswoman	139	101
Domestic servant	107	91
Tobacco processor	80	88
Midwife	96	86
Seamstress	76	83
Cook	88	82
Chambermaid	82	81
Weaving loom operator	103	79
Precious stone modeler	118	77
Agricultural employee	57	75
Farmer	103	73
Housekeeper	57	75
Cleaning woman	94	71
Spinning loom operator	117	70
Knitter	92	67
Ribbon weaving operator	107	67
Yarnmaker	104	66
Lingerie seamstress	88	63
Dressmaker	59	61
Hawker	56	49
All employed women, including other occupations	112	118

Source: Käthe Biske, "Women's Work in Occupation and Household," Zürcher Statistische Nachrichten, XLIV (Zurich 1968), 193.

TABLE 26

Principal Female Occupation, Part-Time Work,
and Household Duties, 1960
(per thousand)

Marital Status	Employed Full-Time	Employed Part-Time	Housewives
Spinster	920	38	42
Married	151	125	724
Widowed	415	155	430
Divorced	825	87	88
All women	393	102	505

Source: Käthe Biske, "Women's Work in Occupation and Household," Zürcher Statistische Nachrichten, XLIV (Zurich 1968), 126.

Part-time employment of women by branch of activity is presented in Table 27. The table shows that nearly half of the women performing part-time work are in agriculture; they may be assumed in practically all cases to be the wives of farmers who help on the family farm. Liselotte Schucan-Grob has investigated the question of part-time employment for female university graduates in Switzerland, and the OECD has also produced a comprehensive study on the whole subject.[35]

Reintegration of Women in
Occupational Activity

It has been illustrated that the employment rate of women declines with marriage and that the view of the majority is still that the mothers of infants should not go out to work because their presence is needed to ensure the most harmonious mental development of the child. Reference has also been made to an alternative that would aim for a considerable expansion of service facilities for working mothers and for their children of preschool and school age. But once the children have reached some degree of independence or are grown up, the mother remaining in a house from which the children have gone may want to resume employment. At present the acute demand for manpower has the effect of making employers more flexible in their attitudes toward the reinstatement of women who have given up their jobs for family reasons, but it seems likely in the long term that other

TABLE 27

Part-Time Female Workers,
by Occupational Group, 1960

Occupational Group	Part-Time Female Workers	
	Absolute	Per Thousand
Agriculture	72,639	444
Industry and handicrafts	26,889	164
Commerce, banking, insurance	12,155	74
Transport	2,401	15
Hotels and restaurants	9,713	99
Other services	25,405	155
Hospitals	392	2
No indication of group	13,208	81
Other	951	6
All part-time female workers	163,753	1,000

Source: Käthe Biske, "Women's Work in Occupation and House-hold," Zürcher Statistische Nachrichten, XLIV (Zurich 1968), 229.

factors will be more important in finding a positive solution to the problem of women wanting to return to employment. Under the influence of the forces moving toward complete equality, the higher standards of education, and the higher vocational qualifications of women, the already disintegrating image of the woman in the kitchen will continue to fade and gradually be replaced by the image of the woman participating fully in life outside the home and thereby in economic events as well.

A study carried out by the Evangelical Women's Association of Switzerland already points to trends in this direction.[36] It is stated in the introduction to this study that the initiators had recognized through their contacts with large numbers of women that the contemporary housewife no longer has a full work load in the second half of her life and is therefore frequently dissatisfied. A survey conducted by the Foundation for Research into Female Employment in 1961-62 showed that occupational associations were fairly uninterested in mothers with older children.[37] In connection with the study carried out by the Evangelical Women's Association, a pilot course was organized to examine whether there was a need to resume

occupational activity, whether the experience gained from marriage
and family life could be used for occupational purposes, and what
opportunities were open to women to resume employment; the initiators
of the study arranged for the return of applicants to suitable jobs.
This pilot course was restricted to 22 women in the Zurich area,
however, and it only covered occupations in the service sector.

It was revealed that women had little knowledge of contemporary
economic conditions, and there were few opportunites for married
women to update their occupational know-how. (Exceptions consist of
schools for social activities and the large banks that make refresher
courses one of the functions of their training centers.) Husbands were
generally unfavorably disposed toward their wives' return to employment but often changed their attitudes subsequently. In many cases
it was found that the fact that the wife again had an interesting job to
perform had a positive effect on family life. Older employers were
often opposed to employing married women, but those who agreed to
do so were satisfied with the results, and it was also found possible
to reach a successful solution for organizational problems involved
in the part-time employment of women. An essential condition for
satisfaction on the part of women employees was that commuting
distances should be neither too long nor too complicated. Otherwise,
the input in terms of time, effort, and money was out of proportion
to hours of work and efficiency. It was confirmed that women performing responsible jobs laid greater store on return to employment
than did the others. There was a general demand for meaningful
activity, but in the generation now in their 40s it was often obscured
by prejudices, worry, inhibitions, and uncertainty. This situation
should change, however, as the image of women evolves, and it may
be assumed that the demand for resumption of occupational activity
will set the tone for the future.

Differences in Remuneration
between Women and Men

Switzerland has not yet ratified the International Labor
Organization's convention concerning equal remuneration for men
and women for equal work (final approval is expected in 1972). There
are in fact considerable differences in wage rates for men and women,
even when the work performed is of equal value. Trends in average
hourly earnings of men and women industrial employees are illustrated
in Table 28. This comparison of wages for male and female employees
is not wholly satisfactory because no distinction is made between the
categories of skilled, semiskilled, and unskilled among women. But
even if all women employees are assumed to be unskilled (which is

TABLE 28

Average Hourly Earnings of Industrial
Employees, 1939-70
(in centimes)

Year	Skilled and Semi-skilled Males	Unskilled Males	Skilled Semiskilled and Unskilled Females	Column 3 per Thousand of Column 2	Column 3 per Thousand of Column 1
1939	140	108	73	676	521
1954	293	245	180	735	614
1966	563	485	336	693	596
1969	686	581	404	695	589
1970	738	631	439	696	595

Source: Statistisches Jahrbuch der Schweiz, 1971, pp. 368-69.

obviously not so) there are substantial differences to be seen in all
four years. The difference diminished between 1939 and 1954 but increased between 1954 and 1969.

A slightly different view of the long-range trend is obtained by
comparing movements in the index of average hourly earnings of the
various categories of employees since 1913 (1913 = 100). In 1969 the
index for skilled and semiskilled men stood at 1,025 and for unskilled
men at 1,211, whereas the figure for women was 1,348 and for young
people under age 18 1,026, resulting in an average index of 1,154.[38]
Over the 56-year period covered there was chiefly a narrowing in the
differences between the wages of skilled and semiskilled male and
female workers in all grades, and to a lesser extent between the respective wages of unskilled male workers and female workers in all
grades.

An inquiry into the wages of men and women teachers shows that
in 1965 the principle of equal wages for equal work was fully applied
in only six cantons.[39] The fact that wages in occupations to which
women have only recently gained access (e.g., the police force and
public transport) are generally the same for men and women seems
to point to increasing recognition of the equal wages principle.

A FORECAST OF TRENDS

Now that women have acquired equality of political rights, the
advance toward economic equality may be expected to increase in

speed.[40] Factors having a positive effect on the rate of female employment and likely to contribute to a further change in the image typifying the situation of women include the higher level of education and of vocational qualifications, the advance of urbanization, and, above all, the spread of rationalization, mechanization, and perhaps even the partial automation of housework. Concerning the return of married women to employment in the second half of their lives, the rising life expectancy is a further factor. In combination, all of these factors will reinforce the desire for return to employment. This of course presupposes prior cessation of occupational activity, which is only one of the possible variants regarding changes in the rate of female employment by age and marital status. There are three possible alternatives in this connection.

The first of these variants corresponds to the situation as of 1960, described at the beginning of this chapter. The peak of female employment lies between the ages of 20 and 24, after which comes a considerable decline due to marriage, with only a very slight rise at around the age of 50.

The second variant consists of cessation of occupational activity during the upbringing of children and the subsequent return to employment. The female employment rate thus has two peaks, one before marriage and one after the completion of children's upbringing. The major implications of this alternative have already been discussed in the section on working mothers.

In the third variant the mother does not cease her gainful activity (except, of course, for a longish period before and after childbirth); the employment rate remains at a constant high level. This variant would entail appropriate expansion of social facilities for mother and child.

The second and third of these variants concern hypotheses that are hardly likely to occur in pure form. The individual decision on the part of mothers whether to work or not will depend on a host of personal factors, so that the most likely probability is a combination of the two in varying degrees.

Concerning demand, the increasing tertiarization of the economy will stimulate the employment of women because many skilled women's jobs come within the tertiary sector. In the long range it will probably become less and less common to talk about women's jobs as such. Areas of employment that are still practically closed to women will open up, and the general decline in physically strenuous activities due to automation will also contribute to this occupational assimilation of women.

Reference must be made finally to an additional factor in the female employment rate that can be freely manipulated and is therefore a useful political instrument for the attainment of whatever effects are desired—fiscal legislation. At present, many women are deterred from going out to work because of the rule applying in many places that a married couple's incomes are added together for tax purposes, which frequently means a considerable jump up the progressive ladder. This attitude cannot be adopted by women in the least well-off classes, who are often obliged to add to their husbands' earnings, whatever the tax situation may be. In view of high rents and the frequent necessity of owning a car in order to get to work, the combining of married couples' incomes for tax purposes may prove a socially unjust measure when the woman really has no choice whether to work or not. In Belgium, for example, similar tax regulations seem to encourage tax evasion, or clandestine employment of women.

In summary, it can be said, on the basis of the previous trends and the aims expressed by the political parties, that a further change in social practice may be expected, leading to the complete emancipation of women.

CHAPTER

6

THE FAMILY

THE PARTIES' VALUES AND AIMS

<u>KCVP</u>:
"Reinforcement of the moral and economic foundations of the family remains the first concern of the conservative Christian social policy. Its aim is to establish a social law of the family. Federal legislation on family allowances for employees should provide an effective means of raising allowances in respect to children, families, and households in the cantons and occupational groups and of achieving a proper balance at a level in keeping with the times. Fiscal policy must give greater consideration to the family. Housing construction should be better adapted to family requirements. Insurance, namely the various branches of social insurance and private insurance arrangements, must take family demands into consideration. The right of parents in regard to education and schooling must be respected."

"The modernization of essential elements in private law should reinforce the unity of the family in its legal aspects as well. Matrimonial property rights, the rights of illegitimate children, the system of guardianship and the rights of women workers should be adapted to present-day social and ethical concepts."

<u>Free Democratic Party</u>:
"The party's demands: protection of the family as the foundation of society and state; support for all efforts aimed at the cultural and moral promotion of the family; promotion of economic measures for protection of the family; provision of accommodation through private initiative and where necessary through public support; introduction of ownership of housing; just fiscal consideration for family responsibilities through the provision of adequate family and social allowances;

adjustment of social insurance benefits to family responsibilities; provision of family allowances (primarily on the basis of the firm or the occupation or, if absolutely essential, on the basis of the canton) in accordance with earnings; promotion of all efforts to lighten the burden of mothers of large families."

SPS:
    "The immediate social aims of the Social Democratic Party of Switzerland are . . . protection of the family . . ."
    "In connection with the promotion of housing construction the needs of large families must be taken into consideration."
    "The family, as the natural shelter for the child, should be effectively supported in its educational functions."
    "Federal social policy should protect every individual against social hardship . . . It serves for the protection and dignity of families . . . the SPS therefore proposes: . . . support for families, particularly by creating the necessary social facilities, day-care centers, and kindergartens, and home help services for sick mothers."

BGB:
    "The BGB supports and encourages the work of the family, the church, and the school in forming attitude and character on the basis of the Christian philosophy."
    "The BGB supports all efforts that it considers appropriate for the maintenance of the family, which has national, moral, and cultural significance in the national community. In this connection it advocates an appropriate balance in favor of families with children through the provision of family allowances; the provision of such allowances is moreover a means of preventing the further loss of the best manpower from mountainous areas."

LdU:
    "The nucleus of any communal attitude is the family. It must again bear the principal responsibility in settling questions of education and welfare. Consequently, the various social insurance and welfare institutions must pass through the family community . . . Healthy family life prospers best in rural family dwellings close to nature."
    "The changes taking place in the world have also affected families and have eliminated the protection offered by kinship. Father and mother, school and church have lost authority."

Evangelical People's Party:
    The party sees foundation of family life to be on the divine demands of love and service. It opposes the destructive powers

threatening marriage and family and supports in legislation and in
legal practice everything that protects marriage and reinforces the
desire to bring up children.

"In addition to remuneration in accordance with work performed,
family allowances should be paid by equalization funds, in order to
avoid harming the competitive ability of employers. This will encourage
the domestic and educational functions of women and mothers, which
are of such importance for society and economy alike."

A glance at the values and aims expressed by the political
parties in regard to the family shows that it is universally recognized
as a fundamental form of human coexistence and therefore deserving
of protection and promotion. Some parties expressly acknowledge
the Christian concept of the family. Economic and legal measures in
the fields of housing and social policy are proposed in order to reinforce the moral, economic, and cultural foundation of the family and
to support it in its educational function. It shall be seen in Chapter 7
how one of the reasons for demanding reduction of hours of work is
that families should be afforded greater opportunity for activity and
leisure together.

The parties' image of the family nevertheless indicates a fairly
static approach, because with one exception there is no recognition
of the fact that the family, and consequently views regarding the family,
are subject to constant evolution. This evolution in relation to a
number of functions of the family shall be considered, taking past
developments together with possible future changes. An analysis of
the way in which the family has developed in different countries shows
that in Western civilization two principal types may be distinguished:
the one corresponds to the rural and handicraft society, whereas the
other corresponds to the urban, industrial society.[1]

THE PEASANT-ARTISAN FAMILY

The family is normally of the extended type. In addition to the
parents and their children, the same household also contains grandparents, unmarried brothers and sisters of the parents, and other
relatives. This is in keeping with the production and welfare function
of this family type: The family members belong to the same production unit, but at the same time the family members who are not yet or
no longer capable of working are also looked after.

The relations between the members of the family are based
principally on the family as a production unit and the various roles in
the production process. The short supply of cash and the uncertainty
of production and selling conditions mean that any sort of innovation

is a risk. Failure in this direction would result in debt and perhaps the dissolution of the extended family. But it would be exceedingly difficult for the individual members of the family then to live on their own, so that respect for tradition becomes a functional value that ensures the survival of the institution. The cardinal virtue instilled in the children is discipline, together with acceptance of the authority of the head of the household. Family solidarity and sense of family are the essential concepts.

Generally speaking, this traditional family lives in a society in which the administrative, political, and economic functions are decentralized. The family is consequently responsible for numerous social functions, such as education and protection in times of sickness and need. The individual, who would barely find it possible to live outside the group, does not regard subjection to the authority of the head of the household as in any way negative, even when he has him-self reached adult years or even married.

Upbringing within this type of family consists primarily of preparing the child from a very early age for his role in the production process. Within the family community the child grows into his pre-destined role. Since social mobility is very restricted, no importance is attached to educating children to become adaptable to new situations. A large number of children is a condition for the survival of the family: children represent additional labor and are also the guarantee of economic security for their elderly parents (it can be prophesied that campaigns for birth control in most developing countries will remain unsuccessful until there is social insurance to look after parents in their old age).

The role of women is entirely circumscribed by the functions of motherhood. They leave the authority of the father only to pass under the authority of the husband. In fact, women have a justification for their existence only as mothers; in this role, however, they also become the symbol of the values revered by the group. Only the husband takes part in life outside the home. The woman exerts her influence on the rising generation within the family, but this influence can be exceptionally strong.

This type of family does not seem likely to be able to resist the changing conditions in the world around it. The view is gaining ground that laws drawn up to protect this type of family do nothing to defend the new type of small family based on a system of partnership and actually run counter to its functions and interests.[2] As one of the authors shows in an internal UN report, the traditional family is regarded by some governments as an obstacle to economic and social development, which explains the action taken under regional and national planning to break up the extended family.

THE FUNCTIONS OF THE FAMILY

With the transformation of society from an agrarian and artisanal pattern to an industrial and tertiary structure the production functions of the family have become very diluted. The cases in which the father's work place is situated near the family dwelling have become increasingly rare. In economic terms, the family has been reduced from a production and consumption unit to no more than a consumption community in most cases.

A possible measure of this trend is provided by the number of family collaborators, as given in Table 29 for the three economic sectors during the period 1941-60. The table does not give a really

TABLE 29

Number of Family Collaborators* in Proportion
to Total Active Population, 1941-60

Economic Branch and Year	Total Number Active	Family Collaborators	
		Total	Per Thousand
Total economy			
1941	1,992,487	150,805	76
1950	2,155,656	130,976	60
1960	2,512,411	117,204	47
Primary sector			
1941	414,936	117,168	282
1950	355,427	99,777	281
1960	280,191	74,958	268
Secondary sector			
1941	860,711	16,963	20
1950	995,855	14,789	15
1960	1,267,250	18,702	15
Tertiary sector			
1941	689,000	16,674	24
1950	795,422	16,410	21
1960	960,843	23,544	25

*People who work within a family enterprise—chiefly, farmers' and artisans' sons, wives, and daughters.

Source: Federal Statistical Office, Federal Census: 1941, Vol. 21, Table 44; 1950, Vol. 25, Table 10; 1960, Vol. 28, Table 13.

satisfactory impression of the trend in question because it had already
passed through its decisive stages by 1941. During the period under
consideration the most vital factor for the loss of economic importance
of family collaborators was the further decline in agriculture. In
the tertiary sector the number of family collaborators increased by
about 7,000 persons between 1950 and 1960, representing a proportion
of 4 per thousand, but their proportion still remains very low. The
increase mentioned was accounted for primarily by hotels and restaurants (up 15 per thousand), health and hygiene (up 21 per thousand),
and other services (up 17 per thousand).

It is difficult to judge to what extent this trend is to be attributed
to necessity (namely, the shortage of manpower) or to personal inclina-
tions. In any event, the possibility is already apparent that in certain
of the professions and among other self-employed persons collaboration by women is likely to play a more important role in the future.
Nevertheless, this possible development in a limited area will in no
way alter the fact that in overall terms the production function of the
family will continue to lose its importance in the future. The break-
up of the extended peasant family in Switzerland has been described
in a number of studies.[3] As demonstrated in the example of Vernamiège
in the Valais, the changes in the economic foundations of the extended
family are accelerated by the influence of new values imported from
the towns.[4] The structure of village solidarity is shaken, and its
strict social norms are felt to be too stringent. They have lost their
raison d'être. Young people in villages are no longer economically
dependent on the extended family and can easily find a livelihood outside the family or the village.

The size and structure of the family have altered under the
influence of changing functions. The multigeneration family or the
family of relatives, which frequently still comprises members of the
artisanal and agricultural production until in the same household, has
now become the conjugal or nuclear family consisting generally of
parents and their children only. If changes in the average size of household over the past hundred years are examined, the pattern in Table
30 emerges. From this it can be seen that, as the number of households constantly increased, the average number of persons living in
a household steadily decreased (with a minor exception in the decade
1860-70). Whereas an average household still consisted of nearly
5 persons around 1850, the figure was only 3.04 in 1970.

This pattern is diversified if a general comparison for 1960
covering all of the cantons is added. Table 31 shows that, as opposed
to a Swiss average of 3.41 persons per household (for all of Switzerland), there were cantonal extreme values of 4.33 (for canton of
Nidwalden) and 2.82 (for canton of Basel). The difference between the
extreme values for 1960 amounts to 1.51 persons, whereas the difference

TABLE 30

Number of Households and Average Number of
Persons per Household, 1850-1970

Year	Households[a]	Persons per Household
1850	485,087	4.93
1860	527,960	4.76
1870	557,018	4.77
1880	607,725	4.66
1888	638,064	4.57
1900	728,920	4.55
1910	829,009	4.53
1920	886,874	4.38
1930	1,002,915	4.05
1941	1,147,029	3.72
1950	1,312,204	3.59
1960	1,594,010	3.41[b]
1970	2,062,727	3.04

[a]Family, individual, and collective households.
[b]Including only persons living in family and individual households, as Swiss average of 3.27 persons per household is obtained for 1960 (as opposed to 3.41 when collective households are included).

Source: Statistisches Jahrbuch der Schweiz, 1971, p. 13.

between the Swiss average for 1850 and that for 1960 amounts to 1.52 persons. In 1960 the average size of household in seven cantons (Nidwalden, Obwalden, Uri, Zug, Fribourg, Schwyz, and Lucerne) was over 4 persons, whereas in three cantons (Basel, Geneva, and Neuchâtel) it amounted to less than 3 persons. In all other cantons it is between 3 and 4 persons. The factors determining the average size of household thus consist for the most part of the degree of urbanization and religion; large households seem to go together with the twin features "rural Catholic," whereas small households may be typified as "urban protestant." This first impression needs to be examined more thoroughly, but it might well be shown that the religion in itself is of less importance than the extent to which it is actually practiced and that this degree is itself closely correlated with the degree of urbanization and the relevant economic structure.[1]

The value consisting of the average number of persons per household by canton can be extended and broken down if the actual distribution of the various sizes of household is considered and not

TABLE 31

Number of Households and Average Number
of Persons per Household, by Canton, 1970

Canton	Family and Individual households	Residential Population	Persons per Household
Zurich	388,277	1,107,788	2.85
Berne	379,338	983,296	3.08
Lucerne	81,292	289,641	3.56
Uri	9,063	34,091	3.76
Schwyz	24,944	92,072	3.69
Obwalden	6,367	24,509	3.85
Nidwalden	6,837	25,634	3.75
Glarus	12,425	38,155	3.07
Zug	18,771	67,996	3.62
Fribourg	50,545	180,309	3.57
Solothurn	69,995	224,133	3.20
Basel	92,878	234,945	2.53
Basel-country	64,320	204,889	3.19
Schauffhausen	24,452	72,854	2.98
Appenzell OR	16,172	49,023	3.03
Appenzell IR	3,641	13,124	3.60
St. Gallen	118,370	384,475	3.25
Graubünden	46,434	162,086	3.49
Aargau	130,552	433,284	3.32
Thurgau	56,822	182,835	3.22
Ticino	84,729	245,458	2.90
Vaud	185,658	511,851	2.76
Valais	59,362	206,563	3.48
Neuchâtel	61,675	169,173	2.74
Geneva	129,868	331,599	2.55
Total	2,062,727	6,269,783	3.04

Source: Statistisches Jahrbuch der Schweiz, 1971, p. 13.

TABLE 32

Private Households in Cantons and Cities, by Number of Members, 1960

Canton and City*	Number of Households	Number of Persons	Members in Household											
			1		2		3		4		5		6	
			Total	Per Thousand	Total	Per Thousand	Total	Per Thousand	Total	Per Thousand	Total	Per Thousand	Total	Per Thousand
Canton														
Zurich	293,649	908,833	43,723	149	83,020	283	64,599	220	51,415	175	27,590	94	23,302	79
Berne	255,508	856,732	33,462	131	66,313	260	51,611	202	45,617	178	28,293	111	30,212	118
Lucerne	62,560	242,165	6,351	102	13,892	222	12,031	192	10,504	168	7,398	118	12,384	198
Uri	7,523	30,539	632	84	1,451	193	1,402	186	1,351	180	1,009	134	1,678	223
Schwyz	18,729	72,750	1,895	101	3,997	213	3,086	188	2,342	125	2,342	125	3,893	208
Obwalden	5,329	21,371	676	127	1,037	195	857	161	808	151	681	128	1,270	238
Nidwalden	5,052	20,712	459	91	994	197	912	180	826	163	665	132	1,196	237
Glarus	11,429	37,496	1,505	132	3,083	270	2,334	204	1,980	173	1,293	113	1,234	108
Zug	12,317	46,651	1,124	91	2,753	224	2,476	201	2,243	182	1,531	124	2,190	178
Fribourg	38,000	147,883	4,168	110	7,772	205	6,900	181	6,379	168	4,874	128	7,907	208
Solothurn	55,448	194,324	5,348	96	14,012	253	11,740	212	10,450	188	6,627	120	7,271	131
Basel-Town	79,450	213,802	16,729	211	25,693	323	16,995	214	11,669	147	5,063	64	3,301	41
Basel-Country	42,037	143,797	4,150	99	10,842	258	9,187	218	8,195	195	4,952	118	4,711	112
Schaffhausen	19,869	63,347	2,680	135	5,441	274	4,299	216	3,525	177	2,145	108	1,779	90
Appenzell OR	14,975	45,484	2,697	180	4,484	300	2,746	183	2,204	147	1,430	95	1,414	95
Appenzell IR	3,328	12,015	465	140	778	234	623	187	520	156	357	107	585	176
St. Gallen	92,640	321,547	12,235	132	23,406	253	17,873	193	15,232	164	10,278	111	13,616	147
Graubünden	36,853	133,385	4,311	117	8,421	229	7,047	191	6,423	174	4,699	127	5,952	162
Aargau	96,552	347,880	9,157	95	23,269	241	19,639	203	18,140	188	12,033	125	14,314	148
Thurgau	45,643	159,412	5,418	119	11,528	253	8,962	196	7,786	170	5,327	117	6,622	145
Ticino	61,339	185,607	10,392	169	16,166	264	13,834	226	10,992	179	5,608	91	4,347	71
Vaud	138,206	407,107	24,639	178	41,228	299	28,233	204	22,830	165	11,870	86	9,406	68
Valais	44,744	166,822	5,204	116	9,105	203	8,497	190	8,222	184	5,821	130	7,895	177
Neuchâtel	49,196	141,538	8,608	175	15,627	318	10,145	206	8,026	163	3,902	79	2,888	59
Geneva	90,624	247,747	18,418	203	29,367	324	19,315	213	13,198	146	5,933	65	4,393	49
Total Switzerland	1,581,000	5,168,946	224,446	142	423,679	268	325,773	206	271,621	172	161,721	102	173,760	110
City														
Zurich	150,453	418,341	28,588	190	46,517	309	34,154	227	24,094	160	10,520	70	6,580	44
Basel	74,217	196,302	16,217	219	24,470	330	15,752	212	10,506	141	4,392	59	2,880	39
Geneva	66,379	169,208	15,371	232	22,599	340	14,021	211	8,737	132	3,595	54	2,056	31
Berne	54,354	155,589	9,401	173	16,365	301	12,362	227	9,309	171	4,382	81	2,535	47
Lausanne	45,587	120,128	9,995	219	14,661	322	9,667	212	7,021	154	2,762	60	1,491	33
Winterthur	24,919	77,328	3,265	131	7,117	286	5,769	231	4,529	182	2,490	100	1,749	70
St. Gallen	23,835	71,700	4,103	172	6,940	291	4,873	204	3,956	166	2,134	90	1,829	17
Lucerne	20,884	63,021	3,085	148	6,139	294	4,762	228	3,624	174	1,911	91	1,363	65
Biel (BE)	19,148	56,387	2,715	142	6,109	319	4,404	230	3,284	172	1,598	83	1,038	54

*Communities with over 50,000 inhabitants in the census of December 1960.

Source: Statistisches Jahrbuch der Schweiz, 1967, p. 31

just the mean figure. This distribution is represented by cantons and
by towns in Table 32. This table shows that, taking the average for
Switzerland, out of every 1,000 households 268 comprised two persons,
206 three, 172 four, 142 one, 110 six or more, and 102 five persons.
When the table is more fully examined the following striking points
emerge:

    1. Only the cantons of Obwalden, Nidwalden, Uri, and Fribourg
constitute an exception to the rule that the highest frequency lies,
as in the national average, among two-person households; in those
cantons households consisting of six and more persons are the most
frequent.

    2. In 12 cantons (Uri, Nidwalden, Zug, Aargau, Solothurn,
Basel-country, Schwyz, Lucerne, Fribourg, Valais, Graubünden, and
Obwalden) the lowest frequency is among single-person households,
whereas in the other cantons, the lowest frequency is found either for
households of six or more persons (Basel, Geneva, Neuchâtel, Vaud,
Ticino, Zurich, Schaffhausen, Appenzell OR, and Glarus) or five-
person households (Appenzell IR, St. Gallen, Berne, and Thurgau).

    3. The nine towns with over 50,000 inhabitants all reveal the
same pattern in regard to the maximum and minimum frequency: the
highest frequency rate is found among two-person households, and
the lowest among six- or more person households.

    Table 33 indicates that the small family consisting exclusively
of parents and children is by far the most common form of household,
together with childless households still, continuously, or again childless and single-person households. The table shows that parents (of

TABLE 33

Persons in Private Households, by Status, 1960

Status	Total	Per Thousand
Heads of family, married couples, and		
children (basic family)	4,483,391	867
Parents, parents-in-law, children-in-law		
grand-children, and other relatives	256,623	50
Foster children	18,872	4
Agricultural employees, commercial		
assistants, domestic servants	142,072	28
Lodgers	229,583	44
Others	38,405	7
Total	5,168,946	1,000

Source: Statistisches Jahrbuch der Schweiz, 1967, p. 33.

the head of the household), parents-in-law, sons- and daughters-in-
law, grandchildren, and other relatives together account for only 50
per thousand of the persons living in private households, so that the
multigeneration family or family of relatives plays only an insignificant role. The same applies to households containing servants or
helpers because agricultural employees, commercial assistants, and
domestic employees together account for only 28 per thousand of the
persons living in private households.

As a result of the introduction of general old-age and survivors'
insurance, firms' pension schemes for old-age, and the further extension of sickness funds and private insurance contracts, the protection
and welfare functions of the family have been largely transferred elsewhere. There are various factors to indicate that private and public
insurance will continue to gain ground. Loss of monetary value offers
little incentive for personal saving (although this does not naturally
have the same effect on all types of investment). Taxes on legacies and
gifts weaken the motivation for working in order to leave an inheritance
for one's descendants. At the same time, the growing importance of
study for which the cost is not paid directly by the student's family also
adds to the currency of this attitude, although from another direction.[5]

The changes in family functions so far discussed have resulted
in the loss of a number of external stabilizing factors. Additional
factors consist of the emancipation of women who, in economic respects,
are less dependent on being married, and the changing position of
children, who were valued in the traditional peasant and artisan family
as workers and were also necessary as heirs and to guarantee their
parents' security in old age, whereas today in economic terms the
child represents primarily a expense to the family. Since the family
now no longer represents a production unit and its existence as a
community for protection and safety is restricted, much greater
importance is attached to it in regard to individual's private search
for personal happiness and recognition as a human being.

The roles within the family have changed, and the patriarchal
family based on the father's authority has become a nuclear family
in which the fundamental equality of rights of husband and wife is
increasingly recognized. Marriage and family are regarded far less
as a means of safeguarding economic security and as a social contract
than as a means toward reciprocal personal fulfillment. The much
greater present-day degree of freedom in choice of spouse is an
expression of this trend. The loss of external stabilizing factors has
thus been accompanied by a movement inward (that is, to personal
psychological needs) of the basis for family stability.[6] The child is
to an increasing extent regarded as an element in the happiness sought

within the private life of the family, as the symbol and fulfillment of
the relationship between man and wife. This also means that children
seen in this light are to an increasing extent "planned children." The
extension of the idea and the various practices of family planning
thus corresponds also to the new value of the child in a functionally
changed family community. Abortion could also be considered in
the same context. Estimates of the number of abortions in Switzerland
fluctuate between 25,000 and several hundred thousand every year.
One gynecologist in Zurich believes, on the basis of her experience,
that since the pill became available the number of legal and illegal
interruptions of pregnancy has fallen.[7]

Family planning is also promoted by the increasing value attached
to sexuality, independently of its procreative function. The change
taking place in this connection can be clearly recognized in Switzerland, as in other countries, by analyzing the contents of mass communication media. This change is not restricted to sexuality within
marriage, because sexual values have been specifically recognized
and are no longer necessarily linked to marriage. More will be
said in this connection later.

The view is often expressed that educational functions have been
transferred from the family to other institutions. It might be closer
to the truth to say that the total need for education has increased to
such an extent as to necessitate the collaboration of institutions outside the family (school, organizations, mass media, and so on) but
without reducing the significance of the family's educational function
in itself.

Scientific investigation conducted in the postwar period has
emphasized the vital importance of education within the family from
the time of birth. Much has also been said about differences in
intelligence that are attributable to variation in the cultural environment in the preschool period: One result is that urban children
normally enjoy a privileged position in relation to rural children.[8]

Opinions diverge concerning the educational role of the mother
in the traditional family. With numerous pregnancies, work about the
household, and sharing in the work of the family enterprise, the
mother normally had little time left to bother about the individual
child. The grandmother, elder sister, or other members of the
extended family often looked after the welfare and education of the
small children, which meant that the elder sister's childhood and
school education were to some extent sacrificed to this function.
This makes it questionable whether the present-day mother (who
relies on nurseries, baby-sitting, neighbors, and similar solutions
within the framework of the small family) really has less time available for her children's upbringing. Depending on how the physical,

mental, intellectual, and emotional needs of the child are satisfied,
its development in each of these areas will be accelerated or retarded,
the consequences often being lifelong and not open to either positive
or negative change subsequently.[9]

In the traditional family the child was fed at its mother's breast
for two or three years, abruptly weaned, and then left to itself in many
cases during the equally critical period between the age of three and
six, when curiosity and interest in its surroundings developed.[10]
Moreover, physical development was often insufficiently taken care of:
the fact that people are becoming taller from one generation to the
next is due to the improved living conditions, including the reduced
size of families, as well as to improved nutrition. As the general
awareness of the physical and intellectual development needs of
children increases, there is a likelihood of more nurseries, kindergartens, day-care centers, and similar institutions (see also the
possible variants on the development of mothers' employment in
Chapter 5). This would lead to a fundamental change in functions:
these institutions would not simply help working mothers but would
also become genuine education centers for small children and would
also be available to mothers who do not go out to work. This would
then constitute not so much a transfer of educational functions as
support for the parents in their task of bringing up their children.

Despite the growing importance of schools, education within the
family remains of great significance. Scholastic success at all levels
depends to a large degree on the knowledge and mental attitude acquired
by the child within the family.[11] It is recognized today that the problem of democratization of studies is not just a matter of providing
education grants: The necessary mental and social requirements must
be created early on in the child's life. The curricula of the various
school levels and specialities are based in a proportion of about 60 to
80 percent on knowledge and concepts assumed as preexisting. If the
child has had no opportunity to acquire these in its family, it is
handicapped at school.

The educational importance of the family is and remains exceptionally great for the assimilation and integration of all kinds of
information (in the street, through the mass media, and so on) with
which the child is confronted in what has been termed the "third
milieu" or the "parallel school."[12] These forms of information and
observation are frequently in contradiction to the knowledge, values,
and behavioral standards inculcated in the child in the family and
school.[13] This conflict is one of the causes of recent protest movements among young people and the tension between the generations.[14]

The state has become democratic; the family has the tendency
to follow that direction as well.[15] In a changing world tradition and

experience become less important and are superseded by adaptability. Older generations' knowledge is no longer adapted to the new situation. Economically, the modern family depends just as much on the person who employs the head of the family as on the head of the family himself. As a parallel movement in the world of employment, paternalism is giving away to trade unionism and various forms of participation and codetermination. The diminishing role of inheritance also helps to undermine the authority of the paterfamilias.

The decline in paternal authority is accompanied by the wife's accession to the role of partner. Where the family used to be represented exclusively by the husband in dealings with the outside world, there is now joint effort by husband and wife together acting as a pair. In the modern family based on partnership children are allowed a say in many things. Where they are not, children rebel against parental authority. This results in the emergence of a separate youth culture (see also Chapter 13). A large number of young people make it their aim to spend their leisure outside the family in the company of other young people. This trend might have certain negative effects on the future demand for second homes, which is described as very important in several other passages in this study. From a certain age onward many children and young people would prefer to spend their leisure time in larger urban centers with companions of their own age rather than with their parents in a second home in the country, unless this second home is in a place where they can escape from their family's surveillance. The same line of thought is followed by youth specialist Peter Kuenstler of the Social Affairs Division of the UN, when he asks whether youth centers should not be created some distance away from their homes, whereas the collective facilities for mothers and infants should of course be as close as possible to their homes.

The small family poses many problems in regard to its style of housing. Will the apartment or house be large enough for the children? Will they be too large once the children have grown up and probably moved to some other place?[16] How will old people live? (One of the characteristics of satellite towns is their uneven age structure.) Most of these and similar questions must remain unanswered in this book, although a possible solution is contemplated in Chapter 10.

FORECASTS ON THE FUNCTIONS OF
MARRIAGE AND FAMILY

Divorce

The trend in the number of divorces since the beginning of this century can be seen from Table 34. Comparison of the number of

TABLE 34

Marriages and Divorces, 1906-69

Year	Marriages	Divorces	Divorces per Thousand Marriages during Same Period
1906-10	27,482	1,490	54
1916-20	27,470	1,824	66
1926-30	30,017	2,543	85
1936-40	31,009	3,215	104
1946-50	38,309	4,245	111
1956	40,488	4,293	106
1960	41,574	4,656	112
1965	45,082	4,977	110
1968	45,711	5,599	122
1969	46,886	5,980	127

Source: Statistisches Jahrbuch der Schweiz, 1971, pp. 41, 45.

divorces with the number of marriages during any particular period
is of questionable value, since divorces normally relate to marriages
contracted in an earlier period. In the absence of any other data, however, this factor may still be of some use because it is certainly more
indicative than the number of divorces in absolute terms without any
reference basis. Moreover, the number of marriages follows a fairly
steady pattern of development, that is to say, without any years with
an exceptional glut or dearth of marriages.

Table 35 gives the same figures for the five largest cities and
three smaller cities in 1965. Bearing in mind that these figures are
used only for expediency, it can be seen from the two tables that the
relative frequency of divorces roughly doubled from the beginning to
the middle of this century but that the increase rate was less in the
last 20 years. This result is rather suspect, however, and might turn
out to be illusory if more thorough investigation were to reveal that
the changes between 1946-50 and 1968 were affected by a sharp rise
in the frequency of marriages or, although this would be of significance
in this connection for only a few years, the attainment of marriageable
age by persons born in years in which the birth rate was especially
high. This question must be left open for the time being. From the
cross section for 1965, however, it can be seen without ambiguity
that the incidence of divorces in the towns is in excess of the Swiss
average. The leading position is occupied by the two large towns in
French-speaking Switzerland. Although Berne and Schauffhausen

do not entirely fit into the picture, it may be asserted that the frequency
of divorce in smaller towns is slightly above the Swiss average and
that in large towns it is higher again than in the smaller ones.

Legal and Sociological Aspects of Divorce

It has already been mentioned that the family is not likely to
regain its lost functions, with the possible exception of a future increase in the family's importance as a center for culture and leisure.
But if marriage and family are to serve primarily as the source of
personal well-being and intimacy, the marriage contract is seen
principally as the means of attaining this aim. If marriage fails in
this function, there should be no obstacle to a dissolution of the contract. This would imply legal approval of divorce by consent, as an
expression of the predominant feeling in society. The most recent
opinion in this connection comes from Max Keller, of the Faculty of
Law and Political Science of the University of Zurich, whose ideas
have been taken as the basis for the following observations.[17]
The system of divorce by consent was recognized under Swiss
law through application of the Marital Status Act of 1874. But when this
failed to produce the desired standardization of divorce practice, it
was dropped with the introduction of the civil code now in force.
Keller now observes that, through the line of action followed by
arbitration judges, divorce by consent is not only permitted, notwith-
standing the requirement of the law, but is in fact often encouraged.

TABLE 35

Marriages and Divorces in Selected Cities, 1965

City	Marriages	Divorces	Divorces per Thousand Marriages during Same Period
Zurich	4,641	674	145
Basel	2,098	322	153
Geneva	1,662	455	274
Berne	1,475	190	129
Lausanne	1,194	254	213
Neuchâtel	295	39	132
Fribourg	256	32	125
Schauffhausen	249	42	169

Source: Statistisches Jahrbuch der Schweiz, 1967, pp. 47, 50

This produces a discrepancy between practice and law, which led a
federal judge as long ago as 1943 to charge the courts with betraying
the spirit of civil law. This discrepancy can be overcome either
by returning to a system of administration of the law that is in keeping
with its requirements or by adjusting existing law to practice. In
order to find out which of these two solutions is to be preferred,
Keller examines the changes that have taken place in attitudes toward
marriage and comes to the following conclusions.

Any stiffening in the divorce practice would encounter very
widespread opposition. State intervention in marriage is felt to be
incompatible with the nature of marriage as a highly personal,
individual, and intimate union. "The conviction has become increasingly
common that it is fundamentally wrong to use the powers of the state
in order to bind a couple seeking a divorce to a marriage that has
ceased in reality to be an intimate personal union," according to Max
Kuler in the Neue Zuricher Zeitung, December 18, 1968. There are two
basically opposed concepts of the nature of marriage: the first sees
it as a religious and moral institution that transcends the individual
interests of the couple; the second sees it as a means invented by
humans for the attainment of individual well-being through a purely
private relationship that can be dissolved at any time. It is the
second of these concepts that is becoming increasingly predominant.
The model of marriage that is today most common is no longer a
spiritual one, and the marriage contract is largely regarded as a
pledge of faith between the partners. Keller refers to the influence
of the churches on these concepts in the following terms: "In reality,
Christianity now has only a traditional and decorative function for
the overwhelming majority of our people. This cannot be concealed
either by the powerful external appearance of our official churches
or by the great display of energy, particularly from the reformed
branches."

Keller then examines the legal situation in a number of other
countries. he notes that, although divorce by consent is still officially
excluded in many countries, it has won legal acknowledgement in the
Scandinavian countries in particular. Subject to certain requirements,
Sweden, Norway, Finland, and Denmark allow divorce by consent. It
must be preceded by separation, but this may not be refused if both
partners wish it. Sweden requires in addition that there should be
an attempt at conciliation first. According to Keller, divorce by
consent is generally regarded as a satisfactory solution, in harmony
with social reality, and has also proved its worth in regard to the
ethical values of marriage.

In view of these facts and observations Keller advocates the
approval and introduction of divorce by consent in Switzerland but
not without effective guarantees against unfounded or hasty applications

for divorce. He suggests a minimum duration for marriages, allowing
the couple to understand their reciprocal relationship fully. In addition,
he suggests that divorce should be preceded by separation lasting more
than one year in order to provide more lengthy proof of the real desire
for a divorce. Prof. Keller attaches particular importance to the
conciliation procedure before separation and before divorce, in which
he refers to the experience in Sweden. Special provisions are called
for when the applicants for a divorce have underage children. Keller
recommends having an expert report to decide which would be worse
for the mental and physical development of the children—to continue
the marriage or to dissolve it.

In conclusion, Keller asks the rhetorical question, "Subject to
these provisions for the protection of marriage, would not legal
recognition of divorce by consent be a better solution than clinging
to a situation that no longer has any but formal validity, because it is
no longer supported by a general social conviction and thus no longer
commands respect?" This situation would, however, finally abandon
the Christian model of marriage, which is still the fundamental basis
of the civil code. Partial revision of Swiss family law is pending,
but the study commission appointed for this purpose does not consider
it feasible to reappraise what it describes as the politically delicate
compromise between advocates and opponents of a mild divorce system
and wishes to keep the possibility of a complete revision in reserve.

In the overall sociological context divorce may be considered
from at least two different aspects. The high divorce rates in cities
(see Table 35), where the living conditions assign new roles to husband
and wife, may be seen as indicating difficulties in adapting to these
new roles. These difficulties can be regarded as structural in that
neither husband nor wife has been prepared for their new roles by
the existing traditional structures of society. According to this
hypothesis, divorce rates may be expected to decline if coming generations are better prepared for their new roles. This would presuppose
elimination of the existing discrimination against women and the
education of children in the light of these new realities and values.

If the interpretation of rising divorce rates as an indication of
inadequate adaptation proves correct, further conclusions follow.
Family law, marriage contract, and divorce procedure, all of which
result in inequality between husband and wife because they were
created for other times and other circumstances, would then appear
in present-day circumstances as institutional factors leading to higher
divorce rates, through their effect of reinforcing traditional behavior
and thereby impeding adaptation. Unless fundamental reforms are
introduced, the future pattern would consist of a further increase in
divroce rates, accompanied by expansion of curative (instead of
preventive) measures (psychiatric treatment and public and private

marriage guidance counselors). This forecast is based on observations of what has happened in the United States as well as in the large
cities of Eastern Europe (Poland, Hungary, and Czechoslovakia). In
these European countries there has been a sharp rise in the number
of marriage guidance counselors since the middle of the 1960s. It
would thus appear that a new type of family will correspond to industrial
society and that social conflict within the country will increase until
thorough reforms make it easier for people to adapt themselves to
the new situation.

From another point of view, divorce may be regarded as a new
value for the well-being of the couple and of the children as well.
This hypothesis is supported by a number of factors. The higher life
expectancy and the fact that grown-up children do not normally live
with their parents any longer mean that the family has generally
completed its biological and educational function at a time when both
husband and wife generally have a considerable span of life still ahead
of them. If there is no longer any link between them after completing
their primary function, there should be no obstacle to dissolving their
marriage. Swiss divorce statistics seem to prove that this hypothesis
is not entirely off the mark because the 5,980 divorces in 1969 break
down in terms of length of marriage as presented in Table 31.

Much the same is suggested by psychological and sociological
research indicating that in many cases the child's well-being is to be
sought in a new family set up through the remarriage of father or
mother or by living together with father or mother following their
divorce rather than in continuing to live against a discordant family
background without divorce. If divorce is looked upon as the best
solution both for husband and wife and for the children, it may be
expected that an increasing number of households will make this choice.

TABLE 36

Divorces, by Years of Marriage, 1969

Years	Number of Divorces
0-1	377
2-5	1,687
6-9	1,271
10-19	1,786
20 or more	859
Total	5,980

Source: Statistisches Jahrbuch der Schweiz, 1971, p. 46.

The Sexual Revolution

The aspirations discussed in connection with divorce aim at adapting the law to attitudes that are becoming increasingly predominant and to what has become the principal function of marriage; there are different demands following very much the same line of development that call for a revision of the existing concepts of sexual morality, which, although not always to be found in the written law, nevertheless exert a powerful influence in society. These trends may be grouped together under the term "sexual revolution." In relation to the view that the principal function of marriage consists of fulfilling the individual's desire for happiness, a further and perfectly logical step is taken in the same direction, with the argument that this striving may also be satisfied outside marriage. The demands advanced in this connection can be summarized as saying that all forms of sexual relations should be allowed between persons responsible for their own actions, provided that no harm is done either to themselves or to anyone else.

This movement has not yet gathered much support in Switzerland, but the germs are there and have contributed, as in other economically developed countries, to unrest among youth. For example, the "First Pamphlet of the Opponents of Authority" (Zurich, 1968) states: "We demand that our authorities discuss this pamphlet with us . . . we shall ignore their inhibited sexual morality" and "What makes us superior to our parents and teachers is not our greater sexual potency but our deeper sensitivity." But the sexual revolution is also felt among adults. Investigations such as the Kinsey report and the work of Masters and Johnson, the mass media, literature, and theater, as well as advertising, show a society that permits increasing sexual freedom. The rebellion of youth is directed against the contrast between this society and the values it upholds. This is further compounded by the biological cause of the sexual revolution among young people in the form of social protraction of childhood (longer schooling) with simultaneous biological shortening of childhood.[18] The anthropologist E. T. Hall mentions that society is eager to maintain a series of taboos while demolishing the technical opportunities for supervision.[19] Quite apart from any moral attitude, the majority of anthropologists and sociologists have come to the conclusion that the sexual revolution is a process that cannot be halted.

When placed in a broader context, these tendencies may seen to correspond to the well-proved finding of sociologists and ethnologists that systems of morals and values in general, including the family specifically, are an expression of the particular type of society. Patterns of social behavior that are apparently accepted at any particular time

cannot be turned into something absolute because they are open to
change just as much as society itself. In the same connection, the
distinction should be noted between "pure ethics" and "simple morals"
(in the meaning of a relative value).[20]

SUMMARY

The preceding observations suggest the following developments
in the family and the values it represents. Marriage as a lifelong
community between a man and a woman will remain the ideal for the
great majority. It is possible at the same time, however, that society
will tolerate other forms of coexistence and may in a later phase even
recognize them in law.* With growing prosperity, resultingly greater
economic independence, and further urbanization, divorce rates are
likely to continue to rise. But at the same time the opportunities for
self-fulfilment within the family will increase because of greater freedom, removal of discrimination, rising prosperity, and greater
leisure. The number of families with a large number of children will
probably decrease, and the average size of a household will at least
for the present continue to decline slightly. Because of the number
and complexity of the factors involved no attempt will be made here
to give any long-range fertility forecasts; it is therefore impossible
to say that a further increase in the average number of children is
necessarily ruled out. As the parents' levels of education rise the
child's needs will be recognized by increasing numbers of people,
and this will lead to the establishment of new institutions. Family
relationships will continue to take on a more democratic pattern. A
problem that will call for a special approach consists of shaping
conditions of life for the growing proportion of elderly persons.

---

*Movements of reaction against the small family as being too
restricted and isolated are specially noteworthy. It would take too
long here to discuss in detail the various new forms of life in a larger
community. What these attempts have in common, however, is their
sincere desire to cultivate mental and emotional relations in a social
framework transcending the small family. It is difficult to predict
whether these attempts are something temporary or whether they
represent the beginning of a deeper transformation of society.

7

WORKING TIME,
WORK-FREE TIME,
AND LEISURE TIME

WORKING TIME

Work-free time as understood today came into existence when, following industrialization, reduction of the hours worked by persons not engaged in agriculture led to a distinction between working time and free time. One of the characteristics of industrial society is the existence of statutory regulations laying down maximum working hours for employees, as well as a minimum age for entry into employment and in many cases a fixed age for retirement as well.

Leaving any more subtle distinctions aside for the moment, the whole life of a gainfully employed person (and of housewives as well, although they are not included under gainfully employed persons in these statistics) breaks down into working time and work-free time. The two are complementary and together they make up the whole of a specified period of a person's life. The fact that the combined duration of working time and work-free time make up the whole of a gainfully employed person's life and that their proportions and their distribution have a decisive effect on the way of life explains the importance of this whole subject. So far these comments have been concerned with the period of gainful activity, but any individual's life breaks down into periods in which he is or is not gainfully employed. The first part of a man's life is normally one without gainful activity (childhood and education), after which comes a period of gainful activity, followed by a second period without gainful activity, which can be termed the age of retirement (without going into any nuances). In a woman's life this pattern is normally complicated by marriage and child-bearing; reference has already been made to the relevant questions in Chapter 5.

The Duration of Gainful Activity

From the economic point of view the most relevant aspect is
really the number of working hours performed in a person's life.
This depends in the first place on the duration of gainful activity and
then on the relationship between working time and work-free time
within the period of gainful activity.[1] In descending order, this
relationship may be seen in terms of the number of working weeks
per year, of working days per week, or of working hours per day,
and from the economic standpoint it is naturally the number of working
hours per year that is of primary significance. The period of gainful
activity depends both on the time when a person enters employment
and on the time of retirement.

Since the beginning of the industrial revolution, when child labor
was still widespread, with the introduction of compulsory universal
education and its subsequent extension, and the steady relative
increase in education after the completion of compulsory schooling,
the average age of entry into occupational life has moved upward.
This means a reduction in the period of gainful activity. As already
demonstrated in connection with education and training, the factors
of longer compulsory schooling and more widespread education after
completion of compulsory schooling will most probably continue to
apply, for a number of reasons, with a likelihood of an increase in
the second of these factors. This will mean a further rise in the
average age of entry into occupational life under the existing educational system. If, on the other hand, the educational system should
be modified so as to integrate lifelong education and advanced education
within the system, which is desirable for a number of reasons, it
would be possible to raise the general level of education without
deferring the time of entry into occupational life. Employment and
education could then be closely interconnected and alternate in a
variety of ways throughout the individual's working career. This
would largely do away with the traditional distinction between the
three phases in a normal individual's life.

In the long range this evolution is not only desirable but also
probable. Joffre Dumazedier mentions that excessive extension of
the school period might result in difficulties (too great a load on the
active population and improvements in productivity would benefit
mostly young people and therefore not provide the expected reduction
in hours of work).[2] Moreover, extension of the school period tends
to isolate young people within society and to withhold from them
rights and responsibilities connected with gainful activity.[3]

The Time of Retirement

Under the influences of the increasingly widespread introduction
of a pensionable age and of the old-age and survivors' insurance scheme

the age of retirement from gainful activity has been gradually reduced, but as a result of the increase in average life expectancy more people are reaching that age and thus extending their own period of gainful activities. It seems most likely that the future evolution will be governed by two contradictory factors. On the one hand, the rising standard of prosperity will add fuel to the demand for a lower pensionable age, whereas on the other hand the improvement in the physical and mental capacities of older people will reinforce the desire to remain active beyond the present retirement age, although demands to up the latter are unlikely to be accepted.

Reduction of the pensionable age is demanded not only by the trade unions but in some other countries by certain employers as well. The legal possibility of early retirement could well grow into a social problem. Various investigations have shown that certain undertakings prefer at a time of rapid technological change to pension their employees who are over age 50 rather than to retrain them. The pretext advanced in this connection, that it is hardly possible to acquire new knowledge at that age and that productivity declines after the fortieth year, is tied to the myth of youth imported from the United States and ought to be seriously examined. In Europe the problem has been dealt with in particular in a polemical essay.[4] The problem will become more acute with the increase in life expectancy.

The solution allowing for both of these conflicting tendencies will probably lie in a more flexible attitude toward pensionable age.[5] This recommendation—although probably conceived under the pressure of the present acute manpower shortage—had already appeared in the election manifesto issued by the Free Democratic Party for the 1967 parliamentary elections. It has considerable prospects of being put into effect, especially in view of the change in the age structure of the Swiss resident population mentioned in Chapter 3 (an increase in the proportion of persons over age 65, with a critical phase around 2020). It is questionable, however, whether this more flexible approach to pensionable age will be sufficient in itself to overcome the future problem of the elderly.

Only a partial answer can be expected from such solutions as a gradual reduction of working hours for persons over age 40, leading up to a gentle transition to retirement (as practiced, for example, by some Canadian firms) or opportunities for voluntary activities in clubs or charitable organizations for the elderly. Investigations into the problems of the "third age" show that this is a fundamental problem of the times (and, as the demographic forecasts suggest, an increasing problem in the future as well), calling for the most thorough attention.[6]

Reduction of Hours of Work

Since the mid-nineteenth century the relationship between working time and free time has been characterized by a steady reduction in

working hours and a corresponding increase in free time. Figures
permitting a historical comparison for Switzerland are not available;
thus, changes in the number of working hours in industry will be
illustrated through the case of the United States and France, as presented in Table 37. Although hours of work in the United States have
steadily been reduced except immediately after World War II, the
pattern in France was seriously disturbed by the economic crisis of
the 1930s, the war, and the special circumstances of the postwar
period. There can be no doubt, however, that the long-term trend is
toward a reduction of hours of work. It may be safely surmised in
regard to Swiss figures that they run, although at a slightly higher

TABLE 37

Average Number of Weekly Working Hours
in Industry, 1850-1965

| Year | Country | | | Index (1900 = 100) | |
	France	U.S.	Switzerland	France	U.S.
1850		63.0			114
1870		61.0			110
1880		59.0			108
1890		56.4			102
1900	64.5	55.3		100	100
1910	60.0	52.9		93	95
1920-29	47.5	49.1		74	89
1930-35	45.7	43.9		71	79
1937	40.0	41.2		62	74
1946	43.0	40.4		67	72
1949	44.3	40.4		68	72
1952	45.0	40.7		70	74
1958	45.8	38.6		71	70
1965			45*		

*Includes overtime, according to a survey by the Federal
Office for Industry, Trades and Labor (BIGA).

Source: Jean Fourastié, La civilisation de 1975, Collection
"Que sais-je?," No. 27 (Paris: Presses universitaires de France,
1959), p. 17.

level, roughly parallel to the U.S. trend, because the reduction of
hours of work is an international phenomenon and follows approximately
the same course in countries with different degrees of industralization.

The Swiss Labor Act of 1964, which came into force on February
1, 1966, fixes the maximum weekly hours of work for wage-earners
of either sex at 46. This applies to industrial workers, clerical staff,
technical, and other salaried employees, including sales staff. For
all other employees the maximum hours of work per week are 50. In
practice, collective agreements often provide for shorter hours of
work than laid down in these federal minimum requirements. For
example, the 44 hour week has already been introduced for several
categories of wage-earners. Concerning holidays, by the end of 1962
12 cantons had introduced laws on the subject. At that time, only 3 of
these 12 cantons (Geneva, Neuchâtel, and Vaud) had laws allowing all
employees three weeks' paid holidays irrespective of age or length of
service. Since then the number of these cantons has slightly increased.[7]
Reduction in hours of work has been possible thanks to substantial
improvements in productivity brought about by technological and
organizational innovations. Table 38 uses U.S. sources to give an
idea of long-term improvement in productivity in the three economic
sectors. During the period of 67 years covered by the table productivity in the primary sector rose nearly three-fold, in the secondary,
sector more than three-fold, whereas the increase in the tertiary
sector was insignificant.

Higher productivity raises the question whether it should be
converted into greater output or shorter working hours, which means,
in practical terms, in what proportion it should be distributed between
these two. Although it is true that increased productivity permitted
working hours to be reduced, the fact that this possibility became a
reality is due primarily to the success of trade union pressure.

When one considers the future development of the two main
factors—namely, productivity (a further increase)* and the working
man's desire for more leisure time (see the parties' views and aims,
in this chapter)—one comes to the conclusion that the most likely
trend consists of further reduction in working hours. Examination
of the parties' statements on the subject of working time and free
time shows that there are considerable differences, depending on the
background circumstances. Some see the reduction of working hours

---

*The comparison study on the economy forecasts a 120 percent
increase in productivity for the period 1967-2000, namely, an average
annual rate of 2.8 percent until 1979 and 2.3 percent for the rest of
the period.

TABLE 38

Changes in Productivity in Three Economic
Sectors, United States, 1870-1937

Year	Real per Capita Income from 2,500 Working Hours (in U.S. dollars)		
	Primary Sector	Secondary Sector	Tertiary Sector
1870	260	515	2,250
1925-34	660	1,560	2,280
1937	700	1,850	2,765

Source: Jean Fourastié, La civilisation de 1975, Collection
"Que sais-je?," No. 279 (Paris: Presses universitaires de France,
1959), p. 26.

as one of their essential aims and campaign actively for it; others
simply accept the trend as a fact; yet others are reluctant to recognize
any such demands. There are also differences in views as to the way
in which reduction of working hours should be institutionalized: Some
parties call for statutory provisions, whereas others prefer agreement
between those concerned. The actual principle of further reduction
of working hours is not, however, directly challenged as such by any
of the parties.

In the long term the question arises whether reduction of hours
of work will be an unending process or whether it is subject to certain
predictable limits. Here again, analysis of the two main factors at
play can provide an answer, but the second factor, the working man's
desire for more leisure, is more difficult to appraise in absolute terms
than the productivity factor.

Work may be regarded as alienation or as an opportunity for
personal development. In both cases, however, the reduction of
working hours seems to correspond to a genuine need, but it is
difficult to say precisely where the border lies. Appraisal of the
productivity factor should in fact prove much more simple. It will
continue to grow in the primary and secondary sectors, while the
economy will develop to an increasing extent into a tertiary structure.
Naturally, there are limits on productivity increases in the tertiary
sector. The time can be foreseen when man's demand for goods
produced by the primary and secondary sectors will be satisfied,
but there seems to be virtually no limit to the need for goods and

services relating to the tertiary sector. Jean Fourastié therefore predicts the continuation of the fundamental conditions of our economy, in the form of a relative shortage of certain goods and the consequent need for work.[8] But it remains difficult to say precisely where the limits of reduction of working hours will lie and what the pace at which it will progress will be.

Table 39 attempts to give some possibilities of yearly working hours around the year 2000, together with the distribution in weeks and days. If these figures are compared with Fourastié's,[9] it is found

TABLE 39

Alternative Possibilities for Yearly Working Hours
and Distribution per Week and Day, Assuming
Continued Long-Term Reduction
of Working Hours

Working Hours per Week and Day	Public Holidays	Weeks of Holidays	Working Days	Work-Free Days	Working Hours
5 x 8.0 = 40.0	10	2	240	124	1,920
5 x 8.0 = 40.0	10	3	235	129	1,880
5 x 8.0 = 40.0	10	4	230	134	1,840
5 x 8.0 = 40.0	10	6	220	144	1,760
5 x 7.5 = 37.5	10	5	225	139	1,687
5 x 7.0 = 35.0	10	4	230	134	1,610
5 x 7.0 = 35.0	10	6	220	144	1,540
5 x 7.0 = 35.0	10	8	210	154	1,470
4 x 8.0 = 32.0	10	4	182	182	1,456
4 x 8.0 = 32.0	10	6	174	190	1,392
4 x 7.5 = 30.0	10	4	182	182	1,365
4 x 7.5 = 30.0	10	6	174	190	1,305
4 x 7.0 = 28.0	10	4	182	182	1,274
4 x 7.0 = 28.0	10	8	168	196	1,096

Note: The first figure gives the assumed number of working days per week; the second figure gives the assumed number of working hours per day; the product (third figure) gives the number of working hours per week.

Source: Herman Kahn and Anthony J. Wiener, L'an 2000 (Paris: Robert Laffont, Paris Match, 1968), p. 259, and authors' calculations.

that the 30 hour week and the 40 week year, producing an annual total of working hours of about 1,200, would correspond to a good half of the present working time in the industrial countries of Europe. This sort of reduction would require that productivity double in order to maintain even the present-day living standard. At the same time, the progressive tertiarization of the economy must be borne in mind. In major centers there are already tertiary firms that operate on a 7 hours per day, 5 days per week, and 48 weeks per year schedule, which comes to somewhat less than 1,700 working hours per year. If absences for various causes are included, a resulting figure of 1,450-1,500 actual hours of work performed per year is often considered satisfactory in such cases, according to Fourastié.

In determining which of the possible work schedules is most likely to be followed for a given number of working hours per year, there are a number of factors at play, of which only two will be described here as being of particular importance in connection with national planning.

The number of hours of work per day will depend primarily on the average commuting distance. If this figure can be kept within reasonable bounds, the number of daily working hours can be relatively high; on the other hand, if a considerable time is needed for the daily average commuting journey (two hours or more each day), the effect will be to compress the number of daily working hours. In regard to the distribution of the daily working hours, further extension of the so-called English working schedule is to be expected (starting work relatively late and finishing relatively early by having a fairly short midday break at or near the workplace).

Once the five-day week has been introduced on a more extensive basis, the possibility of going on to a four-day week will depend partly on how common it becomes to own a second home outside the city. In 1971, however, the women in the major French trade unions took a stand against the four-day week, arguing that the daily schedule should be modified instead. Similar positions have been taken by women members of German trade unions. There will be an interrelationship between the two factors (desire for a four-day week and possession of a second home). If a relatively large number of people have a second home, they will want to be able to make proper use of it and will therefore demand a four-day week. But once the four-day week has been introduced, many people who hitherto had no second home will want to acquire one in order to enjoy the long weekend to the full, which means that there will be a second wave of buying or renting of second homes.

In basic terms, quite apart from the question of the division of the working schedule, the extent to which a second home is desired will be determined primarily by the average living conditions in

people's first homes (although in the higher income brackets ownership
of a second home seems today to be less a matter of living conditions
in the first home than a question of social prestige). In other words,
if the average first home already fulfills a number of the demands
normally made on a second home (tranquility, proximity to nature, a
garden, and so on), the desire for a second home will be less strong
than otherwise. The general subject of second homes is of considerable
importance for national city and country planning; therefore, it is
referred to at various other points in this book.

THE PARTIES' VALUES AND AIMS

KCVP:
        "Greater promotion of meaningful leisure activities is a priority
need."

Free Democratic Party:
        "The party's demands: promotion of meaningful leisure activities
in connection with the reduction of hours of work. Working hours and
working conditions appropriate to the times, allowing for the special
needs of small-scale industry and agriculture. Promotion of contractual arrangements concerning free days and annual holidays for
wage-earners and salaried employees. Creation of increased opportunities for leisure activities and promotion of appropriate sports."
        "We proclaim the following principles: The transition from
occupational life to retirement should be made as flexible as possible;
the opportunities for partial further employment after completing a
regular employment relationship should be used to the full."

SPS:
        "The rising productivity of the economy brought about by
rationalization, automation, and so on, should be used for the benefit
of the workers in the form of wage increases, greater leisure, and
price reductions."
        "Labor law should be developed on a uniform basis, with partic-
ular attention to respect for human personality, reduction of working
hours, and provision of holidays with pay."
        "We strive toward adult education, promoting personal independ-
ence and encouraging meaningful leisure activities. In addition to the
development of knowledge and ability, human and cultural relations
should be developed. Extra leisure can create the external conditions
needed for humans to recover their internal values and to have time
for their families, for activities within free communities, and for
pastimes. It is the function of the public authorities to promote private

noncommercial efforts directed toward popular education and leisure activities."

The SPS proposes a "general implementation of the claim for three weeks' paid holidays through cantonal legislation and the gradual introduction of the fourth week of holidays with pay by means of collective agreements."

BGB:
"Increases in real wages and further improvements in conditions of work, particularly through reduction in working hours, should remain within the limits of productivity increases in order to combat inflation."

"Hours of work should be so governed as to ensure that the competitivity of small-scale enterprises is not affected."

LdU:
"Healthy family life prospers best in rural family houses closely linked to nature. These also offer the most desirable form of leisure activity and counteract the unhealthy growth of the towns."

"The meaningful use of leisure time is also an element in public health. Opportunities must be created whereby the individual can engage in mental or handicraft activity, pursue sports, and enjoy restful holidays."

Evangelical People's Party:
Support for meaningful holiday and leisure activities is given, as is support for the extension of legislation on rest periods, public holidays, and holidays with pay.

PdA:
"The increasing tempo of work and its greater intensity expose every worker to extreme physical and mental tension. Reduction of working hours is therefore one of the most urgent present demands on the part of all workers."

"Reduction of hours of work is essential in order to raise the standard of health of people. It is only men and women in a good state of health, physically and mentally rested, who can perform the maximum productive work in a given time. The demand for a 44 hour work week is a minimum, while the aim is the 40 hour, five-day week. Working time must be laid down by law in order to avoid divergences between regulations according to the particular canton or industry."

"The right to holidays: A solution applying to the whole of Switzerland is needed—a minimum of three weeks of paid holiday for everyone and four weeks for young workers."

FREE TIME

The right to free time is recognized in the Universal Declaration
of Human Rights of the UN (1948) and in the various texts adopted by
the International Labour Organization (ILO). Indirectly, it is also
acknowledged by national legislation on employment and holidays.[10]
The growing significance of free time as a basic value in human
existence may be attributed to various factors: to the physical and
mental need for rest, which is perceived, on the one hand, as an
individual right and, on the other hand, as a condition for the satisfactory productivity of the work force, as well as to the change in the
value of work in human life.

A number of sociological trends may be distinguished in this
connection, according to the different attitudes expressed. Adam
Smith and Karl Marx show that man's relationship to his work has
been changed by the industrial division of labor.[11] Work lost its
existential content and its significance as a form of human creativity;
in view of the alienation resulting from industrial work, Marx demanded
the right to free time as such.

A second direction is represented by Max Weber, R. H. Tawney,
Erich Fromm, David Riesman, and their schools.[12] They base their
attitudes on the hypothesis that the development of capitalism goes
back to the values of protestantism (especially Calvinism), glorifying
labor and thrift and deploring idleness as a vice. Their respective
analyses of the decline of the protestant ethic are different, but they
agree that of this decline is fact and that the significance of labor as
a basic value is being supplanted by other values (conformism, consumption, leisure). This is the same trend of ideas represented by
the Swiss theologist Joseph Pieper, who draws from Thomas of
Aquinas to show that effort is not necessarily a condition for knowledge.
He would want free time and leisure to be integrated within Catholic
ethical values, rather than putting them at the same level with sloth,
which is one of the seven deadly sins. In Pieper's view leisure is
a mental attitude during free time.[13]

A third trend is represented by empirical investigations into
free time in the various socioeconomic classes. The results are
perfectly clear: Even members of the professions and top managers,
who like their work and find fulfillment in it, complain of the excessive
hours of work, which, in their own estimation, they do not themselves
choose but which are imposed upon them by circumstances. Wage-
earners and salaried employees have less feeling of being able to
develop creativity in their work, even if they do not dislike it.
"Industrial man seems to perceive his life history as having its center
outside of work for his intimate relationships and for his feelings

of enjoyment, happiness and worth," as Dubin observed on the basis
of his investigations in three American firms.[14] The same findings
were expressed in connection with the centenary of the Corning Glass
Company: "Creating an industrial civilization is essentially a problem
of social invention and creativity in the non-work aspects of life."[15]
Numerous investigations have been made in Europe as well. A comparative study conducted in 1963 in both Eastern and Western Europe
(Poland, Yugoslavia, Finland, Denmark, France, and West Germany)
came to the conclusion that "leisure and the remainder of nonwork
time are generally of greater significance for the worker than his
work".[16]

Based on demands advanced in the various parties' programs,
it will be briefly recapitulated here what somebody seeking a reduction
in his hours of work expects from the extra free time. The demand
for meaningful leisure, which is to be found in almost all of the party
programs, is not particularly significant in itself except through the
recognition that leisure is regarded as a necessity and as a means of
providing a fuller life. In more specific terms, it is expected that
leisure will permit education, which promotes personal independence
and gives due prominence to human relationships and cultural activities
alongside mere acquisition of knowledge; it should enable people to
know themselves and to have time for their families; it should provide
opportunity for creative intellectual or manual activity; and finally
it should help to raise the standard of public health.

These demands reflect the fact that a large number of people
find a decreasing amount of satisfaction in their work, so that the
latter is sought in their free time. As already pointed out, this
change in the significance of work in human lives goes back to the
industrial division of labor. It is possible that with a greater emphasis
on the tertiary sector of the economy more people will find part of
their personal realization in their work. But free time will lose none
of its importance as a compensatory factor. People will have greater
opportunity in the future to enrich their lives by means of both active
and passive cultural activities, through leisure within their families,
through creative activity, and through contact with nature. The
importance of the factors underlying these aims will grow in the future.

THE DISTINCTION BETWEEN FREE
TIME AND LEISURE

Sociologists used to equate work-free time with leisure. Today,
this oversimplified view is rejected. It does not make allowance for
the true circumstances and has little to offer for the purposes of
leisure policies or national city and country planning. According to

this traditional concept, for example, engaging in a second job or
moonlighting would be lumped together with free time. Normally,
however, these activities are not regarded as a hobby; they are a
matter of demonstrable financial need.[17] Second jobs are much more
common than is frequently imagined: In a sample survey carried out
in the town of Annecy in Savoy, Joffre Dumazedier found that 25 percent of the workers had a second job.[18] The traditional view also
fails to allow for the fact that longer commuting journeys are not
regarded as free time but as a source of nervous tension. Dumazedier
writes:

> It would therefore be both incorrect and dangerous to define
> leisure simply by opposition to occupational time, as is
> done by most economists and sociologists who have dealt
> with the question. Almost all of them seem to labor under
> an excessive theoretically formula: the three eights—
> eight hours of work, eight hours of sleep, eight hours of
> leisure.

The traditional view is also unfair to housewives. It may have been
true of the higher bourgeoisie described by Veblen at the turn of the
century that the lady of the house, surrounded by plenty of servants,
led a life of leisure, but it was certainly not true for the majority of
women even at that time and is even less so now.[19] The "three-
eights" concept was dispatched for good by time-budget studies, which
consist of systematic and meticulous observation of the daily course
of activities.

For a long time, and even now to a certain extent, studies on
leisure consisted principally of questions such as, "What are your
leisure activities?" or "What leisure activities do you prefer?"
Dieter Hanhart demonstrated through his investigation among workers
in Zurich that these two questions are by no means synonymous,
because the most common and important leisure activity is often not
the same as the one that is preferred.[20] It is often possible to devote
very little time to the preferred leisure activity. That means that
the results of traditional investigations can be misleading and may
result in questionable decisions in the sphere of national city and
country planning. Certain leisure institutions might remain practically
unused, whereas others corresponding to a genuine need might not be
provided at all.

In contrast to the traditional style of surveys, time-budget studies
note the distribution and duration of all activities (often recorded every
six minutes for several periods of 24 hours) among representative
samples. The results of such studies are of considerable significance
for decisions in regard to leisure and national planning. In the

countries with planned economies time-budget studies have long since become a permanent instrument of the various planning authorities (city and country planning, leisure, and social policy); the first such study conducted in the Soviet Union, by S. Strumilin, goes back to 1924.[21] The growing interest displayed by various industrialized countries in time-budget studies is based on a number of factors—higher life expectancy, larger proportion of elderly people in the population, the greater importance of commuting, long weekends, the significance of television, and the interest in gaining more precise knowledge of female work in the home.

This growing interest, which is only natural in view of the importance of the decisions to be taken, was revealed in a major international study in which 11 countries representing Eastern and Western systems participated (Bulgaria, Czechoslovakia, East and West Germany, Hungary, Poland, France, Belgium, Yugoslavia, USSR, and the United States; Switzerland did not take part).[22] This survey was conducted under the leadership of A. Szalai and was sponsored by the United Nations Educational, Scientific and Cultural Organization (UNESCO) European Research and Documentation Center for the Social Sciences in Vienna. National research authorities carried out the actual survey in their countries in 1964-65; a total of over 130,000 persons were covered. The results were communicated to the World Congress of Sociology in 1966 in Evian in a large number of reports, and there have been numerous publications on the subject since then. This congress represented a turning point in the short history of the sociology of leisure. Whereas it was previously largely a matter of speculation, it has now become an applied science.

Since there are no results available for Switzerland, some of the conclusions produced by this international survey will now be presented. They almost certainly correspond to the situation in Switzerland. Actual leisure time is not identical to work-free time. The various daily activities were grouped under the following four major categories, each of which was subdivided into a number of subsidiary categories. (a) principal and subsidiary occupation; (b) housework and care of children; (c) sleeping, eating, and personal care; and (d) available leisure time. This division entirely does away with the three-eights concept.

At the Evian congress France Govaerts systematically distinguished between "tied" and "untied" free time. "Tied" free time is the time used to perform "essential" activities (primarily sleeping, eating, commuting, personal care, and so on); "untied" free time is the remaining period available to the individual, or leisure time. From this it is clear that an increase in total free time does not necessarily mean an increase in the "untied" free time, or leisure time, because extra free time may, for example, be spent on a longer

commuting journey and thus become "tied" free time. The following
observations have been derived from publications by France Govaerts.[23]
In regard to the available leisure time, the following is observed:
(a) available leisure time varies with the degree of economic development of countries; (b) within individual countries there are substantial
differences between different social classes in regard to the leisure
time available; and (c) in all countries employed women are under-
privileged in regard to free time. Concerning the type of free time
activity, these factors are noted: (a) television occupies a predominant
place in leisure time; (b) activities for personal fulfillment, participation in political or social events, and active sports are on a small
scale; (c) a major part of leisure time is spent in the family; and (d)
the household work of women, even if they do not go out to work, takes
up so much of their time that they have very little left for playing with
the children or to devote to personal fulfillment. These observations
apply to all eleven of the countries that took part in the international
survey. The only time-budget study for Switzerland that is known of,
which Käthe Biske conducted in Zurich among married women workers,
seems to confirm these observations.[25]

The observations are rather disquieting. If the social differences
in regard to leisure time increase, there is a danger that money that
could have been invested in a leisure policy at the proper time will
have to be spent for therapy. However praiseworthy the activities of
an organization such as the Pro Juventute Foundation may be in
providing holiday homes for overfatigued mothers, it cannot be denied
that preventive reforms of the social organization would be more
appropriate. Inequality in regard to leisure time may lead to social
tension, both within the family and between different social strata and
socioeconomic groups. The fact that little leisure time is devoted to
personal fulfillment or to political and social participation and information, whereas mass communication media (especially television) occupy
such an important place, may prove a threat to the functioning of
democracy. That relatively little time is devoted to further education
is disturbing if it is true that the economy will need manpower capable
of adapting to technological change. The fact that mothers have no
time for information or for personal fulfillment is disquieting both in
itself and in regard to the upbringing of children.

SOME FURTHER INTERSECTORAL RELATIONS

Leisure is still largely an area that tends toward passive
acceptance of decisions made in other sectors rather than benefiting
from an active and coordinated policy geared to its specific requirements. Following are a number of areas in which decisions are taken

that may have an influence on leisure patterns, often without having
the latter as the direct aim: school (education to a passive and con-
formist attitude or to an active and creative attitude), housing (size
of dwelling, arrangement of rooms, organization of kitchen), preservation of water and forest resources, number and type of service
facilites, and transport.

Conversely, if the leisure infrastructure is well balanced it can
have an influence on the location of industries. For example, a city
in the U.S. Midwest wanted to diversify its range of industries and
attract new firms. The chairman of the committee in charge of this
operation explained its success in the following terms: "We are
attracting companies with our new recreational and cultural facilities:
two new swimming pools, seven new playgrounds, a story-land zoo, a
much enlarged supervised recreation program including a senior
citizens' recreation program and an adult education center."[26] There
are also negative examples in which cities have failed to attract new
firms largely because they lacked the necessary leisure infrastructure.[27]

8

Knowledge of the quality of life and the standard of living is of fundamental importance in understanding a society. This is particularly true in connection with city and country planning, because options and decisions in this area are not only affected by such knowledge but also generally have a direct influence on the standard of living of particular regions or social strata.

In this book no special importance will be attached to a theoretical definition of the standard of living or to the distinction between the standard of living and the quality of life; however, some general comments on this subject are called for as a preliminary. The standard of living gives some indication of the extent to which the material and cultural needs of the population are satisfied. It can be said that in the postwar period higher living standards have become, under popular pressure, a national aim in practically all countries, both in the west and in the east.

In the economic context this aim is furthered by the recognition that economic and social development are not so much in competition with each other as had been thought for a long time. In fact, they progress together and are interrelated. "Human investment" is no longer regarded by economists as in any way subsidiary. There is increasing recognition today that for both political and economic reasons the first priority must go to the human being.

The standard of living and the quality of life, that is, the degree of prosperity enjoyed by any population, reflect that people's philosophy of life. Consequently, there are no absolutely satisfactory indicators of the standard of living that apply in all instances. The significance of any indicator is liable to vary from one country to another and within the same country as well.[1] For example, one of the most common factors used to indicate the standard of living—income— can be very deceptive if taken in isolation. Young people's purchasing

power is often higher than might be suspected from their income when
they still live at home and therefore have to pay a fairly small amount
for rent and food. In the Eastern European countries a genuine difference in the standard of living is often due less to any major variation
in cash income than it is to the provision of relatively luxurious official
accommodations, cars, and other items extraneous to actual income.
Under the influence of the sharply rising tax scales these forms of
indirect income are also becoming more important in the Western
countries, including Switzerland.

In making international comparisons it is also important to
consider the difference in the role played by the state as guardian of
the citizen's welfare. For example, Sweden and Switzerland are both
countries with a high standard of living, yet in this latter respect they
differ very widely.

PER CAPITA INCOME AND DISTRIBUTION OF
WORKING POPULATION

In the study of the prospects for the Swiss economy by the year
2000, undertaken by the City and Country Institute at Zurich at the
same time as the social analysis on which this work is based, the
average income of a gainfully employed person in 2000 was forecast
at either 50,000 or 41,000 francs at constant prices (under two separate
hypotheses), compared with 23,000 francs in 1967. Income per capita
amounted to 11,250 francs; for the year 2000 it was forecast at 25,000
francs in the principal hypothesis and at 20,000 francs in the subsidiary
hypothesis, compared with 11,250 francs in 1967. This means that in
both cases income will more or less double.

It was also pointed out in the study on the economy that there
are no reliable data available in regard to the distribution of households by income class. One must therefore take the corresponding
distribution of gainfully employed persons. Since the figures are
also significant for the purposes here, Table 40 is taken from that
study. In 1960, with a gross national product of 37,055 million francs
and a gainfully employed population of 2,512,000 persons, income per
gainfully employed person amounted to 14,750 francs. If this is rounded
up to 15,000 francs, the income of 89.5 percent lay below the Swiss
average in 1960, and that of 10.5 percent above.

For the year 2000 the corresponding figures, taking the forecast
of an income of 50,000 francs, will be 83.8 and 16.2 percent.* According

---

*According to the forecast, in the year 2000 the income of 83.8
percent of gainfully employed persons will be below the Swiss average,
and the income of 16.2 percent will be above it.

TABLE 40

Distribution of Gainfully Employed Population, by
Income Class, 1960, and Forecast for 2000

Income Class (thousand francs)	Number of Persons (in thousands)		Percent	
	1960-61	2000	1960-61	2000
0-5	950	175	36.3	5.1
5-10	1,020	250	38.9	7.4
10-15	375	325	14.3	9.5
15-20	127	425	4.9	12.5
20-25	57	475	2.2	14.0
25-50	63	1,200	2.4	35.3
50-100	19	350	0.7	10.3
100 or more	9	200	0.3	5.9
Total	2,600	3,400	100.0	100.0

Source: Schweizerisches Institut für Aussenwirtschafts und
Marktforschung, Hochschule St. Gallen, Teilleitbild Volkswirtschaft
(Zurich: Institut für Outs-, Regional- und Landesplanning an der
Eidgenössichen Technischen Hochschule, 1968), p. 18. (Mimeo.)

to the study on the economy, therefore, income distribution in the
future will be somewhat less uneven that at present. In the year 2000
approximately half the employed population will earn between 20,000
and 50,000 francs, whereas in 1960 these amounts were earned by
less than one-twentieth of the employed population (apart from the 1
percent of high-income persons). About one-third of employed persons
in the year 2000 will still be in the income classes in which the overwhelming majorty, 94.4 percent, were situated in 1960. In the year
2000 about one-seventh of the employed population will come within
the highest income classes, which in 1960 were occupied by only one-
hundredth.

These figures for the whole of Switzerland are both filled out
and illustrated by the results of a survey conducted by the People's
Family Movement in French-speaking Switzerland in 1968.[2] This
survey is restricted to wage-earners' households. Of the six volumes
covering the results of the survey, only two had appeared at the time
of writing this book, so that the survey can only be included in part.
The average monthly income of the heads of family covered by the
survey amounted to 1,380 francs. The following differences appear
according to occupational situation: wage-earners, 1,090 francs;

salaried employees, 1,350 francs; public servants, 1,660 francs; and managers, 2,060 francs.

Differences in the average monthly income may also be seen in the size of cities, the figures being 1,470 francs in Geneva and Lausanne, as opposed to only 1,250 francs as the mean figure for towns with less than 3,000 inhabitants. The average monthly income for an employee in the various French-speaking cantons or regions reveals the following differences: French-speaking Switzerland, 1,380 francs; Geneva, 1,460 francs; Vaud, 1,430 francs; Neuchâtel, 1,320 francs; Fribourg, 1,300 francs; Valais, 1,270 francs; and Jura, 1,240 francs.

OWNERSHIP OF VARIOUS APPLIANCES AND MACHINES

Although the per capita income in combination with population distribution according to the various income classes is one of the most common criteria for measuring the standard of living and therefore for comparison between different times and places as well, it remains largely abstract and fails to provide a graphic image of the situation. It makes one curious to know how a change in the per capita income specifically affects the ownership of various articles or the residential situation, that is, how the way of life is altered as a result of changes in per capita income. The Schweizerischer Beobachter has conducted a number of interesting surveys among its subscribers; here, the third of these, dating from 1965, will be referred to.[3]

The survey covered 2,000 subscribers' households, providing a representative sample of the total of about 410,000 subscribers. It cannot be said with any certainty whether the approximately 1.5 million people living in these 410,000 subscribers' households constitute a representative selection of the whole population of Switzerland. Although the survey is restricted to German-speaking Switzerland, there are other factors that indicate that the sample is a fairly good approximation of the overall population of Switzerland: the 2,000 subscribers' households covered in the sample comprise 7,040 persons, which gives an average of 3.52 persons per household. This figure is quite close to the average of 3.41 persons (or 3.27, excluding collective households) that was calculated for the overall population of Switzerland in 1960. If the sample is applied to the total readership of the journal, the age structure of those concerned breaks down as follows:

	Number	Percent
Adults	985,000	68.3
Young persons, 10-18 years	205,000	14.2
Children, 4-9 years	142,000	9.8

	Number	Percent
Infants under age 4	111,000	7.7
Total	1,443,000	100.0

In determining distribution by income level, the survey uses the concept of "purchasing power class" (PPC), and it is pointed out that in practice "classification was left to the common sense of our well-trained field staff. . . moreover, the experience accumulated over a number of years shows that the estimates are generally correct." Distribution of the persons covered by the survey according to the four PPCs provides the following pattern:

		Percent
PPC I	High income	13
PPC II	Upper middle class	33
PPC III	Lower middle class	44
PPC IV	Low income	10
Total		100

The survey makes a further distinction according to the type of residential area, using the categories of "urban," "semiurban," and "rural."

The great advantage of this survey is that, as the third in the series after the previous ones conducted in 1950 and 1960, it offers an opportunity to follow up the growth of prosperity over the period of 15 years (1950-65). It would of course be wrong to accept the results of this survey blindly as representative of the whole population of Switzerland, but it may be assumed that the trends emerging can justifiably claim general validity. In any case, apparently there are no comparable periodical surveys providing essential details for an evaluation of the standard of living.

Table 41 attempts to summarize some of the results of the survey (generally speaking, figures exist for all three of the years covered only in respect of the major categories, which explains the large number of blanks in the table). The following observations may be made on the basis of this table. During the period 1950-65 ownership of all the appliances and machines included in the table increased. This applies equally to the general average and, as far as information is available, to the various residential areas and purchasing power classes. In regard to the various residential areas, the ownership or use of refrigerators, television sets, and additional transistor radios shows a slight decline in 1965 from "urban" to "semiurban" and "rural"; for the ownership or use of washing machines and private cars the differences are slight, but in both cases the peak is found in semiurban areas. As is only natural, there is in some cases a

TABLE 41

Ownership of Various Appliances and Machines as
Indicator of Standard of Living, among Subscribers
to Schweizerischer Beobachter, 1950-65

Appliance or Machine	Percentage of Subscribers Owning or Using		
	1950	1960	1965
Refrigerator	10.5	54	81
Urban			86
Semiurban			84
Rural		40	72
PPC I			96
PPC II			91
PPC III			76
PPC IV		21	45
Washing machine	36	75	85
Urban			87
Semiurban			89
Rural	13	69	81
PPC I			98
PPC II			92
PPC III			82
PPC IV			64
Television		8.1	34
Urban		10	39
Semiurban		9	30
Rural		5	30
PPC I		16	46
PPC II			40
PPC III		9*	31
PPC IV		4	10
Radio		97	100
One or more additional			
transistor sets			29
Urban			35
Semiurban			31
Rural			22
PPC I			54
PPC II			37
PPC III			20
PPC IV			14
Electric grill	6	9.1	10.3
PPC I			31.6
PPC II			13.4
PPC III			4.4
PPC IV			0.5
Two-wheeled motor vehicle		14.6	15.6
Telephone		70	83

Appliance or Machine	Percentage of Subscribers Owning or Using		
	1950	1960	1965
Electric polisher	3	11.6	13.5
PPC I			41.7
PPC II			14.1
PPC III			7.6
PPC IV			1.5
Electric iron	1	1.6	5.6
PPC I			15.6
PPC II			6.0
PPC III			3.4
PPC IV			1.5
Sun lamp			14.9
PPC I			34.7
PPC II			20.6
PPC III			8.0
PPC IV			1.5
Electric sewing machine	19	50	61.6
PPC I			80.2
PPC II			68.8
PPC III			57.5
PPC IV			32.2
Typewriter			56.7
PPC I			90.4
PPC II			74.6
PPC III			43.6
PPC IV			14.3
Electric record player		38	51
Tape recorder		6	14.2
Piano		18	19.3
Slide projector		7.5	16.0
Movie camera			8.5
Camera			67
Automobile	9.7	21.9	45
Urban			44
Semiurban			47
Rural			45
PPC I			88
PPC II			63
PPC III			28
PPC IV			7

*In 1950 and 1960 only three purchasing power classes were used.

Source: Schweizerischer Beobachter,

TABLE 42

Household Accounts: Families by Number of Children, Income Grades, Composition of Income, and Composition of Expenditure

Income, Expenditure	Families, Total	Annual Income (in francs)					Married Couples by Number of Children			
		Up to 18,000	18,000-22,000	22,000-26,000	26,000-30,000	30,000 and More	1	2	3	4 and 5
Number of families	412	20	88	136	84	84	76	177	109	45
Number of persons per family	4.32	3.55	4.06	4.23	4.77	4.44	3	4	5	6.22
Consumption units per family	2.68	2.29	2.51	2.58	2.85	2.97	2.18	2.54	2.91	3.54
Per Thousand Distribution of Income										
Income of head of household	886	849	906	906	859	877	855	896	892	910
Earnings of other members of household	41	12	27	26	56	59	72	32	33	33
Income from insurance	18	8	16	17	27	15	2	20	19	7
Assistance of all kinds	2	36	0	1	2	0	7	0	0	4
Net profit from business	2	6	3	2	2	1	1	2	2	4
Miscellaneous income	51	89	48	48	54	48	45	50	54	42
Per Thousand Distribution of Expenditure										
Food	202	272	231	208	204	167	184	196	213	222
Alcoholic beverages	33	41	34	36	28	31	36	35	30	26
Clothing	85	62	76	85	94	85	81	83	88	92
Rent	132	153	138	127	125	136	138	129	129	137
Household decorations	43	29	34	45	47	49	42	44	41	45
Heating, lighting	31	41	36	31	30	27	30	32	31	30
Cleaning of clothes and household	12	11	12	12	11	11	11	11	12	11
Health care	55	53	56	58	58	51	60	56	57	48
Education, recreation	123	97	113	124	125	132	125	125	124	117
Travel*	65	65	62	62	61	73	68	70	58	57
Insurance	125	101	123	129	124	126	124	126	129	118
Taxes, rates	58	42	50	49	56	77	66	57	53	59
Miscellaneous	36	33	35	34	37	39	35	36	35	38

*Including vehicle taxes and insurance.

Source: Statistisches Jahrbuch der Schweiz, 1971, pp. 346-47.

considerable decline from the highest to the lowest purchasing power
class in 1965. Regarding the way in which the greater ownership of
appliances and machines affects the way of life, four categories may
be noted: (a) mass communications media (televisions, radios); (b)
household equipment (refrigerators, washing machines, electric grills,
electric polishers, electric irons, electric sewing machines); (c)
individual means of communication (private cars, two-wheeled motor
vehicles, telephones); and (d) implements serving the purposes of
culture, entertainment, or active leisure (televisions, radios, record
players, tape recorders, pianos, slide projectors, cameras). The
first and the second of these categories are discussed in further
detail below.

The first point to be mentioned is that the number of television
owners or users has risen sharply since 1965 as compared with the
figure given in the table, because the millionth television set was
installed in Switzerland before the end of 1968. If it is assumed that
the number of television sets will continue to rise until they become
just as common as radios are today, the influence of these two mass
communications media on the way of life of the population can be
estimated. (The relevant questions are discussed in fuller detail
in Chapter 7.)

The figures given in the table in regard to the mechanization
of the household and the consequent liberation of housewives from
certain duties show that this trend is still in full swing. Certain
kitchen and household appliances, such as mixers or vacuum
cleaners, have now come to be taken for granted in most households.
Although such items as refrigerators, washing machines and electric
sewing machines are also very widespread, this is not yet the case
for other mechanical household appliances. In 1967, however, a total
of 76,000 freezers were installed in Switzerland, including 70,000 in
private homes. This led to a 16.3 percent increase in the consumption
of frozen products in that same year, which brought Switzerland, with
a consumption of 6.7 kilograms per person, directly behind Sweden,
which was by far the largest consumer of such products among the
European countries, with 10.3 kilograms per person.[4]

Growing prosperity and technological progress will undoubtedly
have further effects in this field and will be very important for the
housewife's pattern of life. Together with other factors discussed
elsewhere, the mechanization of many household jobs will help to
raise the employment rate of married women, while also allowing
housewives more time for their other duties (bringing up their children)
and generally giving them more free time.

TABLE 43

Household Accounts in Wage-Earners' and
Salaried Employees' Families, 1920-69

Expenditure	1920	1922	1936/7	1943	1945	1950	1955	1960	1964	1965	1969
					Wage-Earners' Families						
Number of families	128	147	741	399	237	184	216	234	233	227	210
Number of persons per family	4.5	4.4	3.9	3.94	4.0	4.2	4.2	4.39	4.40	4.36	4.29
Consumption units per family	2.74	2.67	2.37	2.37	2.40	2.45	2.50	2.65	2.64	2.66	2.70
			Per Thousand Distribution of Expenditure								
Food	449	395	329	388	376	331	322	289	259	250	220
Alcoholic beverages	38	37	37	34	37	29	33	34	36	37	35
Clothing	122	118	89	92	96	107	92	97	96	94	84
Rent	94	123	178	141	137	121	123	116	114	116	122
Home improvement	50	48	32	32	38	39	41	48	48	49	44
Heating, lighting	59	56	53	50	48	44	44	41	38	37	33
Cleaning of clothes and home	19	16	15	16	15	16	15	15	14	14	12
Health care	22	22	33	32	32	44	47	55	54	53	56
Education and Recreation	34	46	58	48	56	67	75	86	100	110	122
Travel*	19	18	20	18	23	23	31	37	47	55	63
Insurance	27	45	92	72	69	107	110	116	122	112	124
Taxes, rates	24	33	30	44	41	37	30	28	35	37	48
Miscellaneous	43	43	34	33	32	35	37	38	37	36	37

Expenditure	Salaried Employees' Families											
	1920	1922	1936/37	1943	1945	1950	1955	1960	1963	1964	1965	1969
Number of families	97	189	713	124	37	142	113	150	245	191	186	202
Number of persons per family	3.8	3.9	3.6	3.91	4.2	4.1	4.1	4.25	4.21	4.30	4.41	4.35
Consumption units per family	2.44	2.45	2.27	2.30	2.26	2.52	2.39	2.57	2.56	2.48	2.61	2.67
	Per Thousand Distribution of Expenditure											
Food	362	300	248	307	306	263	256	233	225	215	209	186
Alcoholic beverages	27	29	27	27	32	21	26	27	28	28	29	31
Clothing	139	119	95	96	90	111	98	98	99	96	95	85
Rent	106	134	183	134	130	122	131	117	121	123	121	140
Home improvement	53	57	41	40	46	48	48	46	48	56	52	42
Heating, lighting	57	54	52	52	53	45	43	39	40	36	33	29
Cleaning of clothes and home	22	19	18	18	19	18	15	15	14	13	13	12
Health care	30	32	46	42	57	55	47	58	58	57	61	55
Education and Recreation	58	72	81	65	68	82	96	106	102	106	118	125
Travel*	21	23	27	25	21	30	35	43	47	52	61	66
Insurance	43	62	86	80	79	108	117	129	127	129	119	126
Taxes, rates	37	51	51	69	65	58	50	49	50	48	49	67
Miscellaneous	45	48	45	45	34	39	38	40	41	41	40	36

*Including vehicle taxes and insurance.

Source: Statistisches Jahrbuch der Schweiz, 1971, pp. 344-47.

TABLE 44

Consumer Expenditure of Private Households,
1966, and Forecasts for 2000*
(at 1966 constant prices)

Consumer Expenditure	Total Consumer Expenditure (million francs)	
	1966	2000
Total consumption by private households	37,600	111,000
Expenditure without regional connection	2,140	11,100
Holidays and relaxation in Switzerland, second home	957	4,290
Expenditure abroad	1,183	6,810
Expenditure with regional connection	35,489	99,900
Retail expenditure	21,430	58,840
Items connected to the locality	11,314	24,430
Food	9,246	19,660
Alcoholic beverages	709	2,000
Tobacco	859	1,660
Cleaning	500	1,110
Items connected to the center	10,116	34,410
Alcoholic beverages	2,166	5,880
Shoes and shoe repairs	680	2,000
Clothing	2,195	6,660
Clothing accessories	217	780
Household goods	2,371	10,660
Personal care	745	2,550
Purchase of vehicles	1,207	3,880
Entertainment	535	2,000
Other expenditure	14,059	41,060
Rent ·	4,372	11,430
Heating and lighting	1,620	4,110
Health	1,657	5,330
Maintenance of vehicles	1,830	6,660
Public transport	467	2,000
Post, Telephone, Telegraph	389	1,330
Education	1,351	4,660
Insurance	748	2,000
Servants' wages	587	210
Miscellaneous	1,038	3,330

*Any differences in the totals of sections or subgroups are due to rounding off.

Index Changes (1966 = 100)		Changes in Percentage of Consumption		Consumer Expenditure per Inhabitant (percent)		Index Changes per Inhabitant (1966 = 100)	
1966	2000	1966	2000	1966	2000	1966	2000
100	296	100.0	100.0	6,268	14,800	100	236
100	519	5.7	10.0	367	1,480	100	415
100	448	2.5	3.9	160	572	100	358
100	576	3.1	6.1	197	908	100	460
100	281	94.4	90.0	5,916	13,320	100	225
100	274	57.0	53.0	3,572	7,845	100	220
100	216	30.1	22.0	1,886	3,257	100	173
100	213	24.6	17.7	1,541	2,620	100	170
100	282	1.9	1.8	118	267	100	226
100	193	2.3	1.5	143	222	100	155
100	222	1.3	1.0	83	148	100	178
100	340	26.9	31.0	1,686	4,588	100	272
100	272	5.8	5.3	361	784	100	217
100	294	1.8	1.8	113	267	100	236
100	304	5.8	6.0	366	888	100	242
100	360	0.6	0.7	36	104	100	289
100	449	6.3	9.6	395	1,421	100	360
100	342	2.0	2.3	124	340	100	274
100	322	3.2	3.5	201	517	100	257
100	374	1.4	1.8	89	267	100	300
100	292	37.4	37.0	2,344	5,475	100	234
100	262	11.6	10.3	729	1,525	100	209
100	254	4.3	3.7	270	548	100	203
100	322	4.4	4.8	276	710	100	258
100	364	4.9	6.0	305	888	100	291
100	428	1.2	1.8	78	267	100	347
100	342	1.0	1.2	65	177	100	272
100	345	3.6	4.2	225	622	100	277
100	268	2.0	1.8	125	267	100	214
100	36	1.6	0.2	98	27	100	23
100	321	2.8	3.0	173	444	100	257

Source: Schweizerisches Institut für Aussenwirtschafts- und Marktforschung an der Hochschule St. Gallen. Teilleitbild Volkwirtschaft (Zurich: Institut für Orts-, Regional- und Landesplanung an der Eidegenössischen Technischen Hochschule, 1968). (Mimeo.)

HOUSEHOLD ACCOUNTS

The Federal Office for Industry, Arts and Crafts, and Labor
and the Federal Statistical Office have for several decades conducted
surveys of household accounts in employees' families. Table 42
represents the income and expenditures of 412 families according
to the number of children and income levels for 1969. It is not necessary to go into each of the items of income separately, but an analysis
of expenditures shows that food is by far the largest item in all cases.
As the income level goes down and the number of children goes up,
the proportion of expenditure represented by food also rises. The
second, third, and fourth places are occupied by expenditures on
rent, insurance, and education and recreation. The proportion represented by rent increases as the income rises; the proportion represented by education and recreation likewise rises.

Table 43 presents the relative trends in the various expenditure
items in the household accounts of wage-earners' and salaried employees' families in the period 1920-69. This table indicates that in
the last 49 years the proportions of most of the staple items, such as
food, clothing, heating and lighting, and cleaning (of clothes and home),
have declined, and in some cases substantially (in the case of food
from 449 to 220 per thousand in wage earners' households, and from
362 to 186 per thousand in salaried employees' households). An
exception among primary items of expenditures consists of rent, the
proportion of which went up from 94 to 122 per thousand in wage
earners' families and from 106 to 140 per thousand in salaried employees' families. This relative reduction in expenditure on primary
items permitted a relative increase in other items, the most spectacular cases being the 122 per thousand for expenditure on education and
recreation in wage earners' families and 125 per thousand in salaried
employees' families, and the 124 and 126 per thousand, respectively,
for insurance. There was also an increase in the relative outlay on
travel (rising from 19 to 63 per thousand in wage earners' families
and from 21 to 66 in salaried employees' families), and for health
care and taxes and rates. The proportion spent on alcoholic beverages
and on the home remained virtually unchanged in both categories.

Regarding the probable future proportional development of the
various items of expenditure, one may refer to Table 44, from the
study on the economy, which forecasts the consumer expenditure of
private households. This table covers all private households, which
means that comparison with the previous statements on wage-earners'
and salaried employees' households is subject to certain restrictions.
This table shows the continuing decline in the proportions represented
by food, cleaning, and heating and lighting. There is a switch in primary

expenditure in regard to rent (the previous relative increase is replaced by a slight reduction in the future) and for clothing (the previous
decline gives way to a slight increase). Another change relates to the
proportional movement of expenditure on insurance, for which the
previous sharp increase is replaced by a slight decline. For education
and recreation, health care, and travel the previous trend toward a
further relative increase in the proportion of expenditure will continue.
In contrast to the previous stagnation the item of home improvement
will rise in relative terms.

HOUSING CONDITIONS

In a study of social development, which is designed as a contribution to the way in which the national territory is to be used in
the future, information on housing conditions is of special interest.
Table 45 indicates the number of inhabited buildings, the number of
households, the number of households per inhabited building, and the
number of persons per inhabited building during 1850-1960. The table

TABLE 45

Inhabited Buildings, Households, and Households and
Persons per Inhabited Building, 1850-1960

Year	Inhabited Buildings	Households	Households per Inhabited Building	Persons per Inhabited Building
1850		485,087		
1860	347,184	527,960	1.52	7.23
1870	387,148	557,018	1.44	6.86
1880	400,322	607,725	1.52	7.07
1888	400,284	638,064	1.59	7.29
1900	434,084	728,920	1.68	7.64
1910	471,216	829,009	1.76	7.97
1920	494,816	886,874	1.79	7.84
1930	545,330	1,002,915	1.84	7.46
1941	604,272	1,147,029	1.90	7.06
1950	672,883	1,312,204	1.95	7.01
1960	759,979	1,594,010	2.10	7.14

Source: Statistisches Jahrbuch der Schweiz, 1967, p. 12.

shows that the number of inhabited buildings and the number of households have steadily risen. Except for a slight decline in 1860-70,
the number of households per inhabited building also rose constantly
from 1.52 in 1860 to 2.10 in 1960. Such a slight rate of increase might
seem surprising, because it is accompanied by a sharp increase in
the degree of urbanization. (See Chapter 10.)

The figures show that the change in area of residence reflected
in urbanization has largely taken place without any corresponding
change in forms of construction. This provides statistical evidence
for the familiar fact that Swiss cities have mainly grown through the
addition of unchanged elements. Traveling through Switzerland today,
however, one has the impression that since 1960 there has been a new
trend in certain places that suggests that the next census will reveal
a sharper increase in the number of households per inhabited building.
It can only be mentioned in passing that this number of households
per inhabited building expresses an essential element in social coexistence, and that any changes in it also affect social patterns of
behavior. The future forms of construction will have a direct influence
on the number of households per inhabited building and consequently
on social patterns of behavior. As will be seen from the proposals
for further action, this range of problems is considered so important
that separate investigation should be devoted to it.

What seems even more surprising at first glance is the fact
that the number of persons per inhabited building has barely changed
in the course of the last 100 years. It has been subject to certain
fluctuations, having fallen from 7.23 in 1860 to the lowest point of
6.86 in 1870, but thereafter it rose again until it reached the maximum
of 7.97 in 1910, then declining to 7.01 in 1950, subsequently rising
again, to 7.14 in 1960.

If the number of households per inhabited building and the number
of persons per household are included in the calculation, it is seen
that the virtually unchanged number of persons per inhabited building
during the 100-year period conceals a dual movement: the number of
households per inhabited building becomes greater, while the number
of persons per household becomes smaller. In very simplified terms,
that is to say, considering only the average and not the actual distribution, it can be said that the seven persons who inhabited a house 100
years ago belonged to a large household, whereas the seven persons
inhabiting a house in 1960 were split up into two small households
(see also Chapter 6). To supplement this comparison in time, Table
46 presents the position for the various cantons. The table shows
that, with an arbitrary borderline of ± 25 percent of the two average
values, both in regard to the number of households and in regard to
the number of persons per inhabited building it is only the two decidedly
urban cantons of Geneva and Basel that lie considerably above that line.

TABLE 46

Inhabited Buildings, Households, and Households and Persons per Inhabited Building, by Canton, 1960

Canton	Inhabited Buildings	Households*	Households per Inhabited Building	Persons per Inhabited Building
Zurich	111,299	295,958	2.66	8.56
Berne	133,224	257,327	1.93	6.68
Lucerne	28,715	63,040	2.20	8.83
Uri	4,614	7,602	1.65	6.94
Schwyz	11,266	18,923	1.68	6.93
Obwalden	3,728	5,394	1.45	6.21
Nidwalden	2,993	5,122	1.71	7.41
Glarus	8,463	11,525	1.36	4.74
Zug	5,933	12,490	2.11	8.85
Fribourg	24,218	38,378	1.58	6.57
Solothurn	31,405	55,858	1.78	6.39
Basel	22,089	79,955	3.62	10.21
Basel-country	23,638	42,278	1.79	6.27
Schauffhausen	10,560	20,007	1.89	6.25
Appenzell OR	9,976	15,134	1.52	4.90
Appenzell IR	2,618	3,361	1.28	4.94
St. Gallen	52,711	93,512	1.77	6.44
Graubünden	24,052	37,541	1.56	6.13
Aargau	61,609	97,190	1.58	5.86
Thurgau	28,630	45,992	1.61	5.81
Ticino	36,589	61,899	1.69	5.34
Vaud	56,561	139,639	2.47	7.59
Valais	27,423	45,290	1.65	6.48
Neuchâtel	17,255	49,550	2.88	8.57
Geneva	20,440	91,045	4.45	12.68
Total	759,979	1,594,010	2.10	7.14

*Family, individual, and collective households.

Source: Statistisches Jahrbuch der Schweiz, 1967, p. 12.

In regard to the number of households per inhabited building Neuchâtel
and Zurich also come slightly above this line. In the same field
(number of households per inhabited building), the cantons of Aargau,
Fribourg, Graubünden, Appenzell AR, Obwalden, Glarus, and Appenzell
IR are below the lower limit, although only in the case of the first four.
The lower limit of 5.35 persons per inhabited building is undershot,
in descending order, by the cantons of Ticino, Appenzell IR, Appenzell
OR, and Glarus.

        The figures quoted so far in regard to living conditions (house-
holds per inhabited building and persons per inhabited building) give
information on certain aspects of the style of life but do not permit
any direct conclusions as to the actual quality of life. An important
indicator of this consists of the volume of living space per person.
In the Schweizerischer Beobachter survey the changes in this indicator
over the period 1950-65 were established, although only actual living
quarters were considered. It was found that in 1950 one person had
an average of 1.09 rooms; by 1960 this figure had risen to 1.23,
whereafter it remained stationary until 1965. Compared with 1960,
however, the lower income categories had less living space.[5]

        The Federal Census of 1960 provides comprehensive information
on population density. Table 47 presents the population density according to the date of construction of the house, its ownership, and
the size category of the community. The table shows that, taking the
average of all dwellings, the population density in the buildings constructed before 1947 is lower in all size categories than in the dwellings
built after 1947. This is true of all categories of ownership, with the
single exception of rented and cooperative dwellings in communities
with less than 1,000 inhabitants, but in the overall context this exception
is not significant. This means that greater comfort in other respects
is in some ways purchased through greater population density. Taking
the criterion of ownership, the lowest population density rate appears
in all cases in owner-occupied houses. The middle position is occupied
by rented dwellings, while cooperative dwellings show the highest
population density in all size categories of communities. These
differences in population density according to ownership status are
greatest in large cities; they generally become less noticeable as the
size of the community declines.

        Table 48 again considers population density, but this time ac-
cording to social position. In addition, the average annual rent per
room is shown in conjunction with the social position of the occupants.
Thus, three main types of social position can be distinguished according
to population density: the average density among self-employed persons
and public servants is approximately at the same level and is slightly
below the general average. The density among wage-earners is substantially above the average, while for pensioners it is decidedly

TABLE 47

Dwellings, by Period of Construction, Ownership,
and Population Density, by Size of Community, 1960

| | Inhabitants per Room | | | |
Size of Community	All Dwellings	Owner- Occupied Dwellings	Rented Dwellings	Cooperative Dwellings
100,000 or more	0.90	0.64	0.94	1.00
dwelling built before 1947	0.86	0.63	0.91	0.91
dwelling built after 1947	1.02	0.75	1.02	1.08
50,000-99,999	0.81	0.67	0.84	1.01
dwelling built before 1947	0.77	0.65	0.81	0.89
dwelling built after 1947	0.94	0.77	0.94	1.08
20,000-49,999	0.86	0.71	0.92	1.03
dwelling built before 1947	0.82	0.68	0.88	0.86
dwelling built after 1947	0.96	0.80	1.00	1.06
10,000-19,999	0.84	0.69	0.93	1.01
dwelling built before 1947	0.79	0.67	0.88	0.85
dwelling built after 1947	0.95	0.77	1.00	1.06
5,000-9,999	0.84	0.74	0.93	1.01
dwelling built before 1947	0.80	0.72	0.89	0.85
dwelling built after 1947	0.94	0.82	1.00	1.05
2,000-4,999	0.86	0.80	0.94	1.03
dwelling built before 1947	0.84	0.78	0.93	0.86
dwelling built after 1947	0.91	0.86	0.98	1.06
1,000-1,999	0.86	0.82	0.96	1.05
dwelling built before 1947	0.85	0.81	0.95	0.98
dwelling built after 1947	0.90	0.87	0.97	1.06
Under 1,000	0.86	0.83	0.98	1.01
dwelling built before 1947	0.86	0.82	0.98	1.04
dwelling built after 1947	0.88	0.86	0.97	0.99
Total	0.86	0.77	0.93	1.01
dwelling built before 1947	0.83	0.76	0.91	0.90
dwelling built after 1947	0.95	0.84	1.00	1.07

Sources: Federal Statistical Office, Eidgenössische Volkszählung 1 Dezember 1960, Vol. 29, "Switzerland," Pt. III, "Housing" (Berne, 1964); Statistische Quellenwerke der Schweiz, Vol. 379, pp. 162-63.

TABLE 48

Dwelling, by Social Position, Population
Density, and Rent, 1960

Social Position	Occupants per Room	Average Rent per Room (in francs)
Self-employed	0.85	547
Salaried employees in private firms	0.85	622
Public servants	0.82	588
Wage-earners in private firms	1.03	423
Wage-earners in public services	1.03	455
Pensioners, persons not gainfully occupied, and unemployed	0.60	467
Switzerland Total	0.86	505

Source: Federal Statistical Office, Eidgenössische Volkszählung
1. Dezember 1960 Vol. 29, "Switzerland," Pt. III, "Housing" (Berne
1964); Statistische Quellenwerke der Schweiz, Vol. 379, pp. 190-91.

below it. The average annual rent per room is highest among salaried
employees of private firms followed by public servants and self-
employed persons. Pensioners and wage-earners come below the
general average.

The distribution of households of different sizes among dwellings
of different sizes, as well as the equipment of dwellings in regard to
cooking facilities, baths and showers, and heating are shown Table 49.
The distribution of households by size of dwelling will not be examined
in further detail here. Regarding the equipment of dwellings, the table
shows that in 1960 less than one-tenth of households still used wood
or coal. About two-thirds had a bath or a shower, while roughly
one-half were heated with individual stoves, the other half having
central heating or some other system.

Table 50 is set out according to area of settlement and purchasing
power class in order to show the percent of households in single-family
houses and dwellings in multifamily houses, as well as the percent of
families able to use a garden or an allotment. The table shows that
the percentage of families living in single-family houses fell from
39 percent in 1950 to 32 percent in 1965. A comparison between
1960 and 1965 shows that this declining trend applies to urban and
semiurban conditions, whereas in rural areas there was a slight

TABLE 49

Private Households According to Equipment and
Number of Persons and Rooms, 1960*

Number of Rooms in Dwelling	Total Households	Number of Households by Number of Persons in Household					
		1	2	3	4	5	6 or More
1	93,848	65,182	21,377	5,230	1,441	355	263
2	240,337	68,828	100,195	43,367	19,130	5,787	3,030
3	472,145	51,410	154,469	125,027	88,292	35,007	17,940
4	354,832	22,333	80,556	79,671	82,841	50,891	38,540
5	197,898	9,259	37,061	38,552	42,155	33,281	37,589
6	102,221	3,811	15,659	17,047	19,461	17,714	28,529
7	52,671	1,666	7,081	7,987	8,823	8,869	18,245
8	29,623	874	3,505	4,070	4,474	4,561	12,139
9	14,978	368	1,621	1,973	2,048	2,209	6,759
10 or More	21,837	529	1,996	2,730	2,897	3,005	10,680
Total	1,580,390	224,260	423,520	325,655	271,562	161,679	173,714
Equipment							
Kitchen, kitchenette	1,552,290	208,865	417,160	322,974	269,919	160,762	172,610
Wood or coal stove	131,538	22,136	29,184	20,770	17,662	14,286	27,500
Other stove	1,418,994	185,483	387,658	302,095	252,222	146,453	145,083
Bath, shower	997,930	106,461	269,881	222,920	191,174	107,465	100,029
Single stove heating	792,554	118,648	205,053	151,386	124,660	83,564	109,243
Other heating	787,441	105,377	218,393	174,224	146,882	78,104	64,461

*Not including 610 households in caravans, houseboats, and emergency homes.

Source: Statistisches Jahrbuch de Schweiz, 1967, p. 33.

TABLE 50

Some Indicators of Living Conditions
among Schweizerischer Beobachter
Subscribers, 1950-65
(percent)

Indicator	1950	1960	1965	
Single-family house	39	34	32	
Urban		19	15	
Semiurban		38	37	
Rural		38	50	
PPC I			58	
PPC II			37	
PPC III			24	
PPC IV			19	
Dwelling in multifamily house	61	66	68	
Urban		81	85	
Semiurban		62	63	
Rural		62	50	
PPC I			42	
PPC II			63	
PPC III			76	
PPC IV			81	
Garden and/or allotment*	73	66	Garden 59	Allot. 31
Urban			Garden 35	Allot. 14
Semiurban			Garden 66	Allot. 33
Rural			Garden 84	Allot. 51
PPC I			Garden 74	Allot. 28
PPC II			Garden 58	Allot. 31
PPC III			Garden 56	Allot. 34
PPC IV			Garden 59	Allot. 29

*A piece of land used for gardening, situated at some distance (near or far) from the house, rather that around it.

Source: Schweizerischer Beobachter, Wachsender Wohlstand: Wie sie leben—1965, (Basel: Verlangsgesellschaft Beobachter AG), n.d.

relative increase in the number of single-family houses. In the breakdown according to purchasing power class, as expected, the proportion of single-family houses declines as the purchasing power lessens, from 58 percent among the better-off classes to 19 percent among the less well-off in 1965. In contrast to the general trend the comparison in time for the purchasing power class of the well-off shows a continuous rise in the number of single-family houses, although the exact figures are not given.[6]

The information on gardens and allotments permits a precise comparison between the years 1950 and 1960 only, in which the two categories were taken together, but not with 1965, when they were considered separately. In overall terms, the percent of households with a garden or allotment fell from 73 percent in 1950 to 66 percent in 1960; in 1965 59 percent of households were able to use a garden and 31 percent (consisting partly of the same households) had an allotment available. When analysis is made according to social strata, a striking increase in the ownership of gardens is noticeable among the well-off.[7]

The desire for rest and relaxation through contact with nature seems very deep rooted, and increasing prosperity makes it attainable. An alternative solution in fulfilling the same needs consists in having a second home in the country. Table 51 shows the percentage of families with their own country houses. Out of the 410,000 households covered by the Schweizerischer Beobachter survey, 28,000 had their own country home. Assuming that the sample covered by the Schweizerischer Beobachter is representative for the population of Switzerland, this would produce a very rough estimate for 1965 of a total of easily 100,000 country homes owned by Swiss. On the occasion of the federal census of 1970 one of the questions related to second homes, which should throw light on the situation in Switzerland; at the time of writing, however, the results had not yet been published.

An interesting comparison can be made with France in this connection. According to information published by the French Statistical Office, in mid-1967 there were 2.83 million households, or 18.2 percent of the total, with a second dwelling, that is, a holiday or weekend country home.[8] Of these, 1.73 million households, or 11.1 percent of the total, were owners or tenants; the others were mainly accommodated by relatives and friends. The bulk of households with a second dwelling have their principal home either in Paris or in the immediate surroundings. This "luxury" is also very widespread on the Mediterranean, the main dwelling in such cases generally being in Marseilles. The same source goes on to say that this trend has advanced rapidly. This means not only that customs have changed but also that the additional home has become an important factor in economic life. In particular, this has stimulated housing construction,

TABLE 51

Households with Own Country House, by Area of
Residence and PPC among Schweizerischer
Beobachter Subscribers, 1965

Area of Residence and PPC	Percent of Households with Own Country House
Urban	7
Semiurban	9
Rural	4
PPC I	12
PPC II	8
PPC III	4
PPC IV	1
General average	7

Source: Schweizerischer Beobachter, pp. 41-43.

so that old farm houses abandoned by their original occupants have
been restored in large numbers, weekend traffic in the vicinity of large
towns has expanded enormously, the pattern of savings has also been
influenced, and the demand for furniture and consumer durables has
increased.

The fact that in France, with its lower per capita income, a
larger percent of households have a second home than in Switzerland
(although it remains to be seen whether the question regarding second
homes was put in the same way in both cases) and that these households
are largely concentrated in the two largest cities suggests that a
second home is not only a function of income but is equally dependent
on the residential conditions offered by the first home. In other words,
the extent to which the desire for rest and relaxation in contact with
nature must be fulfilled through having a second home is considerably
affected by the circumstances of the first home. The subject of second
homes will be returned to later.

HOLIDAYS AWAY FROM HOME

Table 52 shows the changes in the proportions of people going
on holiday during the period 1950-65, according to the residential
area and purchasing power class. The percent of subscribers who
went away on holiday rose from 53 percent in 1950 to 79 percent in

TABLE 52

Schweizerischer Beobachter Subscribers
with Vacations, 1950-65

| Area of Residence and PPC | Percent Taking Vacation Away from Home | | |
	1950	1960	1965
Urban	76	85	95
Semiurban	51	71	80
Rural	34	42	54
PPC I	79	87	98
PPC II	56*	75**	89
PPC III	34*	45*	67
PPC IV			44
General average	53	68	79

*In 1950 and 1960 there were only three purchasing power classes.

Source: Schweizerischer Beobachter.

1965. This trend applies to all residential areas and purchasing
power classes. In harmony with similar surveys both in Switzerland
and elsewhere, this shows that more urban dwellers went away on
holiday than did those living in semiurban areas, but that holidays
away from home were more common among the latter than among
rural dwellers. In connection with purchasing power classes the
proportion of persons going on holiday naturally enough increases
with the degree of prosperity. This means that, with a further increase
in per capita incomes and a general extension in holiday periods, there
should be a further expansion in the number of holiday travelers. In
regard to the place chosen for holidays there was a change in the
trend from 1960, because the proportion of persons taking their
holidays in Switzerland (as a proportion of all persons going away
on holiday) rose to 72 percent in 1965, following a decline from 82
to 68 percent between 1950 and 1960.

TAXATION IN THE CANTONS

The following figures and comments might well have been
included at some other place in this study, but it would appear that
there is a connection between per capita income and total taxation
in the various cantons (see the comments on Table 53). Taxation

influences the territorial distribution of the population, although it is
no easy matter to distinguish between cause and effect. Does a
particular area (community, canton) attract residents because it has
a low tax rate, or can it reduce its tax rate because it has a high
population density? Of course the same thing applies mutatis mutandis
to areas with a high tax rate that are becoming depopulated. Tax rates
are in any case one of the instruments whereby the territorial distribution of the population can be influenced.

The ensuing comments are based essentially on a statistical
study on the subject of taxation and are designed mainly to illustrate
the differences in the tax situation in the various cantons.[9] The
difficulty involved in assessing the overall weight of cantonal and
municipal taxes from the individual types of tax led in the mid-1950s
to the creation of the taxation burden index of physical persons. The
purpose of this index was to show by means of a single figure the
burden of the various kinds of income and property taxes in comparison to the average total tax burden in all cantons. This index is
of particular importance in listing the cantons in order of financial
potential when federal subsidies are distributed. The basis of calculation consists of the tax burden in the 244 largest communities.

For 1964 the pattern of income and property taxation shown in
Table 53 results (added to the index figures are the order of listing
in accordance with total taxation and per capita income for 1966).
What the table reveals first of all is the existence of considerable
variation in the rate of taxation between the cantons: in Appenzell IR,
for example, the figure is nearly double that for Geneva. In 15 cantons
having an aggregate population of about 3.5 million (estimated average
resident population in 1963) the rate is above the mean for Switzerland,
whereas in 10 cantons with about 2.8 million inhabitants it is below
the mean. Comparison of the order of cantons in terms of taxation
and per capita income does not reveal any really uniform pattern.
In 12 cantons (Appenzell IR, Obwalden, Valais, Solothurn, St. Gallen,
Schauffhausen, Aargau, Zug, Basel-country, Zurich, Basel, and
Geneva) the difference between the respective orders is less than
three, which at first glance suggests a close correlation between
taxation and per capita income. The other 13 cantons, in which the
difference between the two figures amounts to at least three places,
can be divided into two categories: cantons with a relatively high
rate of taxation, although the per capita income is not especially
low (Fribourg, Graubünden, Lucerne, Thurgau, Berne, Ticino, Vaud,
and Neuchâtel) and cantons with a relatively low rate of taxation,
although the per capita income is not especially high (Schwyz, Appenzell OR, Glarus, Uri, and Nidwalden).

The variation in the rate of taxation is a consequence of the
differences in fiscal legislation from one canton to another. This may
be illustrated by means of the following examples:

TABLE 53

Weight of Income and Property Taxation, by Canton

Canton	Total Index of Taxation	Order According to Weight of Taxation, 1964	Inverted Order by per Capita Income, 1966
Appenzell IR	144	1	1
Fribourg	128	2	10
Obwalden	127	3	1
Graubünden	125	4	9
Lucerne	123	5	11
Thurgau	118	6	14
Valais	117	7	6
Berne	116	8	16
Ticino	110	9	12
Vaud	110	9	21
Neuchâtel	109	11	19
Solothurn	107	12	14
Schwyz	106	13	3
St. Gallen	103	14	13
Appenzell OR	102	15	8
Glarus	99	16	5
Schauffhausen	96	17	17
Aargau	96	17	17
Uri	95	19	3
Nidwalden	90	20	6
Zug	89	21	22
Basel-country	86	22	20
Zurich	84	23	23
Basel	81	24	25
Geneva	79	25	24

Source: Eidgenössische Steuerverwaltung, "Steuerbelastung in der Schweiz 1964," Statistische Quellenwerke der Schweiz, vol. 386 (Berne, 1965); Schweizerische Bankgesellschaft, La Suisse en chiffres, 1967 (Zurich, 1967).

Even tax allowances on social grounds vary widely. In the canton of Geneva, for example, the taxpayer can deduct 1,300 francs for each child, which is over five times more than in Appenzell Inner Rhodes [IR] (250 francs). With a deduction rate of 1,000 francs per child the canton of Zurich is also near the top of the

list. The cantons of Basel Town and Vaud also allow 1,000
francs for the first child, and even more in respect of
successive children. The progressive approach to tax
deductions in accordance with the number of children is
also followed in Berne, Schwyz, Glarus, Zug, Fribourg,
Solothurn, St. Gallen, Graubünden, and Neuchâtel. It is
hardly surprising that social deductions are generally
lowest in the cantons with the weakest financial situation.

The variation in deductions, combined with the fact
that the various scales do not begin at the same income
level, mean that the starting point of income tax assess-
ment shows substantial divergences. In Zurich a married
man without children is liable to tax from a gross annual
income of 3,996 francs upward. In Frauenfeld the starting
point is 1,512 francs, while in Geneva it is 5,401 francs.
The differences are even more startling when one takes
the case of a married man with four children: before an
inhabitant of Geneva becomes liable to tax he has to earn
more than seven times as much as someone in Frauenfeld
and nearly four times as much as a person in Appenzell.

The starting point for property tax liability reveals
yet more striking differences. For a gainfully employed
married man without children tax is assessed from 100
francs upwards in Fraunfeld; in Zurich it is 21,000, but
in Geneva 101,001.[10]

Many more examples of differing taxation standards in the cantons
could be quoted.[11]

CANTONAL DIFFERENCES IN LIVING STANDARDS

Table 54 indicates that there are sometimes quite substantial
differences in standards of living as between the various cantons. It
is enlightening to augment this table with two additional measures:
participation in the annual field shooting exercises of 1968 (the number
taking part in the voluntary exercise as a proportion of the number attending the compulsory federal exercise) amounted to 82.76 percent
in the canton of Appenzell IR and in Geneva to 8.74 percent.[12] In
Table 54 Appenzell IR is last in four out of the six columns, whereas
Geneva is first, second, or third in five of the columns.

CRITICISM OF THE PRIORITY GIVEN
TO ECONOMIC GROWTH

It is a declared or undeclared aim of all of the Swiss political
parties to raise the general level of prosperity. Analysis of the

TABLE 54

Selected, Partially Estimated Indicators of Standard of Living, by Canton, 1966

Canton	Per Capita Income (francs)	Banks Savings per Capita (francs)	Automobiles per 1,000 Inhabitants	Telephones per 1,000 Inhabitants	Doctors per 10,000 Inhabitants	Life Insurance Premiums per Inhabitant (francs)
Zurich	10,850	8,770	169	313	12.4	274
Berne	8,000	7,050	141	250	9.7	194
Lucerne	7,500	5,980	125	219	9.6	145
Uri	6,600	5,060	92	139	5.2	143
Schwyz	6,600	7,700	121	171	5.3	140
Obwalden	6,200	5,870	101	164	5.2	117
Nidwalden	7,200	8,580	122	168	5.2	126
Glarus	6,750	5,410	101	182	8.0	213
Zug	9,500	6,200	139	216	10.6	165
Fribourg	7,400	6,240	139	183	7.0	124
Solothurn	7,900	6,540	129	206	7.2	228
Basel	13,700	9,890	162	360	17.8	396
Basel-country	8,600	5,520	166	226	6.5	138
Schauffhausen	8,200	7,150	141	256	8.6	186
Appenzell OR	7,250	4,970	119	204	6.9	157
Appenzell IR	6,200	7,540	82	131	3.6	171
St. Gallen	7,650	9,170	119	208	8.2	183
Graubünden	7,350	5,670	122	228	10.4	184
Aargau	8,200	7,950	150	216	6.6	201
Thurgau	7,900	7,870	131	202	6.2	183
Ticino	7,600	7,240	191	247	12.0	251
Vaud	8,900	5,720	164	287	13.2	182
Valais	7,200	6,110	122	163	7.1	136
Neuchâtel	8,400	5,340	174	286	9.5	204
Geneva	13,000	6,940	254	357	15.8	260
Total Switzerland	8,900	7,280	153	256	10.3	214

Source: "Switzerland in Figures, 1967," leaflet issued by the Union Bank of Switzerland.

evolution of various indicators relating to living standards has shown
that it has steadily risen, and the forecasts point to a further upward
trend. This chapter would remain incomplete, however, if it were
not to make some reference to a factor in social development that is
connected to the standard of living, although new in this context,
namely, the criticism of or even rebellion against a society rated
on performance and consumption. These feelings of revolt are
expressed in the "First Pamphlet of the Opponents of Authority,"
which was put out in Zurich in 1968. One passage reads: "The
fact that we find no satisfaction is the fault of the people who would
have us believe that life consists of nothing except subordination
and advancement, respect and career, study and certificates, work
and payday, diligence and thrift, calm and order, morality and law,
Volkswagen and Opel, sausage and roast potatoes." It is not possible
to examine all aspects of this sort of criticism here, but it must be
pointed out that it is not directed against prosperity in itself but
against the system that turns prosperity into the highest commandment.

According to Herbert Marcuse, the advanced industrial societies
have produced systems of production and culture that have either
relegated alien elements and critical attitudes with dimensions other
than their own to outsider status or have integrated them into the
established system, thereby condemning it to stagnation. This system
gives a privileged situation to certain groups and cements their
economic predominance. The consumer is forced into wastage by
the system.[13] Marcuse argued that the rebellion of youth comes
from its loathing for the affluent society, its vital need to break the
rules of a deceitful and bloody game, and to opt out altogether. In
the younger generation's resistance Marcuse sees the emergence of
a new consciousness with a different instinct for reality, life and
happiness, and the desire for a freedom that has nothing to do with
the freedoms practiced in the "senile" society and that refuses to
have anything to do with them.[14]

In the wave of dissatisfaction that has crystallized in Switzerland
over the issue of excessive foreign infiltration, criticism of unbounded
economic growth seems to have become an essential component. In
the course of development such criticism has even become an acceptable topic in speeches by members of the judiciary or the universities
(for example, an inauguration speech at the University of St. Gallen
in 1970 discussed the subject of "Economic Growth—Progress or
Spoilation?"). The widening range of criticism is closely connected
with the growing awareness of the need for environmental protection.

9

THE PARTIES' VALUES AND AIMS

KCVP:
   "The party acknowledges the principle of private property. In accordance with Christian social beliefs it stresses the social obligations of property and the enhanced responsibility today placed in landownership. The party welcomes the reintroduction of apartment ownership and the timely expansion of building facilities to enable additional sections of the population to own property, to permit better utilization of the land, and to open up new opportunities for social housing construction."

   "The acquisition of a share in the means of production by the workers, together with increased responsibility in a more prosperous economy, are inherent social components in our economic program."

   "It is the task of the family and of society to teach the value and significance of property for the development and protection of economic and moral personality. In occupational life this attitude finds its natural complement in participation by employees in the ownership of undertakings, with all the concomitant advantages and risks. The numerous possibilities offered by such participation should be left for further social evolution, without state invervention."

Free Democratic Party:
   "The party favors the "reinforcement of the economic independence of the citizen through promotion of savings, facilitation of property formation, and its widest possible distribution in all sectors of the population. [The party also supports] fiscal measures to promote savings and property formation."

   "The party favors the principle of the private economy and private property. However, it recognizes the need for general economic institutions to perform public duties."

"The free economy has created prosperity for all, but prosperity
must not be allowed to end with ample coverage of everyday living
requirements and desires for luxury. The possibility of property
formation must also exist. Property means social security, it reduces
dependence on the state and reinforces personal freedom. This should
be possible for everyone. In addition, we demand:

> The promotion of building and the acquisition of moderately
> priced apartments and houses for ownership by families
> with modest incomes and resources, particularly through
> the provision of credit or loan security;
>   the construction and allocation of privately owned
> dwellings at reasonable conditions by employers and
> nonprofit cooperatives;
>   the inclusion of action to promote moderately
> priced, privately owned apartments and houses in all
> future housing construction plans of the Federal and
> Cantonal Authorities."

SPS:
        "In the case of monopolistic undertakings and organizations it
is essential either to create the requirements for fair competition
or to place them under public control or public ownership. Similarly,
private undertakings whose activities lie within the field of public
interest may be converted to serve the general economic interests."
"Private ownership of the land should be restricted to the extent
needed in order to implement a new land policy and carry out effective
local, regional, and national city and country planning."

BGB:
        "The BGB favors a healthy and efficient economy based on
private ownership and free competition within the limits set by the
well-being of the national community."
        "The BGB desires the broadest possible distribution of private
landownership. It decisively rejects socialist nationalization tendencies."

LdU:
        "Hand in hand with this natural attachment to the land goes the
healthy desire of the Swiss for property. Every person has the
economic aim of owning some property, however small or modest it
may be. This natural joy in ownership makes us unsympathetic to
all state socialist tendencies from either the left or the right, and
these therefore have no future with us. We believe that the principal
task of Swiss economic policy consists of enabling every Swiss
citizen to acquire his own property and thereby to attain economic

freedom. In the eyes of the Swiss, extensive property does not endow
the owner with any special prerogatives."

"Principle: Recognition and protection of private property,
promotion of small property."

"Private housing estates should therefore be promoted in every
way."

Liberal Democratic Citizens' Party:

"Although it is undeniably necessary to prevent certain forms
of misuse of private landed property, there can be no question of
doing away with it. Such property creates attachments that are
beneficial to the country and that make it possible to satisfy the
individual's real needs."

Evangelical People's Party:

"All property is a pledge received from God's hand. Ownership
of land or of the means of production must not be misused."

"A fair wage should enable the thrifty worker to acquire property."

PdA:

"In the production and distribution of the goods produced men
enter into specific relationships: production relationships. The
decisive element determining the form of production relationships
is the ownership of the means of production."

"Private ownership of the means of production also results in
the fundamental contradiction of capitalism: the contradiction between
the social character of the process of production and the private
capitalistic form of the acquisition of products. The workers' power
recognizes the legitimacy of property held by peasants, artisans,
and small traders. The workers' power frees the ground of the
cities and farming lands from speculation, it cancels mortgage
charges, returns the ownership of urban land to the community and,
far from depriving the peasants of the land, assigns it to them for
utilization in perpetuity."

This survey of the relevant passages in the parties' programs
and other statements shows that all of the parties normally described
as bourgeois (which would include the National Independent Association
in this context) recognize the principle of private property and
attribute a moral value to property. Consequently, they also call for
measures to facilitate property formation and broad distribution of
property. The two left-wing parties call for statutory restriction
of property rights in certain cases, together with the transfer of
certain enterprises to public ownership or the nationalization of all
branches of the economy, but there are substantial differences between
the two parties.

Although the various party aims are clear enough, the actual
property situation is far from simple. This chapter ought to be able
to turn to statistics of landownership and industrial plant ownership
so that at least the number and character of the owners would be
known according to the size and type of the property at different
times. As far as is known, however, there are no comprehensive and
generally accessible statistics of this kind. Accordingly, one is
obliged to make do with makeshift solutions and partial aspects of
the situation in attempting to arrive at some cautious conclusions.

OWNERSHIP OF AGRICULTURAL LAND

The ten-yearly federal census (of enterprises and farms)
provides information on ownership of agricultural land. The pattern
for 1955 and 1965 is presented in Table 55. Accordingly, the proportion of land belonging to the farmers who work it decreased during
the ten years under consideration by 28 per thousand, while the proportion of rented land increased by the same amount. If the actual
figures for land area were considered it would probably be found
that the decline in the number of farms during recent decades has
led to a reduction both in the number of agricultural landowners and
in the area owned by farmers working the land.

Maurice Erard refers to the growing interconnection of agriculture with other branches of the economy. In 1955, for example,
there were 14,669 farms owned by nonagricultural enterprises.[1]
Since any comprehensive statistics covering nonagricultural landownership are available, some general observations by Erard regarding
the subject follow:

> Communal land is still to be found frequently in rural
> areas, particularly mountain lands . . . In addition, a
> number of municipal authorities pursue a policy of land
> acquisition . . . These factors resulting in a decline in
> the number of individual landowners are compounded
> by the fact that a growing proportion of the land is
> controlled by purely financial interests, owing to the
> emergence of real estate companies (in 1962 there were
> 13,415 such companies with an aggregate capital of
> over 1 billion francs) and of real estate investment
> trusts (controlled to the extent of 80 percent by banks).[2]

OWNERSHIP OF HOUSES AND APARTMENTS

The federal census of 1960 not only gave an inventory of
dwellings but also provided information on the ownership of dwellings

TABLE 55

Per Thousand Distribution of Farmlands,
by Owned Land, Rented Land, and Land Used
by Arrangement, 1955 and 1965

Type of Land	1955	1965
Land owned by user	703	675
Rented land	292	320
Land used by arrangement	5	5

Sources: Federal Statistical Office, Eidgenössische Betrieb-
szählung September 1965 - Landwitschaftsbetriebe: Bodenbenützungs-
systeme, Betriebsformen, Produktionseinrichtungen (Berne) Statistische
Quellenwerke der Schweiz, Vol. 419, 1968, p. 218. The figures for
1955 are from Maurice Erard, "A Sociological Outline of Social
Classes in Switzerland," Cahiers Internationaux de Sociologie (Paris),
XXXIX, (July-December 1965), p. 10.

and the population's housing conditions. Its findings are therefore
a valuable contribution to knowledge of the social, health, and economic circumstances of the people. The 1960 survey was the first
one to cover dwellings throughout the country. Although the following
observations relate only to the 1960 data, it is possible to draw
certain indirect conclusions concerning probable future trends by
means of comparison between the different size categories of communities. This is assuming that the present circumstances in towns
and cities are largely a prefiguration of the pattern to be followed
by further urbanization (this forecast would have to be corrected if
it should be found that private ownership of individual apartments
comes to play a predominant role). Regarding the scope of coverage,
the introduction to the volume of the census relating to this subject
states that it does not cover all dwellings:

> The survey did not include holiday and weekend
> dwellings, dwellings remaining unoccupied owing to
> ownership of more than one dwelling (city and country
> home, mountain and valley farm) or dwellings used
> for other purposes (doctors' surgeries, offices, and
> so on). The premises of collective households
> (monasteries, hospitals, old people's homes, hotels,
> apprentices' hostels, and so on) were also excluded.
> On the other hand, inhabited caravans, houseboats,

and emergency dwellings were included but not under
the heading of dwellings. Information on unoccupied
dwellings was not assessed. Only "true" single-
family houses were reckoned as such. Farmhouses
and buildings with workshops or shops were not
counted as single-family houses, even if inhabited
only by a single household.[3]

Tables 56 and 57 present, in absolute and per thousand figures,
the ownership of dwellings in the various size categories of communities. The tables show that the proportion of dwellings owned by
individuals increases as the size of the community (in population)
diminishes. Moreover, the differences are substantial, because in
large cities only 389 per thousand dwellings belong to individuals,
whereas this proportion rises to 816 per thousand in communities
with less than 1,000 inhabitants. The fact that the corresponding
figure in communities with 50,000 to 99,999 inhabitants is somewhat
higher (586 per thousand) than in the next size of community in
descending order (568 per thousand) is no doubt due to the circumstance
that the population expansion in recent times was in many cases
particularly great in communities with 20,000 to 49,999 inhabitants
and that this expansion was frequently met by means of dwellings
constructed by building and real estate companies. The proportion
of dwellings belonging to such companies in this size category of
community is in fact high, at 130 per thousand. The same thing
applies, though to a somewhat lesser degree, in communities with
10,000 to 19,999 inhabitants, where the proportion of such dwellings
is 101 per thousand, which is more than in the medium-sized cities,
communities with 50,000 to 99,999 inhabitants (74 per thousand).
This exception aside, the rule for dwellings owned by building and
real estate companies is that their proportion declines with the
size of the community. One of the social implications when a dwelling
belongs to a building or real estate company is that the tenant's
relationship to the proprietor is a purely business one and often
largely anonymous. If a large number of adjacent apartments belong
to the same company, this can also have the effect, as recently
illustrated in the western part of Switzerland, of stimulating the
formation of tenants' action groups, resulting in new social relationships, even if based on purely practical considerations.

Much the same trend of a declining proportion as the community becomes smaller is found in the case of dwellings owned by other
companies, cooperatives, associations, or foundations, although the
dwellings belonging to other companies or cooperatives in large
cities account for a relatively small proportion (67 per thousand),
whereas the figure is relatively high in communities with 10,000 to

TABLE 56

Dwelling, by Owner and Size of Community, 1960

Size of Community	Total Dwellings	Dwellings Owned by									
		Individuals	Several Individuals	Building and Real Estate Companies	Building and Real Estate Cooperatives	Other Companies and Cooperatives	Associations and Foundations	Communities	Cantons	Federation	Foreign Countries and International Organizations
100,000 or more	390,700	152,159	41,018	93,801	41,422	26,319	18,690	14,135	1,779	602	1,495
50,000- 99,999	88,771	51,985	8,298	6,536	9,313	6,773	2,850	2,068	567	204	177
20,000- 49,999	72,872	41,412	6,513	9,447	4,772	4,799	2,481	2,388	791	224	45
10,000- 19,999	192,623	117,174	17,465	19,537	8,508	16,687	6,273	4,498	1,278	607	596
5,000- 9,999	186,238	131,154	16,205	10,274	4,742	13,486	4,729	3,680	1,070	662	236
2,000- 4,999	272,315	209,613	24,110	7,309	3,842	16,848	2,857	5,064	1,263	1,106	303
1,000- 1,999	170,329	136,065	16,218	2,348	780	8,118	1,379	3,758	814	781	68
Below 1,000	206,542	168,441	22,475	772	160	5,766	941	6,094	735	1,146	12
Total Switzerland	1,580,390	1,008,003	152,302	149,304	73,539	98,796	40,200	41,685	8,297	5,332	2,932

Source: Federal Statistical Office, Eidgenössische Volkszählung, 1 Dezember 1960, Vol. 29, "Switzerland," Pt. III, "Dwellings" (Bern, 1964), Statistische Quellenwerke der Schweiz, Vol. 379, p. 17.

TABLE 57

Dwelling, by Owner and Size of Community, 1960
(per thousand)

Size of Communities	Dwellings Owned by									
	Individuals	Several Individuals	Building and Real Estate Companies	Building and Real Estate Cooperatives	Other Companies and Cooperatives	Associations and Foundations	Communities	Cantons	Federation	Foreign Countries and International Organizations
100,000 or more	389	105	238	106	67	48	36	5	2	4
50,000-99,999	586	94	74	105	76	32	23	6	2	2
20,000-49,999	568	89	130	65	66	34	33	11	3	1
10,000-19,999	608	91	101	44	87	33	23	7	3	3
5,000-9,999	704	87	55	26	72	25	20	6	4	1
2,000-4,999	770	89	27	14	62	9	19	5	4	1
1,000-1,999	799	95	14	5	48	8	22	5	4	<1
Below 1,000	816	109	4	1	28	4	30	4	4	<1
Total Switzerland	638	96	94	47	63	25	26	5	4	2

Source: Federal Statistical Office, Eidgenössische Volkszählung, 1 Dezember 1960, Vol. 29, "Switzerland," Pt. III, "Dwellings" (Bern, 1964), Statistische Quellenwerke der Schweiz, Vol. 379, p. 17.

TABLE 58

New Dwellings, Classified by Proprietor, 1948-70

	Proprietor				
Year	Public Corpo- rations	Building Coopera- tives	Other Legal Entities	Individuals	Total
	Total Number				
1948	601	8,680	3,551	6,483	19,315
1953	153	3,776	9,169	10,698	23,796
1958	651	2,192	7,686	10,070	20,599
1963	865	3,959	17,537	19,813	42,174
1970	1,127	6,242	18,071	20,080	45,520
	Per Thousand				
1948	31	449	184	336	1,000
1953	6	159	385	450	1,000
1958	32	106	373	489	1,000
1963	21	94	416	469	1,000
1970	25	137	397	441	1,000

Source: Statistisches Jahrbuch der Schweiz, 1971, p. 162.

19,999 inhabitants (87 per thousand). No significant differences, by
size category of community, are found in the case of dwellings
belonging to several individuals, to municipal, cantonal, or federal
authorities, to foreign states, or to international organizations.

The information in tables 56 and 57 is supplemented by Table
58, which presents a survey of new dwellings built since 1948,
classified according to proprietors. The table shows that the share
of the building cooperatives as proprietors of dwellings has fallen
sharply since 1948, whereas the proportion of "other legal entities"
has increased most rapidly, from 184 per thousand in 1948 to 397
per thousand in 1970. This means that "other legal entities" have
become almost as important as proprietors of dwellings as are
individuals, whose share rose by only 101 per thousand, from 336
in 1948 to 441 per thousand in 1970. As already pointed out, these
other legal entities are most active in the cities and in the rapidly
growing medium-size communities, so that a further increase in
their importance is to be anticipated in the housing sector with the
advance of urbanization. Here again, reference must be made to

TABLE 59

Dwelling, by Status of Occupancy and Size of Community, 1960

Status of Occupancy	Total Switzerland	Total Single-Family Houses	Communities of 100,000 and More		Communities of 50,000-99,999		Communities of 20,000-49,999	
			Total	Single-Family Houses	Total	Single-Family Houses	Total	Single-Family Houses
Total Number								
Owner occupied	531,981	213,011	32,380	14,553	15,309	6,641	14,583	7,167
Land-tenant occupied	29,105	–	2,204	–	762	–	882	–
Rented	900,063	40,320	313,554	3,340	63,379	1,050	52,664	1,179
Cooperative	59,522	6,907	35,600	4,420	7,648	705	3,156	216
Service dwelling	31,750	7,657	5,451	503	1,141	188	1,072	238
Supplied free	27,969	4,894	1,511	234	532	80	515	93
Total	1,580,390	272,789	390,700	23,050	88,771	8,664	72,872	8,893
Per Thousand								
Owner occupied	337	781	83	631	172	767	200	806
Land-tenant occupied	18	–	6	–	9	–	12	–
Rented	570	148	803	145	714	121	723	133
Cooperative	38	25	91	192	86	81	43	24
Service dwelling	20	28	14	22	13	22	15	27
Supplied free	17	18	3	10	6	9	7	10
Total	1,000	1,000	1,000	1,000	1,000	1,000	1,000	1,000

162

	Communities of 10,000-19,999		Communities of 5,000-9,999		Communities of 2,000-4,999		Communities of 1,000-1,999		Communities under 1,000	
Status of Occupancy	Total	Single-Family Houses	Total	Single-Family Houses	Total	Single-Family Houses	Total	Single-Family Houses	Total	Single-Family Houses
Total Number										
Owner occupied	49,720	25,372	66,938	30,507	128,373	51,282	92,958	34,491	131,720	42,998
Land-tenant occupied	1,849	–	2,718	–	6,075	–	5,367	–	9,248	–
Rented	129,433	4,093	106,787	5,264	122,064	9,522	61,593	6,654	50,589	9,218
Cooperative	6,596	899	3,260	315	2,729	313	454	33	79	6
Service dwelling	3,008	650	3,577	893	6,352	1,678	4,597	1,388	6,522	2,119
Supplied free	2,017	332	2,958	455	6,722	984	5,360	910	8,354	1,806
Total	192,623	31,346	186,238	37,434	272,315	63,779	170,329	43,476	206,542	56,147
Per Thousand										
Owner occupied	258	809	359	815	472	804	546	793	638	766
Land-tenant occupied	10	–	15	–	22	–	32	–	45	–
Rented	672	131	573	141	448	149	362	153	245	164
Cooperative	34	29	18	8	10	5	2	1	<1	<1
Service dwelling	16	21	19	24	23	26	27	32	32	38
Supplied free	10	10	16	12	25	16	31	21	40	32
Total	1,000	1,000	1,000	1,000	1,000	1,000	1,000	1,000	1,000	1,000

Source: Federal Statistical Office, Eidgenössische Volkszählung 1 Dezember 1960, Vol. 29, "Switzerland," Pt. III, "Dwellings" (Berne, 1964); Statistische Quellenwerke der Schweiz, Vol. 379, pp. 22-24.

ownership of individual apartments; it may be that the other legal
entities will continue to produce dwellings but that once they have
been built they will more commonly be sold as individual apartments.

Table 59 indicates dwellings in the various size categories of
communities by status of occupancy rather than by actual ownership.
The most important feature consists of the trends in regard to owner-
occupied and rented dwellings by size category of community. The
proportion of owner-occupied dwellings rises steadily as the size
of the community diminishes, with quite substantial differences. In
large cities only 83 per thousand of dwellings are occupied by their
owners; this proportion rises to 638 per thousand in communities
with less than 1,000 inhabitants. The trend is the opposite for rented
dwellings, the proportion of which is 803 per thousand in large cities,
diminishing to 245 per thousand in the smallest communities. As
previously shown in Table 58, there is a small exception from the
general trend regarding the order of sequence of communities with
20,000 to 49,999 inhabitants (proportion of rented dwellings, 723 per
thousand); the reasons may be assumed to be identical to those
mentioned in the observations on Table 58. The proportion of land-
tenant-occupied dwellings naturally rises the smaller the number of
inhabitants because these are generally tied to a farm. The proportion
of dwellings owned by cooperatives is highest in the large cities,
where it is 91 per thousand; it steadily declines with the size of the
community. The proportion of service dwellings and those supplied
free increases as the size of the community diminishes.

If ownership of a house or an apartment implies attachment,
while a tenancy relationship, especially with an impersonal company,
means very little involvement, with the possibility of alienation in
extreme cases, then a continuation of the trends noted holds certain
perils if the course of urbanization is pursued. The absence of any
share in ownership may be reflected in attitudes of nonparticipation
that could easily spread to public affairs as well. Alternatives to
this development consist of broad extension of ownership of individual
apartments (which is, however, opposed to some extent by increased
mobility) and the formation of new roots by means of second homes.
As standards of prosperity rise, both of these alternatives really
enter the realm of possibility.

The pros and cons of owning or renting houses and apartments
and of the various kinds of housing cooperatives have been examined
in a number of studies.[4] Table 60, which is based on the three
Schweizerischer Beobachter surveys, shows changes in the proportions
of families living in their own homes, classified according to residential area, occupational category, and purchasing power class.
The table shows that, with one exception only, the percentage of
Sweizerischer Beobachter subscribers living in their own homes fell

TABLE 60

Families Living in Own Homes, by Residence,
Occupation, and PPC among Schweizerischer
Beobachter Subscribers, 1950, 1960, and 1965
(percent)

Residence, Occupation, and PPC	1950	1960	1965
Urban	23	24	16
Semiurban	52	49	48
Rural	68	62	57
Wage-earners		27	25
Salaried employees and civil servants		29	22
Top managers and civil servants		46	37
Self-employed persons		65	59
Farmers	85	85	82
PPC I	80	70	64
PPC II and III		45	27
PPC IV	22	26	24
General average			38

Source: Schweizerischer Beobachter, pp. 19-20.

in all categories. The sole exception was PPC IV, the low-income
group, of whom 22 percent lived in their own homes in 1950, 26 percent
in 1960, and 24 percent in 1965.

It is interesting to analyze ownership of two household appliances
indicative of a high standard of living—refrigerators and washing
machines in tables 61 and 62, respectively. Figures for 1950 and 1960
are not given in Schweizerischer Beobachter, but the commentary on
the survey in regard to washing machines shows that between 1950
and 1960 washing machines were procured largely by households
themselves, whereas between 1960 and 1965 landlords provided for
the installation of washing machines to a greater extent.[5] Washing
machines and refrigerators tend increasingly to be supplied as part
of the equipment of apartments, so that they are less and less commonly owned by the tenants. (This is confirmed by the relatively high
percentage of persons in PPC IV who own the household appliances

TABLE 61

Refrigerators among Schweizerischer
Beobachter Subscribers, by Category of Owner, 1965
(percent)

Residence and PPC	Refrigerator Owned by	
	Subscriber	Owner of Dwelling
Urban	66	34
Semiurban	72	28
Rural	82	18
PPC I	84	16
PPC II	70	30
PPC III	69	31
PPC IV	80	20
General average	72	28

Source: Schweizerischer Beobachter, p. 24.

they use, because for the most part these persons live in old low-rent
dwellings that the landlord does not equip with such comforts as
refrigerators and washing machines.)

Taken together with the probable decline in the number of
individual landowners and the relative decline in the number of house
owners, these figures indicate that, in contrast to the aims of most
of the parties, the rising degree of prosperity in this area is not
correspondingly reflected in greater private property. Rather than
tending toward a society with broad distribution of property, the line
of direction would thus be toward an opulent consumer society paying
high rents for high standards of comfort but not establishing any
roots through ownership. It is difficult to say whether ownership of
individual apartments will bring about any radical change in this
connection. Legislation allowing such ownership came into force on
January 1, 1965. After overcoming a number of initial difficulties,
the system now appears to be gaining ground, but its prospects for
the future are hard to assess.

OWNERSHIP OF NONAGRICULTURAL MEANS
OF PRODUCTION AND CONTROL OF
INDUSTRIAL ENTERPRISES

Just as the description of landownership was incomplete and
therefore unsatisfying, it is equally difficult to give any comprehensive

TABLE 62

Washing Machines among Schweizerischer
Beobachter Subscribers, by Category of
Owners, 1965

Residence and PPC	Washing Machines Used by Beobachter Subscribers		
	Leased or Borrowed	Belonging to User	Belonging to Owner of Dwelling
Urban	1	28	71
Semiurban	1	55	44
Rural	1	75	24
PPC I	1	74	25
PPC II	1	50	49
PPC III	1	42	57
PPC IV	1	48	51
General average	1	50	49

Source: Schweizerischer Beobachter, Wachsender Wohlstand:
Wie sie leben—1965 (Basel: Verlagsgesellschaft Beobachter AG,
n.d.), p. 23.

picture regarding the ownership of nonagricultural means of production.
For lack of full statistics the following observations will be incomplete
and are rather like a mosaic of which important parts exist but others
are missing.

A first indication of one trend affecting the overall picture is
the continuous decline in both the absolute and relative numbers of
self-employed persons, the significance of which for the various
economic sectors and industries has already been described elsewhere
(see Table 7). In regard to the ownership of the means of production
this means a decline in the number of self-employed persons who
normally own their own production equipment, even if only simple
and modest tools and implements. This is yet one more instance of
declining importance in a direct and binding relationship that involves
the establishment of roots.

In contrast to the declining number of self-employed persons the
proportion of stock companies has increased most spectacularly in

the recent past, as shown in Table 63, which gives figures for firms
registered under the various legal provisions during the period 1951-
69. The table shows that the number of individually owned firms,
collective companies, limited partnerships, cooperatives, and associations has remained practically stationary since 1951. The largest
increase was recorded for stock companies, from 21, 949 in 1951 to
60, 746 in 1969. In addition, the numbers of foundations, subsidiaries,
and limited companies either doubled or nearly so.

The nominal capital of stock companies increased from 6.9
billion francs in 1940 to 8.6 billion francs in 1950, 14.6 billion in
1960, and 36.4 billion in 1969.[6] In 1962 the nominal capital of the
then about 40,000 stock companies amounted to about 19 billion
francs. Out of this, 13.5 billion was concentrated in 1,702 companies,
with a nominal capital of over 1 million francs in each case.[7]

No complete statistics regarding the distribution of ownership
of stocks is available. In any case, it would have to be determined
what importance should be attached to the ownership of stocks. It
is of course by no means the same thing if a person posesses an
important stock holding that ties him to the company for better or
worse or at least ensures him an effective say in the company's
affairs or if, on the other hand, it is a matter of just a few shares,
the owner remaining in an entirely anonymous relationship to the
company and seldom bothering to exercise his voting rights in person.
In this sense, apart from providing for economic security, broad
distribution of the ownership of stocks seems to have little to do with
what is described in one party's program as "the value and significance
of ownership for the development and maintenance of economic and
moral personality." Broad distribution of ownership of stocks does
not therefore seem an alternative that would help to overcome feelings
of alienation.

A further trend of significance for the structure of industrial
ownership consists of the rapid increase in the number of holding
companies, as illustrated in Table 64. This table shows that the
number of holding companies increased by roughly six times in the
course of 15 years, while their nominal capital increased by nearly
seven times.

To give a better explanation of the purpose of holding companies
and concerns in general, an economic lexicon that relates specifically
to the legal circumstances in West Germany but also contains principles applicable to Switzerland as well is quoted:

> Concerns are formed either through the acquisition of
> stocks in the enterprises to be brought under control
> or, if the enterprises merge voluntarily, by means
> of exchange of stocks or through the acquisition or

TABLE 63

Registered Firms, by Legal Status, since 1951

Year	Individually Owned Firms		Collective Companies		Limited Partnerships		Stock Companies		Limited Companies	
	Total	Index	Total	Index	Total	Index	Total	Index	Total	Index
1951	72,083	100	9,905	100	3,406	100	21,949	100	1,437	100
1956	76,647	106	10,153	103	3,642	107	27,223	124	1,521	106
1961	77,288	107	10,046	101	3,786	111	36,651	167	1,783	124
1966	81,282	113	10,753	109	3,958	116	51,014	232	2,559	178
1970	84,787	118	11,100	112	3,927	115	65,382	298	2,776	193

Year	Cooperatives		Institutes		Associations		Foundations		Subsidiaries		Total	
	Total	Index	Total	Index	Total	Index	Total	Index	Total	Index	Total	Index
1951	12,309	100	107	100	1,391	100	7,869	100	1,798	100	132,254	100
1956	12,580	102	113	106	1,331	96	9,562	122	2,193	122	144,965	110
1961	13,002	106	120	112	1,371	99	12,591	160	2,734	152	159,372	121
1966	13,470	109	131	122	1,535	110	16,766	213	3,472	193	184,940	140
1969	13,518	110	138	129	1,607	116	18,537	236	3,916	218	200,134	151
1970	13,508	110	140	131	1,643	118	19,104	243	4,078	227	206,445	156

Source: Statistisches Jahrbuch der Schweiz, 1971, p. 386.

169

TABLE 64

Number and Capital of Holding Companies, since 1954

Year	Number	Index 1954 = 100	Nominal Capital in 1,000 Francs	Index 1954 = 100
1954	1,620	100	1,537,865	100
1959	2,414	149	2,224,425	145
1964	5,789	357	6,045,885	393
1966	6,836	422	7,594,908	494
1969	9,610	593	10,277,514	668

Source: Statistisches Jahrbuch der Schweiz, 1970, p. 401.

transfer of the stocks themselves or personal ramifications. The concern generally has a central or
holding company, which may be in the form of a
stock company, a limited company, or a general
trading partnership. The leading company's capital
expenditure is reduced by acquiring only large
minorities (if possible, 25 percent or more), because
the interlocking privilege with its tax advantages
can then be claimed, in addition to which it is possible
to prevent any decisions requiring a three-quarters
majority. In actual practice it is generally possible
to control a company with a smaller share, because
many stockholders can be expected to remain
inactive.[8]

At the autumn 1968 session of the Swiss Business Management
Society, which dealt with the subject of concentration of firms,
W. Niederer stated that it is possible to control a large group of
enterprises with comparatively restricted means, by buying the
share majority in a holding company. "Whoever is able to produce
these resources will be in a position to increase his influence out
of proportion to the capital input."[9] W. Niederer described the
concentration movement as something inevitable. He believed that
the Swiss economy was obliged to avoid fragmentation of its strength
and to increase its own vitality. "For this purpose concentration is
at present the most suitable means, because political reasons preclude
an end to the quotas for foreign labor or the introduction of government
aids."[10] Niederer also discussed the social and political consequences
of concentration: "The control of the economy by a few powerful

forces can lead to alienation and to widespread apathy in social and political affairs."[11] He found it characteristic that young people were at present especially unable to resign themselves to this situation. He asked whether the takeover of Swiss firms by foreign enterprises did not represent a danger for the independence of the country. He did not attach excessive importance to this aspect and believed that problems were more liable to arise if the economic integration of Europe were to produce a political federation that Switzerland could hardly stay outside of in view of its strongly intertwined foreign trading interests.

Another aspect of the concentration of economic power is also worth describing. Maurice Erard, professor of sociology and rector of the University of Neuchâtel, includes in his earlier-mentioned article some information from personal records containing the names of 1,695 important directors of companies, together with their business connections. These records cover 400 enterprises, 16 of them being insurance companies, 5 large banks, 23 finance companies engaging in banking activities, 90 medium-size banks, 270 industrial or trading enterprises, and 56 public utilities, mostly semipublic (electricity and gas). These 1,695 directors who are resident in Switzerland together occupy 2,482 seats on boards. The breakdown is presented in Table 65. According to Erard, the upper stratum of this "bourgeoisie d'affaires" includes most of the persons sitting on more than three important boards. He suggests that actual power in the Swiss economy is largely concentrated in these persons. Erard also constructed a table (Table 66) in which he contrasts the income distribution in the military taxation period 1957-58 with the distribution of gainfully employed persons among the social classes distinguished

TABLE 65

Important Directors of Boards, According to
Number of Seats Occupied by Them, 1960

Number of Directors		Number of Seats Held
Total	Percent	by One Director
6	0.4	8-10
53	3.1	5- 7
118	7.0	3- 4
1,518	89.5	1- 2

Source: Maurice Erard, "A Sociological Outline of Social Classes in Switzerland," Cahiers internationaux de sociologie (Paris), XXXIX (July-December, 1965), p. 12.

TABLE 66

Distribution of Gainfully Active Population by
Income Class and by Social Stratum, 1957-58

Average Income (francs)	Gainfully Active Persons (per thousand)	Social Class	Gainfully Active Persons (per thousand)
150,000 and more	0.8	"Bourgeoisie d'affaires"	0.8
27,000-150,000	21.0	Industrial and trading bourgeoisie	19.4
20,000- 27,000	19.7	Strata assimilated by the bourgeoisie	19.6
9,000- 20,000	268.2	Middle class and large farmers	279.4
Below 9,000	690.3	Proletariat and medium and small farmers	680.8

Source: Maurice Erard, "A Sociological Outline of Social Classes
in Switzerland," Cahiers internationaux de sociologie (Paris), XXXIX
(July-December, 1965), p. 13.

by him. He does not examine whether the actual average incomes
of the corresponding classes do in fact jibe with these figures. It is
impossible here to go into his use of the term "proletariat," to which
he gives a meaning that differs from that applied by other authors
who are against its use in regard to contemporary Swiss society,
although their definitions diverge.[12] According to Erard, therefore,
the level of income is determined by membership of the social
classes as defined by production relationships.

ALTERNATIVES TO THE PRESENT
STRUCTURE OF INDUSTRIAL CONTROL

From the social and political points of view, if the trend to
economic concentration is pursued without any change in the existing
property situation or the structure of economic control, there is
a danger of growing alienation and apathy in national life. It has now
become a very topical subject of debate. Thus, in 1971 the Cartels
Commission regarded its main function as being to investigate the

existing situation and the pattern of concentration. The aim it followed
in its study was to present figures showing the trend toward concentration in the various industries over a period of time, while also
revealing changes in the balance of economic power. Pending the
publication of this study, the trend toward concentration in 1970 can
be illustrated by the following list of some of the most spectacular
mergers: Nestlé with Ursina/Franck (food); Ciba with Geigy (chemicals); Omega/Tissot with a large number of firms (watches); Brown-
Boveri with Maschinenfabrik Oerlikon (metalworking and engineering);
Sandoz with Wander; and Heberlein with Arova. The extension of
activities, for example, of the Swiss Credit Bank in order to acquire
shares in other sectors (e.g. the Jelmoli Department Store chain and
the Electro-Watt Electricity Company). The economic journalist
Carl M. Holliger writes in this connection that it is "impossible to
assess the actual power of the Swiss Credit Bank, but it can be safely
asserted that in Switzerland alone it can control and influence hundreds
of enterprises either as a source of financial resources or through
its personal and financial ramifications "[13]

Another commentator writes of a widely held feeling that
Switzerland has been seized by a trend that is advancing irresistibly
and will eventually result in a completely oligopolistic or even
monopolistic economic structure. Views vary considerably regarding
these trends: they range from unreserved approval of what is held
to be an economically and socially indispensable concentration of the
means of production, to resignation in the face of material constraints,
and to the demand for a stiffer anticoncentration policy. The striking
divergence in views concerning the question of concentration is
undoubtedly due in part to different sets of values, for example,
concerning the importance of a "healthy middle class," although it
is the great complexity of the subject that causes the greatest
variation in attitudes.[14]

Economic concentration is an example of a process whose
intersectoral effects are of the greatest significance. In addition to
the previously mentioned connections there is also a possibility of
a change in attitudes toward ownership as a result of the far-reaching
elimination of owner-entrepreneurs. In the political sphere there
might be serious upheavals and the very foundations of pluralistic
democracy might be endangered by the financial and fiscal power
and the commanding market position of a handful of major firms.
Moreover, these firms consolidate their position as landowners and
partners in the housing market through their pension funds' and
welfare funds' investments.

There is an increasingly widespread belief that unrestricted
economic concentration represents the shortest way to oligopolistic
and monopolistic economic structures, which will lead to the demand

for nationalization, and that is a result that is either desirable or undesirable depending upon the individual's system of values. Yet a return to a broad distribution of ownership of the means of production in the sense of increasing the number of independent entrepreneurs would be turning back to the preindustrial era and is entirely out of the question for economic reasons.

In close relation with the question of economic concentration is the demand for workers' codetermination (consultation) at plant level. Several parties demand such rights but their views about the specific nature of these rights are sometimes distinctly vague. In August 1971 the Swiss Trade Union Confederation, the Christian National Trade Union Confederation, and the Swiss Association of Protestant Employees submitted an initiative that had the exceptionally large number of 160,000 signatures and called for an addition to Article 34, paragraph 1 of the Federal Constitution in the following terms: "The federal authorities are empowered to establish provisions concerning codetermination of the workers and their organizations in undertakings and administrations." The president of the Swiss Trade Union Confederation defined codetermination in this context as "a counterbalance to concentration of corporate power resulting from the continuous process of mergers."[15]

The codetermination program of the Swiss Trade Union Confederation (published early in September 1971) defines its concept and aims as follows:[16]

> By codetermination at enterprise level may be understood
> all efforts, activities, and arrangements that contribute
> to the improvement of the situation and the rights of the
> workers and permit their participation in the process
> of decision in enterprises. Democracy is indivisible.
> A society is truly democratic only if it is so in all
> of its elements and democratic attitudes also rule
> where orders have to be followed. Despite its
> shortcomings and imperfections political democracy
> in Switzerland is established on a broad and well-
> secured base. This makes the absence of democratic
> principles and customs even more painfully noticeable
> in economic matters. Simple and evident as the aim
> of workers' codetermination may be, it can be defined
> and motivated in a variety of ways:
> The need to overcome personal alienation;
> Human fulfillment for the worker;
> Equal rights for labor and capital;
> Democratization of the rules of operation of under-
> takings.

According to the same program, the right to codetermination also presupposes corresponding rights to information. The demand for codetermination relates in principle to the whole of the undertaking. This also entails the cardinal demand that the workers should participate in all major decisions of principle affecting the undertaking (investment, policy, transfer of operations, mergers, and so on). Whereas works councils' present functions relate primarily to organization, the program calls for an extension of competence to commercial and financial matters. It advocates joint and equal membership of the boards of the major undertakings in the private sector. The next demand it makes relates especially to the greatly expanded importance of holding companies, as already described in this chapter: "Economic concentration and formation of concerns mean that powers tend increasingly to be transferred from subsidiaries to the central concern. The workers' demand for representation on the boards of major undertakings relates not merely to subsidiaries but also to central organizations and holding companies."

Employers are against the codetermination initiative. The president of the Swiss Small-Scale Industries Association rejects it out of hand as "an ill-conceived action" and "an imported product bearing an alien stamp" contributing nothing to the workers' self-fulfillment and liable to result in loss of productivity.[17] In the view of the Board of the Central Federation of Swiss Employers' Organizations, the trade unions' codetermination initiative "is based on false social concepts and artificially created ideological conflict; it is liable to bring attitudes of class warfare and consequent unrest into undertakings. In the view of the employers contractual solutions adopted under legal coercion are in contradiction to the spirit of social partnership."[18] The chairmen of the boards of such companies as Brown, Boveri, and Sulzer took advantage of the 1971 annual general meetings to reject the codetermination initiative. The chairman of Sulzer said that

> the dangers conjured up by using catch-phrases like concentration of power or search for profits do not stand up to close examination. Mergers of firms may also be in the general interest. The larger an economic entity within a democratic state, the more closely it is linked to the community and responsible to it; in a large working community the dividing line between employers and workers vanishes. This offers proper safeguards against any misuse of power. It is in fact the urge for power that impels the would-be ideological world reformers.[19]

The final example is that of an address given by an employer to the delegate assembly of the Employers' Federation of the Swiss Engineering and Metal Industries under the title of "Codetermination: An Attack on Industrial Peace." He stated that the initiative was being used in order to achieve by legal means what the militant Communists sought to reach through direct action, namely the socialization of firms.[20]

The most important question, which only the future can answer, concerns the relationship between ends and means: Will the means consisting of codetermination make it possible to attain the end of overcoming alienation and achieving self-fulfillment for the worker? Nationalization of ownership of the most important means of production under forms of state capitalism, as indicated by the experience of Communist and other countries, does not seem to put an end to feelings of alienation.

These alternatives were presented to the economy in its stage of industrial development. Any long-range consideration must be based, however, on the changes probable in the economic structure. It might well be that problems in the forefront at present will spontaneously become less important. According to Jean Fourastié, the economy is heading toward a structure in which 10 percent of the working population will be engaged in the primary sector, 10 percent in the secondary, and 80 percent in the tertiary. This would imply a great decline in the importance of industrial capitalism and its related problems.[21] A more precise view of the tertiary economy will make it possible to examine this assertion more precisely. Herman Kahn and Anthony Wiener see the future in much the same light: Since jobs in the tertiary sector and the quaternary sector (services supplied not to the primary or secondary sectors but to other service enterprises) will be performed largely by various state institutions, the professions, nonprofit organizations, and the like, there will be a shift away from the present-day private economy to them.[22]

DEMOGRAPHIC GROWTH OF SWISS CITIES

By way of introduction, it is worthwhile tracing the phenomenon of urbanization back to its beginnings, because old cities and city quarters that have retained their original nucleus are among the places in which one is today confronted with part of history in the most obvious and familiar manner. Until the end of the twelfth century the present-day territory of Switzerland did not contain more than 24 places that would be classed as cities according to the standards obtaining at that time. Cities appear to have sprung up around a nucleus of tertiary activities;[1] this holds equally good for the head-quarters of the Roman legion, the castle of a feudal lord, a monastery or a bishopric, or, most common of all, the location of a regular market or fair. From the tenth century onward cities also began to an increasing extent to be the places where artisanal production was concentrated.[2] In the territory of present-day Switzerland (and elsewhere) the thirteenth century was the century of the founding of cities by the feudal lords of the day, so that by the end of the century instead of 24 there were now 170 cities.

After that developments did not follow the same course in Switzerland as in the surrounding countries. Whereas in France, Italy, and Germany cities continued to be created in considerable numbers both during and after the Renaissance, in Switzerland only five new cities were founded from the Middle Ages until 1960.[3] The present-day urban and rural image of Switzerland still reflects this pattern of development very clearly.

Table 67 indicates the demographic development of certain Swiss cities under the ancien régime, at the beginning of the Industrial Revolution, and over the last 110 years. Thus, most of the cities expanded only very slowly under the ancien régime, and in most cases

TABLE 67

Demographic Growth of Selected Cities under
Ancien Régime, at Beginning of Industrial Revolution,
and in 1850-1960
(in percent)

City	Under Ancien Régime*	From 18th until Middle of 19th Century	1850- 1960
Basel	15th-18th ~ 68	82	638
Geneva	15th-18th ~ 208	56	464
Zurich	15th-18th ~ 76	48	2483
Berne	16th-18th ~ 140	130	492
Lucerne	14th-18th ~ 43	134	570
Fribourg	15th-18th ~ 0	74	259
Schauffhausen	16th-18th ~ 120	40	301
Solothurn	-	57	243
Chur	15th-18th ~ 68	137	318
St. Gallen	-	124	579
Herisau	-	68	71
Lausanne	-	242	638

*Rough estimates of demographic growth in a given period, e.g., from fifteenth to eighteenth century.

Source: Michel Bassand, "Quelques aspects de l'urbanisation et de ses conséquences politiques—le cas de la Suisse" (Geneva: Centre de Recherches Sociologiques, University of Geneva, 1966). (Mimeo.)

their population barely even doubled over three or four centuries. Only Geneva, whose population increased by 208 percent from the fifteenth to the eighteenth century, and to a lesser extent Berne and Schauffhausen are exceptions to this rule. In the eighteenth century only four cities had more than 10,000 inhabitants. The growth rate picked up with the beginning of the Industrial Revolution. During the 100 or so years before 1850 the population of most cities rose by at least the same percentage as in the preceding three or four centuries. Only in Geneva and Schauffhausen was the growth rate substantially less during this period. But it was not until the beginning of the nineteenth century that actual urban growth set in on a major scale. From 1850 to 1960 the population of Zurich rose by 2,593 percent; this was followed by Basel and Lausanne with 638, St. Gallen with

579, Lucerne with 570, Berne with 492, and Geneva with 464 percent. Although the other cities grew less rapidly, they also tripled or quadrupled their population during the same period.

Table 68 shows how the number of Swiss cities grew the past 100 years. This means that in 1850 Switzerland had only eight cities in the modern meaning (communities with more than 10,000 inhabitants), of which three had between 20,000 and 49,999 inhabitants and five between 10,000 and 19,999. Between 1860 and 1870 for the first time a city rose above the 50,000 mark, and shortly before the turn of the century two cities reached the figure of 100,000 each. More recently the most striking development has been the rapid increase in the number of communities with 10,000 to 19,999 inhabitants; the number increased from 17 in 1941, to 27 in 1950, and to 49 in 1960. Between 1960 and 1966 an additional 20 communities topped the 10,000 mark.

Table 69 presents the growth rates of all communities with over 10,000 inhabitants in 1960 over the period 1850-1960 (Davos, whose population has fluctuated around 10,000 for a considerable time, is included in the list).

TABLE 68

Changes in Number of Cities, by Size, 1850-1960

Year	Size of City				
	More than 100,000	50,000 99,999	20,000 49,999	10,000 19,999	Total
1850	—	—	3	5	8
1860	—	—	4	6	10
1870	—	1	5	7	13
1880	—	2	6	10	18
1888	—	2	6	10	18
1900	2	2	7	10	21
1910	2	2	9	12	25
1920	3	3	8	14	28
1930	4	3	6	18	31
1941	4	4	6	17	31
1950	5	3	7	27	52
1960	5	4	8	49	66

Source: Michel Bassand, "Quelques aspects de l'urbanisation et de ses conséquences politiques—le cas de la Suisse" (Geneva: Centre de Recherches Sociologiques, University of Geneva, 1966). (Mimeo.)

TABLE 69

Distribution of Cities, by Size, 1960, and Growth
Rate between 1850 and 1960

| | Growth between 1850 and 1960 | | | |
Size of City	Slight— 0-400 Percent	Average— 401-1,000 Percent	Strong— over 1,000 Percent	1960 Total
100,000 and more	–	4	1	5
50,000-99,999	–	2	2	4
20,000-49,999	6	1	1	8
10,000-19,999	21	19	9	49
Total	27	26	13	66

Source: Michel Bassand, "Quelques aspects de l'urbanisation et
de ses conséquences politiques—le cas de la Suisse" (Geneva: Centre
de Recherches Sociologiques, University of Geneva, 1966). (Mimeo.)

The most remarkable fact is that, out of the 49 communities with a
population between 10,000 and 19,999 in 1960, 19 experienced a population increase of 401 to 1,000 percent during the period under consideration; 9 had an increase of over 1,000 percent. Altogether, out
of the 66 communities with more than 10,000 inhabitants, 39 had an
increase of over 400 percent between 1850 and 1960, which means that
their character changed to a decisive degree, although this does not
exclude the possibility that some of the 27 communities with a growth
rate of less than 400 percent also underwent such far-reaching changes
as well.

Table 70 indicates that during the postwar period relative growth
was greatest in the communities that had between 10,000 and 19,999
inhabitants in 1960: nine of them grew by more than 60 percent, six
by 45.1 to 60 percent, and thirteen by 30.1 to 45 percent, which means
that over half of the communities in this size category grew by more
than 30 percent. Of the 17 towns with more than 20,000 inhabitants
only 1 experienced growth of such magnitude, whereas all the others
had a growth rate of less than 30 percent.

These figures become more significant if communities with more
than 10,000 inhabitants are subdivided not according to size categories
but according to their geopolitical situation or function. In this
connection Michel Bassand distinguishes between three categories:
cantonal capitals, suburban communities (i.e., belonging to an
agglomeration with a larger nucleus), and independent centers that

are not also cantonal capitals.[4] Using these categories, Table 71
indicates the pattern for growth between 1950 and 1960. The table
shows that between 1950 and 1960 the suburban communities experienced by far the greatest growth. This reflects the progressive
concentration around major centers, because the principal function of
such suburban settlements is to provide homes for people whose jobs
are geared to the center, together with their families.

The degree of urbanization may be defined as the quotient of
people living in communities with more than 10,000 inhabitants divided
by the total population of the geographic unit concerned. Bassand quite
correctly points out that it is somewhat arbitrary to draw the line at
10,000 inhabitants because the phenomenon of urbanization is not
necessarily tied to this limit. Nevertheless, this is a simple and
convenient definition for the degree of urbanization.[5]

In Table 72 the last column shows the evolution of the degree of
urbanization in Switzerland, as earlier defined; it also illustrates the
distribution of the nonurban population among the different size
categories of communes. The table shows that in 1850 the bulk of the
Swiss population, 677 per thousand, lived in communities with 100 to
1,999 inhabitants. During the period under consideration this proportion steadily declined and amounted to only 268 per thousand by 1960.
In 1850 only 64 per thousand of the population lived in towns; after that
the proportion of urban dwellers steadily rose, until by 1960 it had

TABLE 70

Distribution of Cities, by Size, 1960, and Growth
Rate between 1950 and 1960

Size of City	Growth between 1950 and 1960					
	0-15 Percent	15.1-30 Percent	30.1-45 Percent	45.1-60 Percent	60 Percent and More	Total
100,000 and more	3	2				5
50,000-99,999	2	2				4
20,000-49,999	1	6	1			8
10,000-19,999	10	10	13	6	9	48
Total	16	20	14	6	9	65

Source: Michel Bassand, "Quelques aspects de l'urbanisation
et de ses conséquences politiques—le cas de la Suisse" (Geneva: Centre
de Recherches Sociologiques, University of Geneva, 1966). (Mimeo.)

TABLE 71

Distribution of Cities, by Geopolitical Situation, and
Growth Rate between 1950 and 1960

Geopolitical Situation	Growth between 1950 and 1960					
	0-15 Percent	15.1-30 Percent	30.1-45 Percent	45.1-60 Percent	60 Percent and More	Total
Cantonal capital	10	7	2	1	—	20
Suburban community	—	—	5	5	9	19
Independent center	6	14	6	1	—	27
Total	16	21	13	7	9	66

Source: Michel Bassand, "Quelques aspects de l'urbanisation et de ses conséquences politiques—le cas de la Suisse" (Geneva: Centre de Recherches Sociologiques, University of Geneva, 1966). (Mimeo.)

reached 419 per thousand. Thus, urban dwellers have become the largest group; but it was not until after the war that they reached this leading position, because in 1941 there were still more people living in communities with 100 to 1,999 inhabitants (351 per thousand) than in places with over 10,000 inhabitants (329 per thousand). The proportion of people living in communities with 5,000 to 9,999 inhabitants has also increased, rising from 55 per thousand in 1850 to 122 per thousand in 1960. Thus, in absolute terms the number of urban dwellers increased from the 1850 figure of 154,197 to a total of 2,279,760 in 1960, while the number of inhabitants in other communities rose from 2,238,543 to 3,149,301 over the same period.[6] The essential shift in the territorial distribution of the population over the last 100 years has therefore been the substantial increase in the degree of urbanization, together with its corollary, the dramatic decline in the proportion of the population living in communities with less than 2,000 inhabitants.

Between 1960 and 1968 an additional 22 communities rose above the 10,000 mark, so that the situation at the end of 1968 was as follows: a total of 2,777,500 people were living in 87 communities with over 10,000 inhabitants, which corresponds to a degree of urbanization of 453 per thousand, with an estimated total population of 6,147,000. Departing from the previous definition of the degree of

urbanization and considering all communities belonging to what are
termed agglomerations as urbanized, irrespective of size, the following
picture is obtained: at the beginning of 1969 there were approximately
2,856,000 people living in 27 agglomerations.* If one then adds the
approximately 486,700 people not included under the agglomerations
and living at the end of 1968 in the 26 communities with more than

TABLE 72

Distribution of Population, by Size of Community,
1850-1960

Year	Population in Communities of (per thousand)				
	0-99	100-1,999	2,000-4,999	5,000-9,999	More than 10,000
1850	5	677	199	55	64
1860	4	643	205	63	85
1870	4	604	218	74	100
1880	4	558	235	70	133
1888	4	538	226	81	151
1900	3	476	217	84	220
1910	3	414	218	111	254
1920	3	396	216	109	276
1930	3	370	219	103	305
1941	3	351	200	117	329
1950	3	315	200	117	365
1960	3	268	188	122	419

Source: Michel Bassand, "Quelques aspects de l'urbanisation et
de ses conséquences politiques—le cas de la Suisse" (Geneva: Centre
de Recherches Sociologiques, University of Geneva, 1966). (Mimeo.)

---

*Aarau (9 communities); Arbon (2); Baden (8); Basel (16);
Bellinzona (8); Bern (12); Biel (2); Burgdorf (2); Fribourg (6); Geneva
(29); Grenchen (2); Langenthal (3); Lausanne (16); Liestal (4); Locarno
(4); Lugano (19); Lucerne (8); Montreux (2); Neuchâtel (8); Olten (11);
Rorschach (3); Schaffhausen (8); Solothurn (7); Thun (6); Vevey (4);
Winterthur (6); Zürich (40). Statistisches Jahrbuch der Schweiz,
1969, p. 18.

10,000 inhabitants,* it is seen that 3,342,700 people lived in agglomerations or in nonagglomerated communes with more than 10,000 inhabitants, which corresponds to an urbanization degree of 544 per thousand, with a total resident population of 6,147,000.

A new variation on what had so far been said in regard to the evolution of the degree of urbanization comes from considering urbanization separately in respect to the individual size categories of urban communities, which means that the definition of the degree of urbanization is adapted to the particular size category for each case. Table 73 indicates the evolution of these urbanization degrees in cumulative terms. The table shows that the degree of urbanization has increased in all forms during all periods. The only exception consists of the degree of urbanization relating to major cities during the period 1950-60, which declined from 206 to 199 per thousand. But these figures are deceptive insofar as they relate to the politically delineated major urban communities and fail to reflect the phenomenon of agglomeration around those nuclei. As previously pointed out, however, this form of agglomeration is one of the most salient developments in the postwar period. The table also shows that the degree of urbanization in relation to cities with 20,000 and more and those with 50,000 and more inhabitants continues to grow but less rapidly than before the World War II.

Up to now the concern has been with urbanization for the whole of Switzerland; Table 74 presents the degree of urbanization by canton. Some of the effects of urbanization on the structure and forms of political life are described in the section of political participation.

FACTORS CAUSING OR AFFECTING URBANIZATION

Thus far, the course of urbanization has been described in statistical terms, but an attempt will now be made to give at least a partial explanation of this process. As in the case of the statistical material, these comments will also be largely based on Bassand.

It has already been mentioned that cities originally came into being for the most part in connection with tertiary activities and, seen in political terms, largely through the action of feudal lords. But under the ancien régime the urban guilds never succeeded in

---

*Baar, Bülach, La Chaux-de-Fonds, Chur, Davos, Délémont, Frauenfeld, Gossau SG, Herisau, Horgen, Illnau, Kreuzlingen, Le Locle, Morges, Nyon, St. Gallen, Schwyz, Sierre, Sion, Uster, Wädenswil, Wetzikon (ZH), Wil SG, Wohlen AG, Yverdon, and Zug.

TABLE 73

Evolution of Urbanization, by Size of Community,
1850-1960

Size of Community	Degree of Urbanization (per thousand)											
	1850	1860	1870	1880	1888	1900	1910	1920	1930	1941	1950	1960
100,000 and more	—	—	—	—	—	78	86	115	156	177	206	199
50,000 and more	—	—	—	21	42	116	142	166	204	240	246	257
20,000 and more	36	51	64	88	104	179	211	228	249	278	292	301
10,000 and more	64	85	100	133	151	220	254	276	305	329	365	420

Source: Michel Bassand, "Quelques aspects de l'urbanisation et de ses conséquences politiques—le cas de la Suisse" (Geneva: Centre de Recherches Sociologiques, University of Geneva, 1966). (Mimeo.)

concentrating crafts or commerce entirely in the cities, so that there was always a comparatively large number of craftsmen and traders in the rural districts of Switzerland. Although the Industrial Revolution brought about an upswing in urban growth, industrialization and urbanization have never been so directly interconnected in Switzerland as to mean that industry has settled principally in the cities and thereby attracted industrial manpower.

Industry grew up much more in the form of widely dispersed and generally smaller enterprises, of which two striking examples are the watch industry in the Jura and the textile industry in the canton of Glarus. Home workers and "factory farmers" (industrial workers continuing to work a small landholding) were also very important. The geographic dispersal of industry was also due partly to the wealth of streams, which were originally very valuable sources of power. In the early days the location and form of industry depended to a substantial extent on where labor was to be found. To nowhere near the same

TABLE 74

Degree of Urbanization, by Canton, 1960

Canton	Degree of Urbanization (per thousand)
Basel	997
Geneva	729
Zurich	676
Schauffhausen	624
Neuchâtel	583
Basel-country	454
Vaud	453
Lucerne	388
Zug	377
Berne	370
St. Gallen	294
Appenzell OR	293
Solothurn	281
Thurgau	234
Graubünden	233
Ticino	222
Fribourg	205
Schwyz	141
Valais	94
Appenzell IR	0
Nidwalden	0
Obwalden	0
Glarus	0
Uri	0

Source: Michel Bassand, "Quelques aspects de l'urbanisation et de ses conséquences politiques—le cas de la Suisse" (Geneva: Centre de Recherches Sociologiques, University of Geneva, 1966). (Mimeo.)

extent as other countries did Switzerland go through the mass departure of people from rural areas attracted by industrial centers. This explains why, at the time of the 1888 census, there were already 406 per thousand of gainfully employed persons engaged in the secondary sector (in 1960, 504 per thousand), at a time when there were only 18 cities (communities with more than 10,000 inhabitants), in which only 151 per thousand of the population lived (in 1960, 419 per thousand).

Bassand has pointed out that in Switzerland there is no relationship
between the degree of urbanization and the proportion of gainfully
employed persons engaged in the secondary sector. (Glarus, for
example, has always been one of the cantons with the highest proportion
of people in the secondary sector, but its degree of urbanization continued to be 0 in 1960.)

Nor is there any high correlation between the degree of urbanization and the proportion of gainfully occupied persons in the whole
of the tertiary sector in the cantons, but for a considerable time the
degree of urbanization and the proportion of persons employed in the
tertiary sector have been growing on approximately parallel lines,
taking a time comparison for the whole of Switzerland. The highest
correlation between degree of urbanization and proportion of employed
persons, in a cross section of all the cantons, is for selected tertiary
branches, and in particular banking and commerce. As is to be
expected, the cantonal cross section also shows a fairly close connection between a low proportion of persons engaged in agriculture
and a high degree of urbanization.

The Sociological Institute of the University of Zurich is at
present engaged in research within the framework of the theories of
Peter Heintz, which may prove of great interest in connection with
this book.[7] Without going into the range of concepts, an attempt is
made below to interpret the hypotheses produced by Jean-Pierre Hoby
and the "development scheme" derived from these. Using a correlation
analysis consisting of 31 variables, Hoby formulates the following
hypotheses (certain symbols have been replaced by the corresponding
concepts):

1. Less-developed cantons show a marked tendency to
   expand their educational system, or the development
   of a system begins with mobility on the prestige-
   status line.

At first sight this first hypothesis is very surprising indeed, and it
might be useful to examine to what extent it may be based on a rather
erroneous interpretation of the role played by private secondary
schools, such as alpine establishments, institutes, or schools of a
religious nature.

2. Where urbanization is insufficient the mobility of a
   system is ensured by means of considerable extension
   of the secondary and tertiary sectors.
3. Urbanization (actually rural migration) presupposes
   centers with a (high) per capita income in Switzerland.

If the above hypotheses can be confirmed, the following "development scheme" may be valid for Switzerland:

> The development of a system runs from the disintegration of rigid structures, through the extension of the educational system to the extension of the employment structure. The thesis advanced by Clark/Fourastié does not apply, to the effect that the extension of the tertiary sector in developed contexts is at the expense of the primary and secondary sectors, because the tendency is for the secondary sector to be pursued with greater energy than the tertiary sector. [In the long term, however, the development thesis stated by Clark/Fourastié will most probably come into the fore in Switzerland as well. The extension of the employment structure results in mobility along the income-status line, and only this is effective enough to cause actual rural migration, leading to urbanization.[8]

Concerning the political, economic, and cultural preponderance of city and country in Switzerland in the course of historical development, it has so far been possible to distinguish mainly between two distinctly different phases. During the first phase, lasting until the French Revolution, the rural areas held sway in economic terms, while the towns were politically and culturally dominant. After the collapse of the ancien régime all communities obtained their autonomy de facto in 1803 and de jure in 1848. This change introduced a period of political preponderance for the rural areas, which was particularly noticeable because, as has already been seen, the overwhelming majority of the population then lived in communities with less than 2,000 inhabitants. But at the same time there began a decline in the economic importance of rural areas, which continues today. Thus, the second phase is characterized by the political predominance of the rural areas (farmers' pressure groups attempted and continue to attempt to use this political preponderance to slow down their loss of economic importance, but without being able to stop the actual process), with simultaneous economic and cultural domination by the cities. The present process of urbanization now going forward points to a third phase, characterized by the political, economic, and cultural domination of the cities, which would eventually lead to the virtually complete urbanization of the Swiss population.

THE PARTIES' POSITIONS ON THE INTERPLAY OF CONCENTRATION AND DEPOPULATION

KCVP:
        Short- and long-range economic policy should be turned toward the equal development of the economy of the whole country: efforts

aimed at the economic promotion of hitherto disadvantaged rural regions should be strengthened. Specific action in favor of mountain farming should be incorporated in an overall concept for the promotion of mountain areas. We endorse the efforts made by organizations representing the tradesmen and middle classes for a decentralized and efficient structure of occupations and enterprises."

"The other promotional measures undertaken by the federal authorities should be directed along more differentiated lines with a view to balanced development; the increasing depopulation of mountain areas should be counteracted."

SPS:
        "Where economic assistance is not sufficient to overcome the subsistence difficulties of small farmers and mountain farmers, social action is necessary. The development of regions particularly disadvantaged in economic terms should be promoted so far as possible through the introduction of industry and handicrafts."

"The SPS therefore proposes the following: . . . Democratic economic planning pursuing the aim . . . (c) reducing the differences in the standard of living between the various strata and between individual regions."

BGB:
        "The party is in favor of an appropriate financial balance between cantons and communities in order to prevent rural migration and the concentration of industry in favored areas."

"The party is in favor of the decentralized introduction of industry."

LdU:
        "In view of the considerable climatic and economic differences in our country we need a regional development policy. In threatened parts of the country, particularly in the mountain areas, new economic opportunities must be created, because action relating to agrarian policy is not sufficient on its own."

Evangelical People's Party:
        "The economic inequality between communities and cantons should be reduced as much as possible by means of appropriate fiscal legislation and other suitable action."

This survey of the parties' attitudes to the problem under discussion shows that by and large they are in favor of the same aims: The economy should be evenly developed throughout the country, differences in standards of living between individual regions should be diminished, and the related trends of the depopulation of certain

regions and the concentration of industry in favored regions should
be prevented. These aims are in contrast to the present trend in
development as described in the first part of this chapter. The
following section will deal with the possible alternatives for development, and the measures feasible in order to attain the aims stated
unanimously by the parties, making a distinction between those that
are "trend-related" from the point of view of probable social and
economic development and those that are not.

It may be useful first of all to distinguish between the phenomenon
of concentration, or agglomeration, and the process of urbanization.
Whereas concentration or agglomeration inevitably leads to crowding
into a small number of cities, with the corollary of depopulation of
certain areas, urbanization can theoretically take place on a decentralized basis, that is, at least partly in smaller centers distributed
throughout the country. With an appropriate territorial distribution
of urban centers of different magnitudes it is possible to conceive of
virtually complete urbanization of the population without altering the
existing regional structure or even with a better balance between the
various regions. The concept of "maintenance of the regional structure" also needs to be spelled out, because there is a difference
depending on whether one is referring, for example, to the maintenance
of all of the enterprises in a region or of all the communities in a
region, or the viability of the region, such as a mountain valley, seen
as a whole. These distinctions are important in considering the
alternatives for development and in examining whether the possible
ways of attaining these aims are trend-related or not.

ALTERNATIVE POSSIBILITIES FOR DEVELOPMENT

The basic variants of development are as follows: (a) maximization of the national product without reference to its regional origin
or other aims (these could clearly be equated with further concentration and the corresponding depopulation of certain regions); (b)
maintenance of the viability of all existing communities; and (c) an
intermediate solution between these two extremes. Existing tendencies
and forecasts as to the behavior of factors influencing the situation
point conclusively to continuing concentration in the future, and the
following factors are likely to reinforce the tendency: (a) the gradual
loss of rural political domination over towns; (b) the increasing
substitution of expenditure in the city for expenditure in the place of
residence as the main category of expenditure; and (c) the increasing
tertiarization of the economy, from which the major cities would
benefit to the greatest extent unless special action is taken. If the
trends so far observed continue to apply it would seem that the only

elements that will be spared from the cities' suction effect will be
the primary activities and part of the service facilities for the tourist
trade; moreover, if the suggestion of concentrating agriculture on the
most suitable land is carried out the depopulation of certain areas
will be further accelerated.

On the other side, as a parallel trend to urban concentration,
there would be an increased demand for second homes in the country,
which would at certain times bring back a rather special form of life
to what would otherwise be increasingly depopulated areas. At various
points, the reasons for the anticipated heavy demand for second homes
in the country have been referred to (shorter work hours resulting in
added leisure in the form of long weekends and extended holidays,
rising per capita income, need for rest and contact with nature, social
prestige). The future importance of the phenomenon can hardly be
overestimated.*

It would therefore be very useful for a study to be made of the
way in which specific numbers of second homes can affect the viability
of specific geographic units, and this should cover both existing houses
that have been sold by their original owners and houses especially
constructed for the purpose. To summarize, it may be said that the
"natural" development not affected by any special action would probably
run in the direction of increased concentration of the population in
the big agglomerations, leaving outside the urbanized areas declining
agriculture, part of the tourist trade, and a new kind of "partial life."
This situation coincides with the aim of maximization of economic
growth "at all costs."

This form of development does not, however, correspond to the
unanimously expressed aims of the parties, although it cannot be said
definitely whether the expression of aims corresponds to the opposite
extreme (maintenance of all existing communities) or whether it might
be fulfilled by means of certain intermediate solutions. What does
appear certain is that the aims expressed by the parties cannot be
satisfied unless measures are undertaken to correct the development
that is anticipated if matters follow their natural course. A number
of measures are examined below that can serve to maintain the
viability of regions tending toward depopulation. These include forms
of action that have already been undertaken as well as others that
appear necessary or possible in the light of social evolution or of
certain values. The measures proposed are based on the assumption
that the increase in the degree of urbanization is a largely irreversible

---

*Chapter 6, however, also analyzes factors that may have a
negative effect on the demand for second homes.

process, so that they are directed essentially to the extension or creation of smaller urban centers in areas of depopulation. Everywhere included in the considerations here are the greatly improved opportunities for communication that should result once the national highway network has been completed, the possibility of new means of transport as a result of technological development has been allowed for.

Assistance for Mountain Farmers

From the social (and certainly also from the economic) point of view the mountain farmer is a problematical matter in many respects. The main reason this assertion is that the solution of problems can seldom be seen in the preservation of existing structures. In this respect, assistance for mountain farmers is a non-trend-related measure. Nor can a whole class of society feel much satisfaction when, to put it in drastic terms, it is only preserved in the long run through a form of collective charity.[9] Moreover, it will probably become increasingly difficult to make the motives at present underlying this form of assistance acceptable to the population as a whole when it does not rely economically on the mountain farmers' production. But what makes the value of the present form of assistance for mountain farmers really questionable is that the aim in view, namely, to prevent the depopulation of certain areas, is not attained.

If sympathy for the necessity of mountain farmers' output declines, a different form of sympathy will grow, namely, for their function in preserving and tending the landscape. As long as their activities in this direction are indispensable, the mountain farmers fulfill a function that is acknowledged to an increasing extent, in the present circumstances of shrinking inhabitable space, by a population seeking relaxation and contact with nature. Perhaps, then, assistance for mountain farmers should not be directed increasingly toward this function and be motivated in this light. The expanding opportunities of part-time employment in the growing tourist trade can also help to solve the problem of the mountain farmers.[10]

Promotion of Local Education Facilities
in Depopulated Areas

The promotion of education facilities in depopulated areas would at the same time satisfy the important demands for equality of opportunity in education and full use of the existing reserve of talent. If this proposal were considered in isolation, it could be argued that it would probably result in the opposite of the desired effect, by causing

more talented people to leave. This effect can never be fully avoided;
but it may then be argued, on the other hand, that, although the specific
aim (prevention of depopulation) is not fulfilled, other important aims
are, namely, equality of opportunity in education and use of the reserve
of talented subjects. But this form of action should be related to the
creation of the necessary jobs. There would be a need for extension
of federal subsidies, thus far granted exclusively at higher education
levels, toward secondary and technical schools in depopulated areas.
Since this proposal is one that will help to satisfy the generally sharp
increase in the demand for education, which is discussed elsewhere,
it should accordingly be described as trend-related.

Establishment of Enterprises in Depopulated Areas

The authorities have the problem of offering enterprises suffi-
ciently attractive conditions; employers face the same problem in
dealing with their own labor force. One means of attracting industry
would be to provide tax relief, allowing for the possibility of restoring
the sorely needed tax revenue to cantons and communities by means
of improved intercantonal financial compensation through the confederation. Similarly, it would be possible to influence the location
of industry by means of "attractive" development of the infrastructure,
which might again demand federal subsidies. In the phase in which
no locally trained suitable employees were available, employers
might have to attract them by means of higher wages or other favorable conditions, such as cheap and pleasant housing. If the centers
concerned offer educational facilities for children (the close interdependence of proposals a and b, p. 190, here becomes evident), a
certain minimum of other cultural institutions (which the schools
could help to stimulate), and easy communications with larger centers,
it may be expected, provided that other specific advantages exist
(e.g., proximity of home to work place), that a good number of workers
would prefer these conditions to living in a large city. In later phases
labor could then be either partly or wholly locally recruited as a
result of having the schools there.

Settlement of Pensioners in Climatically Suitable
Depopulated Areas

In Chapter 3 it was seen that the proportion of elderly people in
the population will probably rise sharply until the year 2020 and that
the importance of the retirement age in the course of the individual's
life will become greater and the general state of health at this age will

improve. It has also been seen that the population density of 0.6 per living unit is very low in the case of pensioners. It is even possible to talk of wastage of living space in some ways.

In the United States, in such areas as Southern California and Florida, actual districts for pensioners have been created to which many people move after retirement. It would be worthwhile examining the extent to which, for example, the canton of Ticino and the shores of Lake Geneva already play much the same role. It might well be possible to promote the settlement of pensioners in climatically suitable areas of depopulation along predetermined lines. Tax facilities would be granted with appropriate compensation for the fiscal revenue foregone. It may be assumed that with the general increase in geographic mobility a large number of people will find no great difficulty in changing their place of residence after retirement. With second homes becoming more common it would be quite possible for people to establish links in advance with the places in which they would settle after retirement. By combining the older generation's home and the grown-up children's second home, it would be possible to establish closer contacts between three generations of the same family. Of course additional implications would have to be examined carefully because it should not be allowed to result in isolation of elderly people, but on face the proposal seems well worth exploring. It would be trend-related because it would help to solve the problem of the growing proportion of older people in the population while also releasing inadequately used living space in agglomerations for other purposes.

All of the measures proposed would entail extra functions for the federal authorities. Moreover, all of these proposals also show the need for a general concept of the settlement of the country that is approved both by the population and by the cantons.

THE PARTIES' STATEMENTS ON NATIONAL CITY
AND COUNTRY PLANNING

KCVP:

"The increase in the population together with economic growth result in more intensive utilization of the land and overbuilding in almost all parts of Switzerland. There is consequently a serious danger not only that the natural beauties will be irrevocably lost but also that the unrestrained extension of areas of building, industry, and infrastructure will be detrimental to decent living standards in very widespread areas of our country."

Cantonal and local building regulations are unable to keep up with this headlong development. Moreover, many legal questions cannot be solved by the cantons or not in any final manner, with particular reference to compensation when agricultural and reserved zones are introduced. Federal legislation governing ownership of the land is vital.

Free Democratic Party:
       "The party demands the protection of city and country against unnecessary encroachment, together with preservation of historical sites and cultural monuments.
       "The extraordinary economic expansion that Switzerland has experienced in recent decades is reflected in far-reaching changes in the external living conditions and the consequent invasion of our landscape. Switzerland is one of the most densely inhabited countries in the world. Taking only the actual inhabited areas, the population density is 465 persons per square kilometer (national average, 145). Since the population is continuing to grow rapidly it is therefore urgently necessary to seek a sensible population distribution policy by means of appropriate physical planning and thus to ensure the most rational utilization of the land. This is made even more necessary by the fact that the demand for land has been further increased owing to the very speedy development of transport. Since 1950 the number of motorcars has increased four-fold. There are already over 1 million motorcars on the roads."
       "The industrialization of our country and the extraordinary rise in standards of personal comfort demand their price. For the public authorities the task of striking a proper balance in external living conditions is becoming increasingly urgent and expensive. Only by means of far-sighted precautions will it be possible to guarantee a relative maximum of freedom for the population. The establishment of effective national and regional city and country planning and the creation of progressive landownership laws adapted to the new circumstances are therefore urgent duties facing a modern liberal movement."
       "National planning must much more than hitherto be conceived as a national task. The motto should be: 'as much freedom as possible, as much planning as necessary.'"

SPS:
       "The SPS advances the following proposals: . . . national planning permitting in particular:
       a) separation of zones of industry, agriculture, building and transport as well as natural recreation zones;
       b) action to combat water contamination and air pollution and to protect natural amenities;
       c) improvement of productivity in agriculture through the promotion of combinations of landholdings in order to

maintain optimum farming conditions and of efforts to
introduce new farming methods."

BGB:
        "The BGB supports all endeavors directed toward maintaining
the characteristics of Swiss national customs and the beauty of its
landscape."
        "The BGB considers the question of landownership as a central
problem of Swiss national policy calling for an urgent solution. The
aim should consist of appropriate settlement and utilization of the
restricted volume of living space in Switzerland while upholding the
rights of property unless public interests demand their restriction
. . . The BGB demands that a properly conceived land policy should
have due regard to the natural, economic, technical, social, and
cultural values and corresponding future requirements. . . ."

LdU:
        "The Federal authorities should be empowered to establish the
aims of national city and country planning and to develop plans on the
basis of which the individual regions can undertake practical action.
New legislation on landownership must ensure that building is restricted
to allocated areas . . . Private ownership must be maintained subject
to any restrictions required ownig to public interest."

Liberal Democratic Citizens' Party:
        "The aims proposed (by national city and country planning) can
be attained without any need or purpose in transferring the land to
public ownership but rather through zonal provisions and building
regulations."

PdA:
        "The PdA demands the establishment and implementation of a
general national development plan concerning the infrastructure of
the country (hospitals, purification plants, highway construction,
education, universities, energy, national physical planning, landownership, development of agriculture, and so on)."

THE REFERENDUM OF JULY 2, 1967, ON THE SOCIALIST
INITIATIVE AGAINST LAND SPECULATION

        This referendum has been selected for consideration because it
deals with landownership and therefore has a direct bearing on national
planning. The referendum asked the confederation to take measures
against unjustified increases of land prices, to prevent a shortage in

TABLE 75

Total Vote and Votes in Favor, Referendum
of July 2, 1967, on Land Speculation by Canton

Canton	Total Vote[a]	Votes in Favor[b]
Zurich	504	389
Berne	320	357
Lucerne	345	211
Uri	444	210
Schwyz	386	137
Obwalden	300	45
Nidwalden	464	138
Glarus	418	235
Zug	323	202
Fribourg	253	204
Solothurn	399	293
Basel	374	495
Basel-country	349	335
Schauffhausen	745	415
Appenzell OR	545	239
Appenzell IR	277	61
St. Gallen	471	243
Graubünden	407	165
Aargau	641	307
Thurgau	564	246
Ticino	194	337
Vaud	218	386
Valais	202	171
Neuchâtel	222	447
Geneva	170	504
Total Switzerland	380	327

[a]Proportion of persons voting per 1,000 entitled to vote.
[b]Proportion of votes in favor per 1,000 valid votes.

Source: Statistisches Jahrbuch der Schweiz, 1967, p. 544.

housing facilities, and to favor national territorial planning as a means
in the service of national health and economic progress. An examination of the results of this referendum in connection with the comments
on urbanization produces some interesting reflections. The vote in
the various cantons is in Table 75.

11

TYPES OF HOUSING
AND SOCIAL RELATIONS

Society and the types of housing are closely interdependent.
The type of housing influences the demographic, economic, political,
social, and cultural structures of a country. The form and the size of
a city affect relations between and within social groups.

There is nothing new about any of this. Plato and Aristotle
described the relationship between the size and arrangement of the
polis and the political structure. History tells of the way in which
medieval cities with their own walls helped to bring on the decline of
the feudal lords when their fortresses were no longer necessary.
Similarly, a widely dispersed rural way of life will have a weak and
necessarily less centralized state as its counterpart, because every
family is a virtually independent producing and consuming unit.
Anthropology shows that among primitive tribes there is a connection
between the spatial organization of the village and the patterns of
kinship and power. What is new is that the relationship between
housing and the other aspects of existence in modern society are
becoming more familiar; that is why attempts are now directed toward
the conscious organization of living space.

This book can do no more than put forward a number of concepts,
together with possible variations, point to problems, and show how
cities were often built on the basis of myth. Nobody seems to have
attempted really to examine the actual circumstances that result.
We shall also refer to the relationship between trends claimed in this
book to be virtually irreversible and regional and national city and
country planning.

THE IRREVERSIBLE TREND TOWARD URBANIZATION

The city is above all a way of life.[1] According to Georges
Friedmann it corresponds to the "technical environment," whereas the

rural world corresponds to the "natural environment."[2] The idea that
better living and working conditions were to be found in the city has
been one of the main reasons why people have left rural areas.[3]

Cities are the pole in which economic power is concentrated,
and to an increasing extent political power as well; they therefore
offer greater opportunities for advancement than do rural areas.[4]
The cities are also the cultural centers in which new ideas are created.
They are above all the place in which standards of living are highest,
where the greatest opportunities are offered for entertainment and
better services (e.g., for health and education), and where traditional
social pressures are weakest.

The population density of cities produces a new style of living
in the family, at work, and in leisure time. They create new possibilities and demand that old habits be rejected.[5] The fact that new-
comers attempt to maintain their old style of living means that a city
is never completely urbanized. Some parts are more so than others.
It is not impossible that the problems of cities are due partly to the
fact that some of the inhabitants attempt to influence local political
decisions on the basis of nonurban attitudes and that this leads to
contradictions in the development of cities.

THE PROBLEMS OF CITIES

The uncontrolled growth of cities has created complex problems
that are more or less alike in all industrialized countries except that
they vary in their degree of intensity (because of the absence of very
large cities many of these problems have occurred in only a relatively
mild form in Switzerland): bad housing conditions; air pollution; slums;
greater incidence of nervous and mental disease; indifference to
fellow human beings and the community as a whole; anonymity;
declining political participation; loneliness; inadequate performance
by certain service facilities; noise and dirt; juvenile delinquency;
bureaucracy; lack of open spaces, parks, and playgrounds; frequency
of accidents; the struggle between people and cars; the time spent on
commuting and other travel, with consequent loss of free time;
special problems of satellite towns.[6]

Suburbs do not bring the desired solution to these problems.
All they do is to provide a breathing space before they succumb to the
same difficulties in their turn. Two reports by American Federal
Commissions (National Commission on Urban Problems and Task
Force on Suburban Problems) submitted in 1968 show that there is
not much point in getting out of the cities and settling in the suburbs
because their respective problems are beginning to resemble one
another.

THE EFFECT OF THE URBAN WAY OF
LIFE ON RURAL AREAS

Despite resistance and the limited purchasing power of rural areas the influence of cities is beginning to extend to them as well. The fact that a proportion of manpower has left increases the need for mechanization and rationalization. Mutual assistance and services among neighbors based on personal obligations are coming to be replaced by paid services, just as in the cities. A form of solidarity that established a balance in the community's political power and formed the foundation of all social relationships is fast disappearing. School education, the need for better agricultural vocational training, radio, television, and contacts with tourists—all of these are bringing the urban way of life into the country and are supplanting tradition and custom to an increasing extent.

In Switzerland the attempt to maintain a rural way of life for reasons of national policy has led to intervention by cantonal and federal authorities. The individual farmer often prefers to circumvent the local authorities in applying for subsidies. In this way, something that is intended to help rural areas to survive contributes at the same time to the weakening of the local institutions and the pattern of social relationships that this aid was supposed to preserve.

The concept of regionalism that is so popular at present both in the East and in the West does not just offer a solution for the problems arising from excessive administrative centralization.[7] Cities constituting regional growth poles today increasingly correspond to the requirements of people living in rural areas that, as already shown, are becoming more and more assimilated to those of urban inhabitants.[8]

THE NEIGHBORHOOD COMMUNITY: A MYTH OF
THE URBANISTS?

With the haphazard growth of cities, C. A. Perry, in 1929, was the first to define the concept of the "neighborhood" as a planning principle. [9] Once this idea had been taken up by outstanding figures in the world of architecture—Lewis Mumford, Walter Gropius, and Frank Lloyd Wright—it was put into practice in such places as Wythenshawe in Great Britain and Radburn in the United States. The same idea was resuscitated in Great Britain after the war and was made the official theme of the Town and Country Planning Act. Although this concept also has its economic and aesthetic aspects, it is most important in its social intention: It is designed to restore the urban dweller's

feeling of belonging to a community and thereby to promote his social
and political participation.

The utility of the neighborhood concept as a planning principle
was quite soon challenged by a dissident faction. Roper-Power
showed how neighborly relations tended to lose their importance;
McClenahan based himself on a suburban study in Los Angeles to argue
that the primary group was no longer bound to a specific restricted
area but was very mobile and that friends and acquaintances were
spread over the whole city; and Isaacs, Dewey, and Churchill relegated
the neighborhood principle to the realm of nostalgia.[10]

The minority that questioned the neighborhood principle seems
now to have become a majority. The whole idea is under heavy fire
both in the East and in the West.[11] It is now regarded more and more
as a myth that should no longer be followed as a planning principle.
The Polish author Janusz Ziolkowski describes the situation in the
following terms:

> Even in this era of tremendous spatial mobility when whole
> nations are 'on the move'—and perhaps because of that—
> there is a deep desire to belong, to have roots somewhere.
> This cannot any longer be a local community based on the
> ideal type of a Greek polis or medieval town. A territorially
> limited microcosm, fully self-contained from a social and
> cultural point of view is irrevocably a thing of the past.
> Modern man cannot be held within the bounds of a small
> territorial community, however perfectly organized and
> cohesive. This is why the efforts of town planners to
> recreate in housing estates, new towns, and so on, social
> relations based on the principle of the classical neighbor-
> hood are doomed to failure; if fully realized they can only
> lead to considerable sociocultural regimentation, to in-
> creased control, if not tyranny, of the group over the
> individual, to the formation of local backwaters—in other
> words, to the creation of precisely those village or small-
> town conditions from which the individual flees to the
> large city. And it is the large city, the metropolis—that
> concentration of heterogeneous, mentally emancipated
> individuals enjoying a considerable margin of personal
> freedom, cultivating their own way of life—which is able
> to fulfill all the multiple and sophisticated needs and
> desires of the contemporary man.[12]

There is now an increasing tendency to take the region rather than
the neighborhood as the pole of assimilation and integration.

If the neighborhood principle is really only a myth that is not borne out by the actual facts, then the sociologists who have been dealing with urbanism for years, not to say decades, bear a fair onus of responsibility.[13] With so small a number of empirical investigations on these matters,[14] one is almost bound to conclude that planners and sociologists worked out hypotheses that were incorporated in building projects but that they then failed to check these hypotheses against the real situation. This also seems to be the case of the ribbon settlement structure at present in such vogue. There are obvious advantages to such a system (easier communications, rapid access to the country-side), but as far as is known nobody has yet seriously investigated whether the people in these cities really do live in the way the planners have it worked out.

If there are myths in urbanism it is not so much the city planners or the architects who are to blame. Lucius Burckhardt has demonstrated in his analysis of the machinery of decision-making that the architect has to make decisions that are not of his seeking, and as a result the political decision-making process is considerably simplified.[15]

OTHER PLANNING ALTERNATIVES

The neighborhood principle discussed above is only one aspect of the comprehensive problem of the relationship between types of housing and society. An additional possibility is the satellite city. The idea was that among other things these should satisfy young couples' desire for independence, and in fact they do it to such an extent that the sociologist Paul Cornière has very effectively dubbed them "towns without mothers-in-law."

An alternative possibility consists of cities that would consciously promote contacts between the generations and thereby return toward the old idea of the extended family. This solution is going through a phase of some popularity in Great Britain at present. It means that less kindergartens and similar amenities have to be built, and at the same time some of the problems of old age are overcome (without going into the pros and cons of an upbringing by grandparents). It also corrects the imbalance in the present age structure of satellite cities.

An additional alternative faced by city planners is whether to combine or to separate social classes. In Great Britain, which has used local, regional, and national city and country planning to influence social structures more consciously than any other country in Europe, the aim was for a long time to blend the social classes. More recently this principle has been applied more flexibly because it tended to leave both the manager and the factory worker equally dissatisfied.

At the other end of the scale is the possibility of having homogeneous districts according to social class.

SOME FUNDAMENTAL CONCEPTS

The following concepts may prove valuable in seeking fuller knowledge of the relationship between city and country planning and social structure. The first three represent different variations in regard to the nature of the decision-making and executive agencies.

1. The individualistic variant (placing emphasis on the authority of the head of the household and family): Most of the social functions are performed directly by the family and the individual. It is the function of the overall legislation regarding national city and country planning to promote and facilitate solutions at this level.

2. "Paternalistic" and/or private enterprise variant: The initiative in building, for example, dwellings, leisure amenities, or kindergartens lies with private enterprise or with private agencies. (In Geneva a private firm supplying part-time and auxiliary manpower provides child-care facilities for mothers working for it.)

3. The public or state variant: Initiative and performance lie with the state agencies responsible to the public (as is already the case for roads and schools, for example). Under this variant the distribution of competence at the various levels (federal, cantonal, local) involves some problems.

The four following fundamental concepts relate to the aims of local, regional, and national city and country planning.

1. Social development aims: The purpose is to overcome social inequalities. Examples include slum clearance and social housing construction. Investment of this kind is regarded increasingly often as justified on economic grounds as well.

2. Social defense aims: The purpose here is to correct social evils, for example by providing leisure facilities and youth centers to combat juvenile delinquency. However, the cause of such social evils is not necessarily to be found in problems of urbanism; if the root cause is situated elsewhere urban solutions will not eliminate the problems. Improvements in sanitation also come within this general category (e.g., garbage incineration, prevention of air and water pollution). By and large the problem here is one of defensive action to overcome the negative effects of the disorderly growth of cities in the past, rather than developing a strategy for the future.

3. Forecasting and long range aims: This consists of assessing future needs and directing planning toward those aims. The aims in view can be illustrated by means of an example from Great Britain, where a new town has been planned, to be completed by the year 2000.

Considerable credit allocations are available and a city-manager is already in office. The unusual feature of this project is that the future social needs are its top-ranking criteria. All other criteria are regarded as purely technical and therefore subordinate. The basic question is: "How would one satisfy the human needs of a person living in the year 2000 and what material, architectural, and physical planning principles would have to be followed to meet that criterion?" It is most significant that, despite the quite exceptional conditions (including salary) and although the search covered the whole world, it was not possible to find a single sociologist capable of meeting the challenge in every respect. It was therefore reluctantly decided at the end of 1968 that the basic idea would have, at least partly, to be shelved.

The idea itself was new, because many planners still refer to the charter of Athens and the four main functions it enunciates. If one now attempts to imagine the future one has to decide, for example, whether the distinction between living and working districts is not liable to lose its significance with the transition to a tertiary economy and society (less people working in less dirty factories). There are sociologists who are already wondering whether tertiary jobs should not be brought into dormitory cities:

> There is a need to overcome the segregation of zones
> reserved for housing, whose pulse is tied to the pendulum
> of going to or returning from work. There is a need for
> various activities that can be introduced by means of
> modern techniques on or around the ground floors of
> housing blocks. Apart from injecting greater life into
> the area this will offer a partial solution to commuting
> problems and it will also provide jobs for women near
> their homes.[16]

It is not so easy as one might imagine to identify the needs of a society or of parts of a society. Social research has shown that the desires expressed in public opinion surveys are often very misleading (people who live in a dark basement long to live in a sunny apartment with a generous view on the tenth floor; once they are there their reply is liable to be very different). The answers given in public opinion surveys are often based on incomplete knowledge and incorrect conceptions of unknown matters; caution is always called for in dealing with the results of the traditional types of such surveys. Considerable methodological efforts are being made to overcome these dangers.[17] It is hard enough to identify existing needs but even more so when it comes to future requirements. Even if certain needs are known, this does not necessarily indicate how they should best be satisfied.

Hypotheses have to be established and checked out. Scientifically reliable knowledge in this field is still very limited (which is why the sociologist for the British town of the year 2000 was not to be found).

4. Aims that specifically consider city and country planning measures to plan the way of life as a means of guiding the development of society along the desired lines: This concept involves two prerequisites, as follows:

1. A clear and conscious vision of the type of future society desired;
2. Tested hypotheses concerning the relationship between types of housing (settlement structure, settlement unit, settlement composition, territorial arrangement, settlement texture, utilization, extension, architectural form, and so on), on the one hand, and social relationships, social roles and forms of behavior, on the other hand.

This fourth concept is now being applied mainly in a number of developing countries (for instance in Tunisia). The situation there is relatively simple in that the desired pattern of society is an industrial one (this is, of course, expressed in very broad terms but is basically accurate). Although the desired pattern of society lies in the future, it already exists in other places. For the industrially advanced societies the situation is more complicated: They have no model that they can possibly emulate. The postindustrial society does not exist in reality;[18] in science fiction it is represented not so much as it should be as in a form that should be avoided.

12

CANTONAL PARTY SYSTEMS,
POLITICAL PARTICIPATION,
AND STRENGTH OF PARTIES

This chapter will not attempt to provide a comprehensive coverage of the subject but will point mainly to various connections between
forms of political life and urbanization. We are concerned first with
seeing how the various cantonal party systems differ from one another.

Roger Girod makes a distinction between four different systems
(the abbreviation for each of the systems as used in Table 76 is added
in brackets):[1]

1. One-party system: All members of the cantonal
   government belong to the same party, without any
   organized opposition (S). In these cases any political
   divergences normally occur between different frac-
   tions of the single party.
2. A single party dominates political life and provides
   the majority of government members (M).
3. Three-party systems: Three parties dominate the
   political life of the canton, but none of them provides
   the majority of government members (T).
4. Multiparty systems: Four or more parties are
   represented in the cantonal government (P).

Table 76 shows what systems existed in the various cantons in
1962. It also shows the proportion voting in the federal referenda of
1960 and polling in the 1959 elections for the National Council. The
polling figures for the cantons in which voting is compulsory, where
elections to the National Council are by tacit agreement, or where
there is only one constituency are not included. The cantons are given
in the order of their degree of urbanization in 1960. The table shows
that there is a connection between the complexity of cantonal party

TABLE 76

Degree of Urbanization, Proportion Voting in Referenda
and Elections, and Party Systems, by Canton
(per thousand)

Canton	Degree of Urban- ization, 1960	Voting in Federal Referenda, 1960	Voting in Federal Council Elections, 1959	Cantonal Party System 1962*
Basel	997	259	603	P
Geneva	729	335	457	P
Zurich	676	688	697	P
Schauffhausen	624	—	—	T
Neuchâtel	583	280	558	P
Basel-country	454	331	615	P
Vaud	453	315	550	P
Lucerne	388	420	850	M
Zug	377	293	635	M
Berne	370	357	653	T
St. Gallen	294	—	—	T
Appenzell OR	293	615	—	M
Solothurn	281	351	833	T
Thurgau	234	—	—	P
Graubünden	233	449	735	P
Ticino	222	183	692	T
Fribourg	205	282	696	M
Schwyz	141	425	750	M
Aargau	135	—	—	P
Valais	94	399	741	M
Appenzell IR	0	387	—	S
Nidwalden	0	499	—	M
Obwalden	0	319	—	M
Glarus	0	431	775	P
Uri	0	534	—	M

*P: one-party system; M: a single party dominates political life;
T: three-party system; P: multiparty system.

Source: Michel Bassand, "Quelques aspects de l'urbanisation et
des ses conséquences politiques—le cas de la Suisse" (Geneva:
Centre de Recherches Sociologiques, University of Geneva, 1966).
(Mimeo.)

systems and the degree of urbanization of cantons. Out of the 7 cantons with the highest degree of urbanization, 6 have a multiparty system
and 1 a three-party system. Out of the 8 least urbanized cantons, 5
have a system dominated by a majority party and 1 has a single-party
system; the cantons of Glarus and Aargau, which are only slightly
urbanized but considerably industrialized, have a multiparty system.
Out of the remaining 10 cantons, which have an average degree of
urbanization, 4 have a three-party system and 2 a multiparty system;
4 have a system dominated by a majority party. It must nevertheless
be borne in mind that the definition of these systems is based on
participation by the parties in cantonal governments; their participation
in cantonal parliaments or the existence of parties without any government members or representatives in the cantonal parliaments is
consequently not reflected. The situation may be summarized by
saying that the complexity of cantonal party systems grows with a
rising degree of urbanization.[2] In terms of future projections this
would mean that in the cantons that still have a simple party structure
(single-party system or a system dominated by a majority party) a
more complex system is liable to take its place as the degree of
urbanization increases.

Another organizational form of political life that is losing its
importance with the rising degree of urbanization consists of the
community assemblies. This trend is already noticeable in the light
of urbanization so far and will continue to apply in the future as well.
With regard to the proportion voting in referenda and elections Table
76, combined with data not included in it, permits a cautious conclusion
to the effect that participation is weaker where the relevant geographic
and political unit is more urbanized. The proportion participating in
referenda is less than for elections, and with a rising degree of urbanization there appears to be a relative shift of interest from local to
national questions.[3] It must be pointed out here, however, that the
degree of urbanization, important as it is, is of course not the only
factor affecting the forms and the intensity of political activity.

Concerning participation in referenda and elections according
to social class, a survey conducted by students of Maurice Erard in
Neuchâtel suggests that the rate declines from bourgeoisie to proletariat (using Erard's expressions) and, within the same class, from
top to bottom of the scale of vocational skills.[4]

Table 77 shows the origins of those voting for the various parties
by size of community. Table 78 covers the same situation from another
aspect. It shows how the voters in the various sizes of communities
voted in regard to the three major national parties the two show that
the SPS is the most "urban" of the three major national parties: 325
per thousand of urban voters chose this party, whereas the corresponding figures for the Free Democratic Party and KCVP are only 236 and

TABLE 77

Distribution of Voters, by Party and Size of
Community, Federal Elections, 1959
(per thousand)

	Size of Community				Total of Com-
Party	100,000 and More	30,000- 99,000	10,000- 29,000	City Total	munities of less than 10,000
BGB	73	14	42	129	871
KCVP	102	46	79	227	773
Free Democratic Party	158	72	119	349	651
Democrat.	145	144	109	398	602
SPS	233	78	120	431	569
Evangelical People's Party	424	55	65	544	456
Liberal Democratic Citizens' Party	454	21	94	569	431
LdU	445	92	95	632	368
PdA	645	58	64	767	233
Others	29	11	61	101	899
Total voting	193	61	96	350	650
Total entitled to vote	221	60	95	376	624

Source: M. Bassand.

151 per thousand, respectively. The difference between these parties
also increases in proportion to the size of cities. But even the SPS,
as the most urban of the major parties, received only 431 per thousand
of its total votes in the cities; the majority, 569 per thousand, came
from communities with less than 10,000 inhabitants. The ratio of
rural to urban votes was 651:349 for the Free Democratic Party and
773:227 for the KCVP. Of the major national parties the KCVP is
thus the most rural. Some smaller parties were even more urban
than the SPS: the PdA with 767, the LdU with 632, the Liberal Democratic Citizens' Party with 569, and the Evangelical People's Party
with 544 per thousand of their votes from the cities. The Swiss
Peasants', Traders' and Citizens' Party, with 871 per thousand of its
votes from rural communities, was even more rural than the KCVP.

TABLE 78

Number of Persons in Various Sizes of Communities
Voting for Three Major National Parties, 1959
(per thousand)

Size of Community	Party			
	SPS	Free Democratic Party	KCVP	Others
100,000 and more	318	194	124	364
30,000-99,000	338	279	175	208
10,000-29,000	328	294	192	186
Less than 10,000	231	237	278	254
Total Cities	325	236	151	288
Total Switzer-land	264	237	233	266

Source: M. Bassand.

There are a number of other points that should also be dealt with
in this context. First, a sociological hypothesis will be referred to
that, as far as is known, has never yet been examined. It is argued
that migration from country to city is accompanied by a change of
political attitude, which often represents a lengthy process, however.
In other words, it is suggested that the change of attitude resulting
from this change of residence is often delayed by the length of a generation. This means that if the father (or the mother) moves from the
country to the city his whole attitude remains "rural" under the influence of his upbringing despite the different environment, so that a
change of attitude only occurs with the children. (Conversely, it can,
of course, be argued that a change of attitude is often the actual cause
of the decision to migrate to a city.) Should the hypothesis prove
correct this would mean in terms of projection that the political
consequences of urbanization still remain largely in the future.

Reference should also be made to the role of associations in the
formation of political decisions and to the problem of political information. With the institution of the processes of consultation, the
weight exerted by associations (largely farmers' and industrialists'
associations and trade unions) in the formation of political decisions
has increased,[5] which has been expressed in the polemical assertion
that "politics is not a matter for the people, but an occupation for
experts, who are mostly identical with those directly concerned or
are guided by them."[6]

The parties attach increasing importance to the problem of political information (which also includes civic instruction). In view of the causes of political indifference, to which reference has been made already in various places, it seems questionable whether improved information is sufficient to overcome the growing extent of political nonparticipation.

THE PARTIES' STATEMENTS ON THE
QUESTION OF FEDERALISM

Free Democratic Party:
    "Federalism is the great bulwark against a trend in modern democracy that is known as democratism and is based on the pure law of numbers, whereby the majority becomes the absolute ruler over minorities. For Swiss liberalism the well-being of the minorities is an important criterion for the health of the state . . . This national requirement is now opposed by the demands of expediency. Following in the wake of technology and industrialization the limits of communities and cantons are transgressed in many areas of public activity. Examples include road-building and protection of the water supply, the universities, and the use of atomic energy. In this situation it is vital to defend federalism with the greatest energy wherever it can continue to operate efficiently, but to replace it or to supplement it by means of other solutions wherever this is essential. At the same time, the point cannot be overstressed that the federal principle is capable of great development provided that the desire to evolve new forms of federalism does not weaken prematurely."
    "The division of functions between the federal and cantonal authorities must be reappraised in the light of the developments that have taken place. In order to eliminate the overlapping of competence that has occurred in past decades, together with the confusion of areas of responsibility, specific functions should be assigned on a greater scale either to the federal or to the cantonal authorities. In the case of functions that can only be performed through the joint efforts of federal and cantonal authorities, the areas of responsibility should be clearly laid down. The cantons should not be forced to perform functions that they would not consider reasonable if they were required to finance them on their own. The same approach should be followed where specific functions are to be performed by the state and industry together. Intercantonal and intercommunity cooperation should be promoted at the same time in accordance with these principles. We propose:

    the establishment of a new concept of federalism;
    the promotion of intercantonal and regional cooperation;

the assimilation of cantonal tax systems, and the standardization of the system of charges;
cooperation by means of intercantonal agreements, where
joint solutions can be found;
the assimilation of local and cantonal building regulations."

SPS:

"The economic and social liberation of human beings calls for
the personal and political freedom of each individual. This freedom
is of the most direct significance in Switzerland in the communities
and the cantons. A democratic and federal national structure is
accordingly the basis for the construction of a socialist society in
our country."

BGB:

"The party recognizes the advantages of ensuring the greatest
possible degree of independence for the cantons. . . . In the belief
that only matters of general Swiss concern, which the cantons are
not competent to solve, should be assigned to the Federal authorities."

LdU:

"Our political institutions must be adapted to modern requirements: on the one hand, the responsible agencies must act rapidly
and be able to assume responsibilites; on the other hand, supervision
by Parliament and people must be more effective. The administration
must be rationalized in accordance with the experience of modern
private firms. Small-minded federalism must not be allowed to
impede progress."

Evangelical People's Party:

"Preservation of democracy . . . the correct relationship between
federalism and centralism, according to historical and practical view-
points, must be maintained."

"The autonomy of the community, as a vital element in our
democracy, must be protected and promoted. In principle, as many
functions as possible should be assigned to the community. The
canton should only assume functions that cannot be performed by
the communities, and the Federation should only assume those that
the cantons cannot perform equally well."

PdA:

"The very character of Switzerland, its three languages, its
three cultures, its 22 cantons with their differing customs and attitudes, demand the maintenance of the federal structure. But a more
fruitful basis and improved conditions must be provided in order to
secure its continuation."

13

EXTERNAL INFLUENCES
ON THE DEVELOPMENT
OF SWITZERLAND

In this book it is not possible to give a comprehensive description of the external influences that affect and will affect Swiss society. But an outline of the future development of Swiss society cannot afford to ignore them.

Because of its neutrality, Switzerland was for a long time regarded as an island immune from external influences, free to choose at its own pace its future destiny and the shape of its society. This viewpoint is being questioned today. If Swiss neutrality once played this role to some extent, is it still the case? Swiss neutrality has a long history and has given internal cohesion to a country with a multiplicity of ethnic, linguistic, and religious groups. This status was first internationally recognized and guarenteed in perpetuity by the Declaration of Vienna and the Second Treaty of Paris of 1815, signed by Austria, France, Great Britain, Portugal, Prussia, Russia, and Sweden. These treaties are the legal international foundation of Swiss neutrality up to this day. The interpretation of Swiss neutrality has, however, changed over time. Whereas Swiss had served as mercenaries since the Middle Ages, after 1927 volunteering in foreign armies was strictly forbidden (with the exception of service in the Swiss papal guard).

Swiss neutrality has served as a means of economic independence from political issues. The Swiss developed a merchant ideology, claiming the right to trade with any nation, granting political asylum, acting as intermediary between belligerent states, and providing universal humanitarian service. Congruent with classical economics, which did not take politics into consideration, the Swiss acted as if any economic decision or trade agreement did not have political and ideological elements.

When entering the League of Nations in 1920 Switzerland modified its view on neutrality through the concept of "neutralité différenciée,"

which applied to wars waged against a nation that had broken the pact.
While, in the ordinary way, Switzerland would follow its rules of strict
neutrality, in the latter case it was obliged to adopt economic sanctions
against the agressors. This new interpretation of neutrality was
applied in 1921 and again in 1935 during the Italo-Ethiopian war. In
1938, however, the Swiss government was released, at its request,
from the obligation of participating in economic sanctions.

Has neutrality now become obsolete with Switzerland's new
position in a changing world? Interdependence between states is
growing as the result of a number of forces—the creation of international
organizations pursuing simultaneously economic and political goals,
the extension of internation corporations, faster communications
between countries, and the possibility of generalized war. Interdependence between states always has existed. The new element is that
through the creation of international organizations this interdependence
has been institutionalized and received a legal framework. This
modifies in depth political and economic relationships, both on a
bilateral and multilateral basis. The close links between Swiss
political neutrality and commercial policy are well known, but does
it today assure economic independence? Walter M. Diggelmann
doubts it:

> The much-vaunted independence of Switzerland simply
> does not exist now, and this is because of economic
> factors—we are in a catastrophic state of dependence on
> other powers, other countries. This dependence is
> especially catastrophic because we are politically un-
> aware of it. The same thing will happen to Switzerland
> as in the past: the upheavals will come from outside.[1]

This statement by a "nonconformist" was confirmed in the revaluation
of the Swiss franc at the beginning of May 1971. The Journal de
Genève, for example, headed a commentary on the revaluation
"Powerless" and pointed out that the Federal Council was aware how
powerless it was in the face of foreign factors influencing the economy.
The Neue Zürcher Zeitung had this to say about the monetary crisis:

> In view of the close international links between financial
> currents the policy to be pursued by Switzerland and the
> other European countries will be governed by whatever
> Germany decides to do. The situation of dependence may
> be deplored, but as long as there is a system of fully
> convertible currencies that can be transferred from one
> country to another at any time and as long as the utterly
> uncontrolled Eurodollar market can further stimulate

waves of speculation, there is nothing that can be done
about it.[2]

It is outside the scope of this study to analyze interdependence
in the economic sphere, but economic theory can be regarded, from
the sociologist's viewpoint, as a statement on the operation of certain
social subareas. Both classical and neoclassical theory are based on
the concept of free competition, and both assume that international
division of labor comes about through objective forces in accordance
with the location of various production factors.
But in recent decades sociological concepts have been brought
into the picture, and the idea of choice of location based on purely
economic criteria has been abandoned. In the light of current economic
theories, which introduce the concepts of political power and national
or supranational aims into economic analysis, the question to be considered in regard to Switzerland is whether small countries can retain
their national structural preferences or whether they will be forced
to give them up under the major powers' economic and political
pressure.
The extent of Switzerland's international economic interdependence is indicated by the following cases. At Expo'64 there were 19
firms that had their headquarters in Switzerland and controlled 921
branches in 80 countries; 64 percent of the employees of these firms
worked outside Switzerland. In 1963 Swiss assets abroad, even leaving
aside landownership and mortgage claims, totaled some 44.5 billion
francs, and Swiss liabilities to other countries were about 23.5 billion
francs. Thus, Switzerland was a creditor to the amount of 21 billion
francs, corresponding to 50 percent of the national income and
equivalent to roughly 3,800 francs per person, an exceptionally high
level.[3] In the early 1960s it was calculated that there were 8 billion
francs worth of Swiss holdings of securities in other countries (excluding the United States). According to U.S. sources, privately owned
Swiss property in the United States at that time amounted to 14.5
billion francs. The total foreign holdings of Swiss financial capital
was then estimated at around 50 billion francs, from which 6 billion
can be deducted as "hot money."[4]
This interdependence has inevitably influenced Swiss attitudes
on political and social issues. Even more significant, Switzerland's
traditional international political isolation is being eroded, in the
specific questions of membership in the UN and relations with the
EEC. A past member of the Leage of Nations, Switzerland has not
yet joined the UN, although it is a member of all the specialized
agencies of the UN—UNESCO, ILO, World Health Organization (WHO),
Food and Agricultural Organization FAO, and so on—as well as
of the UN development program (UNDP) and the children's fund

(UNICEF). For some 25 years Switzerland justified its opposition to entry on the basis of articles 24 and 25, which vest large powers in the Security Council. Article 43 of the UN Charter, however, allows each member state to specify, through a special agreement, the extent of its participation in eventual sanctions directed against a state.

Swiss opinion has evolved during recent years. On June 16, 1969, a report was submitted by the Federal Council to the Federal Assembly on Switzerland's future relationship with the UN. Its conclusions were not entirely unequivocal, and for the time being the Federal Council did not recommend entry. Some members of the Parliamentary Commission dealing with the matter, however, considered that, in view of the fact that no fundamental objections to entry were expressed, a more positive conclusion should have been formed. But a motion calling for action for Swiss membership in the UN without prejudice to the country's neutral status was rejected by 18 votes to 6, with 1 abstention. On the other hand, the Federal Council proposed a number of specific measures to bring about a closer relationship with the UN.

In 1971 the Tribune de Genève held an inquiry among members of parliament. Out of a total of 200, 101 national councilors and 26 state councilors (out of 44) replied. Three-quarters of these members considered that membership in the UN was compatible with Switzerland's principal of neutrality, whereas 12 (including 7 from the KCVP) held that it was not.

In June 1972 a new governmental report was presented to the National Council; with the sole opposition of the Republican Party, most political parties were in full agreement with Switzerland's entry into the UN or resigned to it. It is now no longer a question whether Switzerland will enter the UN or not. Public opinion polls indicate that 45 percent are in favor and 34 percent against. A national vote on the entry of Switzerland to the UN will probably take place, at the latest in 1974.

A similar evolution of governmental attitude and, to a certain extent, public opinion took place concerning Swiss relations with the EEC. In 1970, with the increasing likelihood of a break-up of the European Free Trade Association (EFTA), Switzerland entered into formal negotiations with the EEC regarding the possibility of association. In September 1971 the Federal Council published a report covering all aspects of possible integration. It stated that the constant concern of Swiss integration policy had been to develop a middle-of-the-road European policy between the two main poles of growing international economic interdependence and the need to maintain neutrality and national individuality. The aim of this policy is described as the greatest possible degree of cooperation permitted by the overriding political characteristics of the country. The Federal Council is therefore consistent in pursuing a strategy aimed at a "special and comprehensive relationship" in its negotiations regarding Swiss association with the EEC.

Early in 1971 a federal councilor summarized the government's position in a public speech:

> Why not join the EEC then? The EEC's political aims are not compatible with Swiss neutrality, and barely so with our national structure. It is not the material difficulties that stand in the way of our joining: it is the fundamental elements of our national organization. However, this does not prevent us from helping to construct Europe, without giving up our independence or our identity.[5]

The 1971 poll of members of parliament held by the Tribune de Genève produced the following results in connection with European integration: 77 out of the 109 who replied believed that European integration, even at the political level, would be in Swiss interests; 52 believed that it would be possible to maintain Swiss independence and neutrality in a united Europe; and 11 (including 6 from the SPS) were in favor of becoming a full member of the EEC.

THE PARTIES' VIEWS ON WORLDWIDE INTER-DEPENDENCE, THE UN, AND THE EEC

Free Democratic Party:
"The world has become a single comprehensive field of political power from which no one can entirely opt out."

"Our economic progress is based to a substantial extent on the rapidly growing interconnection of our economy with the rest of the world that has taken place in recent years."

SPS:
"In Switzerland as in the whole of Europe freedom, democracy, social justice, and general prosperity can have no true foundation until mankind throughout the world has been freed from war and poverty, fear and lawlessness."

BGB:
"A foreign policy that recognizes only national aims no longer corresponds to the demands of our time, in which the whole of mankind has become a single community sharing the same destiny."

PdA (youth section):
"It is a fact that the material interests of the Swiss worker do not depend on the individual and sovereign branches of the Swiss

economy but rather on the interweaving of the Swiss economy and Swiss capital with the economies of capitalist and developing countries ... It is vital therefore for our thinking and our activities to be directed toward a broader perspective than the national or European level."

On the issues of joining the UN and relations with the EEC, the following statements were made:

KCVP:
       "A foreign policy of worldwide solidarity and service based on the tested principle of lasting armed neutrality demands that possible means and aims should be clearly formulated."
       "Membership in the United Nations is conditional upon recognition of Swiss neutrality,"
       "Insistence on neutrality and maintenance of our distinctive federalist and direct democracy are essential in the event of our joining the EEC."
       "Switzerland's armed neutrality remains a national principle that must not be touched."
       "The spirit of understanding is also the key to our efforts to help to overcome the economic division of Europe into two integrated blocs. The political unification of Europe, which we feel as an ever more pressing necessity, can then be more easily attained. Switzerland has a contribution to make toward such unification, which must respect the diversity of the continent and the individuality of its national forms, traditions, and cultures."

Free Democratic Party:
       "The fact that Switzerland continues to uphold that policy of lasting armed neutrality that the founders of the Federal state regarded in 1848 as 'the most appropriate means to the desired end' does not in any way mean that neutrality has since then become a rigid and immobile dogma. The reality is that when all factors and risks inherent in the present situation are carefully appraised this remains the best possible instrument to attain our supreme national purpose, which is to maintain our free society of free people."
       "The question of Switzerland's membership [of the United Nations] cannot at present be answered with a yes or a no. It requires thorough examination. We demand:
       extension of Swiss participation in the specialized
           agencies of the United Nations;
       examination of ways and means of permitting Switzer-
           land to join the United Nations without affecting its
           neutrality;

consideration of all political, legal, and technical problems that would arise from participation by Switzerland in United Nations peace-keeping activities.

"European collaboration: The desire to overcome the commercial division of Europe remains one of our principal concerns.
At the same time all attempts directed toward integration must be
regarded as part and parcel of efforts to remodel world trade on the
basis of free action. At present certain members of EFTA are seeking
links with the EEC. If their efforts succeeded this would bring about
a radical change in the situation regarding integration, and Switzerland
would also have to consider the question of closer relations with the
EEC. Our country must prepare itself for this eventuality in both
its domestic and its foreign policies just as it must for the possibility
of further discrimination within a Europe that continues to be divided."

SPS:

"The Social Democratic Party of Switzerland supports the efforts
directed toward the unification of Europe and the world within a free
and democratic federation. The Social Democrats firmly uphold the
need for Switzerland to join the United Nations, without affecting our
country's military neutrality."

"The SPS proposes that contacts should be increased at the level
of international organizations and that the obstacles that have thus
far opposed Switzerland's membership in the United Nations should
be gradually removed."

"The SPS proposes action to overcome the division of Western
Europe into two economic blocs, by encouraging the EFTA states'
efforts to create a major economic area either through association
with the EEC or through entry."

"The SPS also proposes promotion of economic and cultural
collaboration between Western and Eastern Europe."

BGB:

"The party sees the main function of Swiss foreign policy in
the preservation of our country's independence. It is in favor of the
unconditional maintenance of our neutrality."

"The party advocates active participation by our country in
efforts to improve international understanding, to reduce political,
economic, and social conflict in the world, and to extend international
law."

"Full membership in the United Nations is not possible, however,
in the party's view until our status of lasting neutrality has been expressly recognized; in any event the question of membership would
have to be put to the vote before the people and the cantons."

"Regarding economic cooperation in Europe the party is in favor of bridging the gap between the two economic blocs of EFTA and EEC. The provisions of the Treaty of Rome seem to rule out the possibility of full membership in the Common Market, since it would be incompatible with out independence, our neutrality, our federalism, our popular rights, and the needs of economic self-defense."

LdU:

"Principle of foreign policy: absolute neutrality toward foreign countries in all political and economic matters."

"We support the efforts directed toward European unification and want to take an active part in them. Since Switzerland has close connections with its neighbors we wish to promote collaboration between EFTA and EEC with a view to a subsequent combination."

"Switzerland's entry into the United Nations should be pressed forward. We wish to maintain our neutral status and refrain from entering into any obligations entailing sanctions, because this attitude can enable us to contribute to a proper balance while helping to solve world problems."

Evangelical People's Party:

"The Party sustains the following principles: Determination to uphold the country's political and military neutrality. Determination to preserve and promote peace among the nations by means of active collaboration in all areas that are not contrary to the principle of neutrality. Extension of international law on a Christian basis and strengthening of the influence of international arbitration."

PdA:

"The interests of monopolies, cartels and trusts, and capital investment in foreign countries, including loans by the Confederation, govern Switzerland's foreign policy. . . . In this way the bourgeoisie violates the fundamental principle of neutrality, which does not consist just in keeping out of other people's quarrels but also of maintaining peaceful and friendly relations with all countries and all peoples."

"The PdA stresses the need for Switzerland to conduct an effective and positive policy of peaceful initiative, within the framework of genuine national neutrality . . . this means that Switzerland must give its consent to the formation of atom-free zones and the creation of a European security system and must accept the treaty on nonproliferation of atomic weapons; it should only join a united, peaceloving Europe free of military and economic blocs. If Switzerland should join the United Nations, it should be principally in order to support this form of policy."

CHAPTER 1

1. This scheme of confrontation was first published in A. Gretler, Values and Evolutionary Trends in European Cultural Foundation: Citizen and City in the Year 2000 (Deventer: Kluwer, 1971), pp. 213-20.

CHAPTER 3

1. Working Group on Long-Range Projections (F. Kneschaurek chairman), Entwicklungsperspektiven der schweizerischen Volkswirtschaft bis zum Jahre 2000, Pt. I: Bevölkerung und Erwerbstätigkeit (St. Gallen, March 1969), pp. 20, 32, and 53.

2. Ibid., p. 20.

3. Kurt Fricker, "Basis of Calculation for the Old-Age and Survivors' Scheme, a Semidynamic Model: Mean Forecast," Schweizerische Zeitschrift für Volkswirtschaft und Statistik (Bern), CI, 2 (June 1965), 122.

4. Ellen Hülsen, "Results of stochastic and biometric models," Schweizerische Zeitschrift für Volkswirtschaft und Statistik (Bern), CI, 2 (June 1965), 114.

5. Wilhelm Bickel, "Results of Extrapolation of Previous Long-Range Population Trends," Schweizerische Zeitschrift für Volkswirtschaft und Statistik (Bern), CI, 2 (June 1965), 107.

6. Ellen Hülsen, "Probable Trends in the Resident Population and the Labor Force," Schweizerische Zeitschrift für Volkswirtschaft und Statistik (Bern), CII, 3-4 (September-December 1966), 270-71.

7. Fricker, "Basis of Calculation."

8. Otto Messmer, "Preliminary Comments on Probable Population Trends in Switzerland," Schweizerische Zeitschrift für Volkswirtschaft und Statistik (Bern), CI, 2 (June 1965), 106.

9. Statistisches Jahrbuch der Schweiz, 1967, p. 46.

10. Käthe Biske, "Women's Work in Occupation and Household," Zürcher Statistische Nachrichten (Zurich), XLIV, 3, p. 122.

11. Statistisches Jahrbuch der Schweiz 1967, p. 46

CHAPTER 4

1. Swiss Bank Corporation (SBC), Schweizerische Wirtschaftsentwicklung 1939-1964 (Zurich: SBC Economic Studies Department, 1964), p. 9.

2. Federal Statistical Office, Federal Census, 1960, "Schedule of Jobs" (mimeo., Bern, 1961).

3. Commission Appointed to Study the Foreign Manpower Problem [Holzer Commission], Le problème de la main d'oeuvre étrangère (Bern: Federal Office of Industry, Arts and Crafts, and Labor, 1964); Michel Hagmann, Les travailleurs étrangers, chance et tournant de la Suisse—problème économique, social, politique, phénomène sociologigue (Lausanne: Payot, 1966); A. H. Gnehm, Ausländische Arbeitskrafte—Vor- und Nachteile für die Volkswirtschaft (Bern: Verlag Paul Haupt, 1966); Klaus Huber, Die ausländischen Arbeitskräfte in der Schweiz (unpublished Ph. D. dissertation, Bern, 1963); Roger Girod, Foreign Workers and Social Mobility in Switzerland (mimeo.) (Geneva: International Institute for Labor Studies, 1965); Klaus Huber, "Future Trends in the Main Factors Determining the Influx of Foreign Labor," Handwerk und Gewerbe, XLIII, 3 (1963), 36-45; "Foreign Workers in Switzerland," International Labour Review (Geneva), LXXXVII, 2 (1963), 133-55; and G. Lucrezio, A. Perotti, and N. Falchi, "Italian Emigration in the 1970s" (Rome: Centro Studi Emigrazione), Prospettive No. 1 (Morcelliana, 1966).

4. Hans-Joachim Hoffmann-Novotny and Jean-Pierre Hoby, "Structural Consequences of Immigration into Switzerland," paper presented at annual meeting of Swiss Sociological Society, Zurich, November 1968 (mimeo.).

5. Ibid., p. 10.

6. Edmond Boissier, "Un problème genevois: L'assimilation des étrangers" (Geneva, 1909).

7. Hoffmann-Novotny and Hoby, "Structural Consequences," pp. 17-18.

8. Ibid., p. 19.

9. Ibid., pp. 23 and 29, respectively.

10. Holzer Commission, Le problème, p. 103.

11. Georges Hartmann, "Needs and Targets of Swiss programming in the Field of Automation", Revue économique et sociale (Lausanne), XXI, 4 (1963), pp. 323-47; Wilhelm Vogt, L'employé et l'automation (Geneva: Imprimerie L. Reggiani, 1966); E. P. Billeter, "Aspects and Problems of Automation in Switzerland," Industrie Rundschau (Zurich), No. 7 (November 1966), pp. 87-89; Georges Hartmann, Die Automation und unsere Zukunft (Stuttgart: C. E. Poeschel Verlag, 1957); Gaston Cuendet, "Growth of Administrative Services in the Enterprise," Revue économique et sociale (Lausanne), XXV, 2 (1967), pp. 143-52; IFO Institute for Economic Research, Soziale Auswirkungen des technischen Fortschritts (Berlin and Munich: Duncker und Humblot, 1962); ILO, "A Tabulation of Case Studies on Technological Change," Labour and Automation, Bulletin No. 2 (Geneva, 1965); ILO, Abstracts of Articles on the Social Aspects of Automation (Geneva, 1964);

Erwin Krause, Automation und Berufsausbildung (Ratingen: A.
Henn Verlag, 1965); Günter Friedrichs, ed., Automation-Risiko
und Chance, contributions to the Second International Meeting of
the Metalworkers' Federation of the Federal Republic of Germany
on Rationalization, Automation, and Technological Progress, Ober-
hausen, March 16-19, 1965 (2 vols.; Frankfurt: Europäische Verlag-
sanstalt, 1965) (See also second meeting, 1968, Computer und
Angestellte); Organization for Economic Cooperation and Development (OECD), European Conference on Manpower Aspects of Automation and Technical Change (Zurich, 1966), Manpower Aspects of
Automation and Technical Change, conference papers, 22 pts.
(Paris: OECD, 1966) and Final Report, 2 vols.; E. Sachse, Technische Revolution und Qualifikation der Werktätigen (Berlin: Dietz
Verlag, 1965); A. Zvorykin, "Methods of Determining the Possible
Consequences of Mechanization and Automation on the Structure of
the Labor Force," in Autorité, technologie et emploi (Paris: Socio-
logical Study Center, 1966), pp. 185-93; C. Vimont and G. Rérat,
"The Influence of Technological Progress on Workers' Skills—a
New Method of Analysis," Population (Paris), XXI, 3 (May-June
1966), 541-62; H. E. Striner, Training in the Perspective of Tech-
nological Change, Seminar on Manpower Policy and Program No. 5.
(Washington, D.C.: Office of Manpower Policy, Evaluation and
Research, 1966); International Labour Office (ILO), Social Aspects
of Automation—a Bibliography of Material Available in the ILO,
ILO/AUT/DOC/2 (rev. ed.; Geneva, 1966); W. Reischeck, Die
Bewaltigung der Zukunft—Technische Revolution, polytechnische
Bildung (Berlin: Volk und Wissen, Volkseigener Verlag, 1966); G.
Friedmann, Où va le travail humain (Paris: Gallimard, 1967); and
J. M. Rosenberg, Automation, Manpower and Education (New York:
Random House, 1966).

    12. Urs Jaeggi, "The Influence of Rationalization and Automation
on Jobs," Berufsberatung und Berufsbildung (Zurich), L, 5-6
(October 1965), 131-37; and Urs Jaeggi and H. Wiedemann, Der
Angestellte im automatisierten Büro (Stuttgart Kohlhamma, 1963.).

    13. Urs Jaeggi, "Influence," p. 132.

    14. Ibid., pp. 132-34.

    15. See also Hans Rudin, "Training of Semiskilled Workers in
the Textile Industry," Schweizerische Arbeitgeberzeitung (Zurich),
No. 4 (January 25, 1968), pp. 68-70. Rudin states that 98 percent
of women and 88 percent of men production workers in the textile
industry are semiskilled and that this structure is attributable to
the degree of automation. The training of these workers involves
familiarizing them with the operation of a particular machine.

    16. See Kurt B. Mayer, "Postwar Migration to Switzerland,"
Migrations Internationales, III, 3 (1965), 125; Kurt. B. Mayer,
"Migration, Cultural Tensions and Foreign Relations: Switzerland,"

Journal of Conflict Resolution, II, 2 (June 1967), 139-52; Marc
Virot, Vom Anderssein zur Assimilation—Merkmale zur Beurteilung
der Assimilationsreife in der Schweiz (Bern: Verlag Paul Haupt,
1968); R. Braun, Sozio-Kulturelle Probleme der Eingliederung
italienischer Arbeitskrafte in der Schweiz (Erlenbach-Zurich:
Verlag Eugen Rentsch, 1970); and P. Schoenbach, Sprache und
Attitüden; über den Einfluss der Bezeichnungen "Fremdarbeiter"
und "Gastarbeiter" auf Einstellungen gegenüber ausländischen
Arbeitern (Bern: Verlag Hans Huber, 1970).

17. Working Group on Long-Range Projections (F. Kneschaurek,
chairman), Entwicklungsperspektiven der schweizerischen Volks-
wirtschaft bis zum Jahre 2000, Prt. IV: Forecasts Regarding the
Swiss Educational System (St. Gallen, May 1971), here quoted from
F. Kneschaurek, "Problems of Occupational Entry in Switzerland—
Some Results of Education Projections until the Year 2000,"
Mitteilungsblatt des schweizerischen Wissenschaftsrates (Bern),
V, 3 (1971), 9-27.

18. Ibid., pp. 20-21.

19. Basel Working Group on Education and Manpower Research,
Bildungswesen, Arbeitsmarkt und Wirtschaftswachstum—Eine
Modellstudie zur langfristigen Entwicklung der Qualifikationsstruktur der Erwerbstätigen in der Schweiz (Basel, December
1969), p. 292 ff. See also B. Blankart, Die Qualifikationsstruktur
des Arbeitskräftebedarfs in der Schweiz (Bern: Verlag Herbert
Lang, 1970).

20. See CIRF, ILO, European Apprenticeship, Effects of
Educational, Social and Technical Development on Apprentice
Training Practices in Eight Countries, CIRF Monographs, Vol. I,
No. 2 (Geneva: CIPF Publications, ILO, 1966). Switzerland is one
of the countries considered.

21. P. Steinman, La formation professionnelle et l'évolution
technique, Seminar on Vocational Training in Switzerland, Vitznau,
October 17-22, 1966 (Geneva: International Metalworkers'
Federation, 1966).

22. Educational Leave in Switzerland (unpublished ms.;
Geneva: ILO, 1969). In November 1969 a motion was introduced
in the National Council by the socialist Wüthrich (Bern) calling
for legislation to institute educational leave, but it was rejected.
The Federal Council also advocated rejection of a Geneva cantonal
initiative calling for the introduction of educational leave. See also
R. Crummenerl and G. Dermine, Educational Leave, a Key Factor
of Permanent Education and Social Advancement (Strasbourg:
Council of Europe, 1969).

23. See F. Hess, F. Latscha, and W. Schneider, Die Ungleichheit
der Bildungschancen (Olten: Walter Verlag, 1966); Kurt Luscher,

Wege zu einer Soziologie der Erziehung—international und in der
Schweiz (mimeo.; Bern: University of Bern, 1968), including
appendix, "Educational Research in Switzerland since about 1965,
with Particular Reference to Sociologically Oriented Studies."

24. A detailed enumeration of these requirements in the form
of a proposal for educational patterns suitable for long-term effort
is to be found in A. Gretler, D. Haag, E. Halter, R. Kramer, S.
Munari, and F. Stoll, La Suisse au devant de l'education permanente
(Lausanne: Editions Payot, Collection Greti-Information, 1971);
a German version is due to appear in 1972.

CHAPTER 5

1. Schweizerisches Jahrbuch für Statistik, 1961, p. 528.

2. Federation of Swiss Women's Associations, Foundation
for Research into Women's Employment, Erhebung über die
Lehrpläne in den Volksschulen (mimeo.; Zurich, 1967).

3. Marion Janiic, "Women's Employment and Conditions of
Work in Switzerland," International Labour Review (Geneva),
Vol. 96, 3 (September 1967), 292.

4. Statistisches Jahrbuch der Schweiz, 1971, p. 460.

5. Käthe Biske, "Women's Work in Occupation and Household,"
Zürcher Statistische Nachrichten (Zurich), XLIV, 3 (1968), 120-40
and No. 4, pp. 187-229. See also H. Thalmann-Antenen, La femme
et la vie professionnelle (Berne), a report submitted by the Swiss
Social Policy Association to the International Association for Social
Progress, 1970.

6. Biske, "Women's Work," pp. 128-29.

7. Ibid., p. 130.

8. United States, Department of Labor, Women's Bureau,
1965 Handbook on Women Workers, Bulletin No. 290 (Washington,
D.C., 1965).

9. Biske, "Women's Work," p. 205.

10. Ibid., pp. 210-11.

11. Walo Hutmacher, with collaboration of A. L. Du Pasquier,
Problèmes de Placement d'enfants d'âge préscolaire à Genève,
1964: les crèches (Geneva: Public Education Department, Sociological Research Branch, March 1966).

12. Biske, "Women's Work," No. 4, pp. 210-11.

13. Ibid.

14. Ibid., p. 213.

15. Ibid., pp. 216-17.

16. Ibid., p. 217. See also P. Hülsmann et al., Gesundheit und
Erwerbstätigkeit der Fran in mittleren Lebensalter (commissioned
by the Ministry of Health of the Federal Republic of Germany)
(Frechen: Bartmann Verlag, 1966).

17. P. H. Chombart de Lauwe, ed., Images de la femme dans la société, Recherche internationale (Paris: Les éditions ouvrières, 1964).

18. Leopold Rosenmayr, "Austrian Women—Their Role and Their Image," in Chombart de Lauwe, Images, Ch. 6.

19. Maria-Immita Cornaz, Le travail professionnel de la mère et la vie familiale (Lausanne: Payot, 1964).

20. People's Family Movement, Aisance et privations, a scientific inquiry into the living conditions of employees' families in French-speaking Switzerland, conducted by the People's Family Movement in conjunction with and under the supervision of the Swiss Public Opinion Institute (6 vols.; Geneva, 1968).

21. France Govaerts, Loisirs des femmes et temps libre (Editions de l'Institut de Sociologie Solvay, Brussels Free University, Brussels 1969).

22. R. Spitz, "Hospitalism, an Inquiry into the Genesis of Psychiatric Conditions in Early Childhood," in Psychoanalytic Study of the Child, (I) (London: Image Publishing Co., 1945); K. M. Wolf, "Anaclitic Depression, an Inquiry into the Genesis of Psychiatric Conditions in Early Childhood" (1946), Pt. II; John Bowlby, Maternal Care and Mental Health (Geneva: WHO, 1951); Léon Duc, "Maternal Love in Early Childhood as a Psycho-Hygienic Problem," reprinted from Bulletin des Eidgenössischen Gesundheitsamtes, Supplement B, No. 2 (May 1, 1954). In Switzerland Dr. Marie Meierhofer has done pioneer work in this field in Zurich.

23. Mary Ainsworth et al., Deprivation of Maternal Care: A Reassessment of Its Effects (Geneva: WHO Public Health Papers, 1962); M. L. Kellmer-Pringle and R. Dinnage, Residential Child Care—Facts and Fallacies, National Bureau for Co-operation in Child Care (London: Longmans, 1967); M. L. Kellmer-Pringle and R. Dinnage, Foster Home Care—Facts and Fallacies, National Bureau for Co-operation in Child Care (London: Longmans, 1967).

24. See, for example, Hungary, Government Order No. 3/1967, January 29, 1967; Veillard-Cybulska, "Aspects of Child Care: Czechoslovakia, Hungary," Revue internationale de l'enfant (Geneva), XXXVII, 3-4 (1967).

25. S. Yudkin and A. Holme, Working Mothers and Their Children, a Study for the Council for Children's Welfare (London: M. Joseph, 1963).

26. In Geneva empirical investigations are being made at present by the Sociological Research Branch of the Department of Education to find what solutions have been found for the 5- to 9-year-old children of working mothers in the Jonction district.

27. See, for example, Leslie B. Tanner, ed., Voices from Women's Liberation (New York: Signet Book, 1970); and Sookie

Stambler, comp., Women's liberation, Blueprint for the Future (New York: Ace Books, 1970).

28. Viola Klein, L'emploi des femmes, horaires et responsabilités familiales, une enquête dans 21 pays (Paris: OECD, 1965).

29. France Govaerts, The Family and Leisure: Masculine and Feminine Roles, SOA/ESOP/1967/4 (Geneva: European Seminar on the Leisure of Workers in Modern Industrial Societies, Semmering, November 2-29, 1967), pp. 33-67.

30. France Govaerts, "Participation by Women in Collective Responsibilities and Protection of the Family in a Civilization of Labor and Leisure" (Brussels: Centre National de Sociologie du Travail), Warsaw Congress of the International Federation of Women in Legal Careers, August 20-26, 1967.

31. Janjic, "Women's Employment."

32. Cf. Wolfgang Lempert, Die Konzentration der Lehrlinge auf Lehrberufe in der Bundesrepublik Deutschland, in der Schweiz und in Frankreich, 1950 bis 1963 (Berlin: Research Institute of the Max Plank Society, 1966), Studien und Berichte, No. 7 (mimeo.). The study shows that Switzerland has a lower concentration of apprentices in a small number of occupations than either of the other countries considered.

33. Biske, "Women's Work," p. 126.

34. Ibid., p. 133.

35. Liselotte Schucan-Grob, "Part-time Employment of Women Graduates," Berufsberatung und Berufsbildung (Zurich), LII, 3-4 (1967); and I. Hillaire, "Part-Time Employment—Its Extent and Its Problems," Employment of Special Groups (Paris, OECD), No. 6, 1968. See also M. I. Cornaz, L'emploi à temps partiel (Paris: International Union of Family Organizations, 1967).

36. Evangelical Women's Association of Switzerland, Boldern Meeting and Study Center, Wiederaufnahme der Berufsarbeit von Frauen in der zweiten Lebenshälfte—Bericht über einer Studienarbeit (Zurich: Evangelical Women's Association of Switzerland, 1968) (mimeo.). See also "Return to Occupational Life," Neue Zuricher Zeitung, No. 779, December 17, 1968; and B. N. Seear, Re-entry of Women to the Labor Market after an Interruption in Employment (Paris: OECD, 1971).

37. Evangelical Women's Association of Switzerland, Boldern Meeting and Study Center, Wideraufnahme der Berufsarbeit von Frauen in der zweiten Lebenshalfte. . . .

38. Statistisches Jahrbuch der Schweiz, 1969, p. 370.

39. Janjic, "Women's Employment," p. 341.

40. See Marga Bührig and Anny Schmid-Affolter, Die Frau in der Schweiz (Bern: Verlag Paul Haupt, 1969). The growing awareness of problems relating to the conditions of women is also

illustrated by the organization of the first major empirical sociological survey on the subject in Switzerland around 1970. The
survey, which was carried out by the Sociological Institute of
Zurich University on behalf of the national UNESCO commission,
is largely financed by the Confederation and is based mainly on
over 3,000 interviews. The results are due to be published in
1972.

CHAPTER 6

1. See, for example, the following: E. W. Burgess, H. J. Locke,
and A. Thome, The Family from Institution to Companionship (2d
ed.; New York: American Book, 1953); D. R. Blitsen, The World
of Family, a Comparative Study of Family Organizations in Their
Social and Cultural Settings (New York: Random House, 1963);
W. J. Goode, World Revolution and Family Patterns (New York:
Free Press of Glencoe, 1963); W. J. Goode, Readings on the Family
and Society (Englewood Cliffs, N.J.: Prentice-Hall, 1964); R. Hill,
"Sociology of Marriage and Family Behaviour, 1945-1956," Current
Sociology, VII, 1 (1958); H. Becker, R. Hill,, et al., Family, Marriage
and Parenthood (2d ed.; Boston: Heath and Co., 1955); J. M. Mogey,
Family and Neighbourhood (Oxford: Oxford University Press,
1956); R. Koenig, Materialien zur Soziologie der Familie (Berne:
Francke Verlag, 1946); H. Schelsky, Wandlungen der Deutschen
Familie in der Gegenwatt (2d ed.; Stuttgart: Enke, 1954); M. D.
Young and P. Wilmott, Family and Kinship in East London (New
York: Free Press of Glencoe, 1957); P. H. Chombart de Lauwe,
"The Birth of Aspirations to New Forms of Family," Recherches
sur la Famille (Tübingen: Mohr, 1956), Vol. I; United Nations,
European Seminar on Social Policy in Relation to Changing Family
Needs, Arnhem, April 16-26, 1961, SOA/ESWP/1961/3 (Geneva),
Renate Mayntz, Die moderne Familie (Stuttgart: Ferdinand Enke
Verlag, 1955); and Hans Ten Dornkaat, "Family in Modern Society,"
Neue Zürcher Zeitung, No. 4044 (September 25, 1966).

2. France Govaerts, "Participation by Women in Collective
Responsibilities and Protection of the Family in a civilization of
Labor and Leisure," Brussels, CNST, Warsaw Congress of the
International Federation of Women in Legal Careers, August
20-26, 1967.

3. H. Beck, Der Kulturzusammenstoss zwischen Stadt und
Land in einer Vororts-Gemeinde (Zurich: Regie Verlag, 1952);
Nicolas et al., Lausanne anthropological research group, Essai de
monographie comparée de deux villages du canton de Vaud: Oppens
et Orzens (Montreux: Imprimerie Gauguin et Laubscher, 1965);
H. Weiss," Vom Bauerndorf zum Industriedorf, Einige soziologische
Aspekte der industriell bedingten Veränderungen einer

Bauerngemeinde," unpublished Ph.D. dissertation, University of
Zurich, 1957; H. Weiss, "Industrialization in Rural Areas: Report
on a Community Study in Switzerland," Kölner Zeitschrift für
Soziologie und Sozial-Psychologie, Special No. 1/1965; E. U. Jäggi,
"Mountain Communities in Evolution," Berner Beiträge zur Soziologie (Berne), ix (1965); J. Nussbaumer, "The Living Conditions of
Farmers' Families in the Homburg Valley; a Study of Agrarian
Sociology and Economics," Kantonale Drucksachen und Material-
zentrale (Liestal, 1963); Schaer Meuirad, et al., "What Is Needed
for Sound Family Development in Mountain Regions?" proceedings
of the 57th meeting of the Swiss Family Protection Commission,
Zurich, March 9, 1967, "Schweizerische Zeitschrift für Gemein-
nützigkeit," No. 6 (June 1967).

4. G. Berthoud, Changements économiques et sociaux de la
montagne, Vernamiège en Valais (Bern: Ed. Francke, 1968).
E. Kobler, La commune de Schiers (Grisons); Etude de géographie
humaine (Geneva: University of Geneva, 1970).

5. The demand that the financing of studies should not be at
the parents' expense has been the leading theme in the "Lausanne
model," advanced by the National Union of Paris Students. See
Union Nationale des Etudiants de Suisse, Modele de Lausanne—
projet d'un nouveau mode de financement des études (Berne:
Edition de l'UNES, 1970).

6. See, for example, Burgess, Locke, and Thome, Family.

7. "Free Pass for Freedom," Weltwoche, No. 1789 (February
23, 1968). The change of values in this connection has become
apparent in the movement launched in June 1971 for a referendum
to legalize abortion. The legal prohibition of abortion (Sections
118-21 of the Criminal Code) would be removed through the proposed new Article 65bis of the constitution, which would read:
"No penalty shall be imposed for performing an abortion."

8. Richard Meili has been most prominent in his investigation
of the subject in Switzerland; see, for example, his "Study of the
Level of Intelligence of Swiss Children," in Berufsberatung und
Berufsbildung, (Zurich), Nos. 1-2 (October 1964).

9. J. Bowlby, "Maternal Care and Mental Health," WHO
monograph series, No. 2 (1951); B. Inhelder and J. M. Tanner,
eds., "Discussions on Child Development: A Consideration of
the Biological, Psychological and Cultural Approaches to the
Understanding of Human Development and Behavior," tape-recorded
discussions between J. Bowlby, F. Fremont-Smith, G. R. Hargreaves,
B. Inhelder, Konrad Lorenz, Margaret Mead, Karl Axel Melin,
M. Monnier, J. Piaget, A. Remond, J. M. Tanner, W. Grey-Walter,
R. Zazzo, B. Buckle, Erik Erikson, Julian Huxley, R. de Saussure,
R. R. Struthers, Bindra Dalbir, J. C. Carothers, and E. E. Krapf;

The Proceedings of the 1st, 2nd and 3rd Meetings of WHO Study
Group on the Psychobiological Development of the Child, Geneva,
1953, 1954, 1955 (3 vols.; London: Tavistock Publications, 1956
and 1958); UNICEF, "Growth and Development of the Young Child
from One to Six Years," E/ICEF/521 prepared for submission to
the UNICEF Executive Board by the International Children's Center,
Paris, May 21, 1965; M. L. Kellmer-Pringle, "Early Learning
and Later Progress," Symposium on Speech, Learning and Child
Health, Proc. R. Soc. Med., LX (September 1967); Deprivation
and Education (London: Longmans, 1965); and M. L. Kellmer-
Pringle, ed., Investment in Children, a symposium on positive
child care and constructive education (London: Longmans, 1965).

10. UNESCO, "Third International Conference on Brain Research" (Paris: UNESCO, May 1968); International Children's
Center, "Recherche comparative internationale longitudinale sur
la croissance et le développement de l'enfant normal, 17th year,"
(Paris). Switzerland is one of a large number of countries participating in this study; several publications have already appeared.

11. R. D. Hess and Virginia Shipman "Early Experiences and
Socialization of Cognitive Modes in Children," Child Development,
XXXVI, 4 (December 1965), p. 21; C. W. Brittain, "Pre-School
Programs for Culturally Deprived Children," Children (Washington,
D.C.), XIII, 4 (1966), pp. 131-34; D. Goldschmitt and I. Sommerkorn,
An Outline of Educational Disadvantages and Deprivation in the
Federal Republic of Germany (Hamburg: UNESCO, Institute for
Education, 1967); P. Bourdieu "Systems of Education and Systems
of Thought," International Social Sciences Journal (Paris: UNESCO),
XIX, 3 (1967), p. 338-58; J. C. Passeron, Les héritiers: les
étudiants et la culture (Paris: Edition de Minuit, 1964); F.
Riessman, The Culturally Deprived Child (New York: Harper and
Row, 1962); J. Floud and A. H., Halsey, eds., Education, Economy
and Sociology: A Reader in Sociology of Education (New York:
Free Press of Glencoe, 1965); and E. Egger, R. Girod, and L.
Pauli, L'Education pour tous et les moins doués, Sixth Conference
of European Ministers of Education, Strasbourg, CME/VI (69)2,
1968.

12. G. Friedman, "L'école parallele," report to Committee IV,
Third International Congress of the European Broadcasting Union
on Educational Radio and Television in the World, Paris, May
8-23, 1967.

13. Ph. Coombs, World Crisis in Education (Paris: UNESCO,
International Institute for Educational Planning, 1968).

14. The special problems faced by young people have been
examined in detail in Switzerland: P. Arnold, M. Bassand, B.
Crettaz, and J. Kellerhals, Jeunesse et société; premiers jalons
pour une politique de la jeunesse (Lausanne: Payot, 1971).

15. J. Lacroix, Force et faiblesse de la famille (Paris: le Seuil, 1957); J. Lacroix, "The Family and the Movement of Ideas," Famille d'aujourd'hui, Chronique Sociale de France (Lyon), 1958.

16. R. H. Hazemann, "Psychological Aspects of the Hygiene of Housing" (in French only), European Seminar on Social Aspects of Housing, Sèvres, October 7-16, 1957, UN/TAA/SEM/1957 (Geneva), pp. 40-54.

17. Max Keller, "Divorce by Consent—the Discrepancy between Law and Practice," Neue Zürcher Zeitung, No. 783 (December 18, 1968).

18. G. Gorer, "Teenage Morals," an education pamphlet with a foreword by Sir David Eccles, Minister of Education (London: Councils and Education Press, 1961).

19. E. T. Hall, The Silent Language (New York: Premier Books, 1961).

20. This distinction is the theme of Wolfgang Binde, Die Revolution der Moral (Zurich: Strom-Verlag, 1968).

CHAPTER 7

1. See United States, Social Security Administration, Office of Research and Statistics, Life-Time Allocation of World and Leisure (Washington, D.C., 1968), which include Switzerland; concerning a particular aspect in this context, see G. Kuehlewind, "Alternativrechnungen zur quantitativen auswirking von Anderungen der Ruhestandsgrenze auf das Arbeitskräfteangebot," Mitteilungen aus der Arbeitsmarkt—und Berufsforschung (Stuttgart), III, 3 (1970), pp. 277-85, 307.

2. Joffre Dumazedier, "L'homme et les loisirs en 1985," La civilisation des loisirs (Verviers, 1967), pp. 251-71.

3. UNESCO, Youth in Contemporary Society, a report written at the request of the Executive Council following the worldwide youth disturbances in 1968 (Paris, 1968).

4. Julien Cheverny, Les cadres, essai sur les nouveaux prolétaires (Paris: Julien, 1967).

5. The OECD has published an interesting study in this connection: Flexibility of Retirement Age (Paris, 1970).

6. UN, European Seminar on the Individual and Social Importance of Activities for the Elderly, Königswinter (Bonn), October 19-28, 1958, Document UN/TAA/SEM/1958/REP.3 (Geneva: United Nations, 1959); European Study Group on Social Welfare Programs for the Elderly, Saltsjobaden, September 1966; E. Shanas, P. Townsend, D. Wedderburn, H. Friis, P. Milhoj, and J. Stehouwer, Old People in Three Industrial Societies (Britain, Denmark, USA) (London: Routledge and Kegan, 1968): UN, European Seminar on Local Participation in Programs for the Elderly, Gummersbach (Cologne), November 2-12, 1971, Document UN/SOA/SEM/42.

7. Marion Janjic, "Women's Employment and Conditions of Work in Switzerland," International Labour Review (Geneva), Vol. 96, 3 (September 1967), pp. 306-7.

8. Jean Fourastié, Le grand espoir du XXe siecle (Paris: Gallimard, 1963), pp. 310, 362.

9. Jean Fourastié, Les 40.000 heures, inventaire de l'avenir (Paris: Laffent-Conthier, 1965).

10. ILO, Annual Holidays with Pay, a World Survey of National Law and Practice, International Labour Conference, 48th Sess. (Geneva, 1964); ILO, Weekly Rest in Industry, Commerce and Offices, a World Survey of National Law and Practice, International Labour Conference, 48th Sess. (Geneva, 1964); and ILO, Holidays with Pay, Report VI(1), International Labour Conference, 53rd Sess. (Geneva, 1968).

11. Adam Smith, An Enquiry into the Nature and Causes of the Wealth of Nations (London, 1776); and Karl Marx, Das Kapital, Vol. I, 1867.

12. Max Weber, Essays in Sociology, translated and edited with introduction by H. H. Gerth and C. Wright Mills (New York: Galaxy, 1958); R. H. Tawney, Religion and the Rise of Capitalism (New York: Mentor Books, 1958); Erich Fromm, Fear of Freedom (London: Routledge and Kegan, 1960); and David Riesman, Nathan Glazer, and Reuel Denny, The Lonely Crowd: A Study of the Changing American Character (New Haven, Conn.: Yale University Press, 1950).

13. Joseph Pieper, Leisure, the Basis of Culture (London: Collins, 1965).

14. Dubin, "Industrial Workers' Work," in Larrabee and Meyersohn, ed., Mass Leisure (Free Press of Glencoe, 1958).

15. Eugene A. Staley, ed., Creating an Industrial Civilization (New York: Harper Brothers, 1952).

16. Joffre Dumazedier, "The Cultural Content of Workers' Leisure in Six European Towns," Revue française de sociologie (Paris), IV, 1 (January-March 1963).

17. Janine Larrue, "Workers' Leisure and Social Participation," Revue de sociologie du travail (Paris), No. 1 (January-March 1963), pp. 45-64.

18. Joffre Dumazedier, Vers une civilisation du loisir? (Paris: Editions du Seuil, 1962).

19. Thorstein Veblen, The Theory of the Leisure Class, an Economic Study of Institutions, with introduction by C. W. Mills (New York: Mentor Books, 1958).

20. Dieter Hanhart, Arbeiter in der Freizeit, eine sozialpsychologische Untersuchung (Bern and Stuttgart: Verlag Hans Huber, 1964).

21. V. D. Patrushev, "On the Practical Use of Time Budget Data," Institute of Economic and Industrial Production, Novosibirsk, 6th World Sociological Congress, Evian, September 1966.

22. A. Szalai, "Introduction: The Multinational Comparative Time Budget Research Project: A Venture in International Research Cooperation," American Behavioral Scientist, X, 4 (December 1966).

23. France Govaerts, "Women's Leisure," Centre national de sociologie du travail, Section loisirs et cultures modernes, 6th World Sociological Congress, Evian, September 1966.

24. See in particular France Govaerts, Loisirs des femmes et temps libre, (Editions de l'Institut de Sociologie Solvay, Brussels Free University, 1969).

25. Käthe Biske, "Statistics of Women's Employment," Zürcher Statistische Nachrichten, Statistisches Amt der Stadt Zürich, No. 66, special ed. (1961 and 1962).

26. George D. Butler, Introduction to Community Recreation (New York: McGraw-Hill, 1959).

27. Nicole Samuel, "Planning for Leisure," European Seminar on the Leisure of Workers in Modern Industrial Societies, Semmering, November 20-29, 1967, SOA/ESDP/1967/4 (Geneva: UN, 1967), pp. 67-83.

CHAPTER 8

1. For a discussion of the theory of indexes of living standards, see J. Drewnowski and W. Scott, The Level of Living Index (Geneva: UN Research Institute for Social Development, Report No. 4, September 1968); J. Drewnowski, The Level of Living Index, New Version (Geneva: UN Research Institute for Social Development, March 1968); J. Drenowski, Studies in the Measurement of Levels of Living and Welfare (Geneva: UN Research Institute for Social Development, 1970); J. Delors and J. Baudot, Contribution à une recherche sur les indicateurs sociaux (Paris: SEDEIS, 1971).

2. People's Family Movement, Aisance et privations, a scientific inquiry into the living conditions of employees' families in French-speaking Switzerland, conducted by the People's Family Movement in conjunction with and under the supervision of the Swiss Public Opinion Institute (Geneva: Mouvement Populaire des Familles, 1968). 6 vols.: "An Outline Sketch of Employees' Households in French-speaking Switzerland"; "Income and Occupational Life"; "Housing Conditions and Household Equipment"; "Food, Clothing, Children's Prospects"; "Holidays, Leisure, Culture, Means of Transport"; and "Social Security, Savings, Social Life."

3. Schweizerischer Beobachter, Wachsender Wohlstand: Wie sie Leben—1965 [hereafter cited as Schweizerischer Beobachter], a survey of the living standards and consumption habits of

subscribers, conducted by the Research Institute of the Swiss
Market Research Society, Zurich, with the advice of Otto Angehton
(Basel: Verlagsgesellschaft Beobachter AG, n.d.).

4. Neue Zürcher Zeitung, No. 701 (November 12, 1968).

5. Schweizerischer Beobachter, p. 15.

6. Ibid., p. 13.

7. Ibid., p. 16.

8. "The Progress of the French 'Consumer Society,'" Neue
Zürcher Zeitung, No. 537 (September 1, 1968).

9. Federal Tax Administration, "Steuerbelastung in der
Schweiz 1964," in Statistische Quellenwerke der Schweiz, vol. 386
(Bern, 1965).

10. "The Burden of Taxation in Switzerland," Neue Zürcher
Zeitung, No. 3052 (July 19, 1965).

11. In connection with this range of subjects, see the following:
"Harmonization of Cantonal Tax Systems," Neue Zürcher Zeitung,
No. 516 (August 24, 1969); Rudolf Rohr, "Limits to Fiscal Harmo-
nization," Neue Zürcher Zeitung, No. 605 (October 4, 1969); B.
Gusberti, "Fiscal Harmonization and Financial Balance—Essential
Features and Connections," Neue Zürcher Zeitung, No. 206 (May
6, 1970); R. Rohr and W. Gut, Bundesstaatlicher Finanzausgleich
in der Schweiz (Zurich: Redressement national, 1970); Dionys
Lehner, Der Finanzausgleich zwischen Bund und Kantonen im
Hinblick auf eine Bundesfinanzreform (Bern: Verlag Paul Haupt,
1971); Walter Wittmann, "Bundesstaatlicher Finanzausgleich—
Eine Globalbilanz" (Zurich: Redressement national: 1971).

12. Neue Zürcher Zeitung, No. 763 (December 10, 1968).

13. Herbert Marcuse, Der eindimensionale Mensch [One-
Dimensional Man], Sociological Texts, No. 40 (Neuried and Berlin:
Hermann Luchterhand Verlag GmbH, 1967).

14. Hans Heinz Holz, "Herbert Marcuse—Philosopher of the
New Left. Background to the Theory of One-Dimensional Man,"
Neue Zürcher Zeitung, No. 317 (May 26, 1968).

CHAPTER 9

1. Maurice Erard, "A Sociological Outline of Social Classes
in Switzerland," Cahiers internationaux de sociologie (Paris),
XXXIX (July-December 1965), 15.

2. Erard, "Outline," p. 9.

3. Federal Statistical Office, Eidgenössische Volkszahlung 1.
Dezember 1960—Band 29, Schweiz, Teil III, Wohnungen, in Statistische Quellenwerke der Schweiz, Vol. 379 (Bern, 1964), pp. 7, 8.

4. See, for example, "Cities and Men," Informations sociales,
Nos. 11-2 (Paris, 1964), special ed.; and "Urban Development,"
Nos. 7-8 (1966), special ed.

5. Schweizerischer Beobachter, p. 22.

6. Statistisches Jahrbuch der Schweiz, 1970, p. 387.

7. Erard, "Outline," p. 11.

8. Heinrich Rittershausen, Wirtschaft (Frankfurt am Main: Fischer Bucherei KG, 1958), p. 65.

9. "Concentration of Firms—Autumn Meeting of ASOS and ASCO in Lucerne," Neue Zürcher Zeitung, No. 745 (December 2, 1968).

10. Ibid.

11. Ibid.

12. See, for example, François Masnata, Le parti socialiste et la tradition démocratique en Suisse (Neuchâtel: La Baccnnière, 1963); and Max Weber, "Social Switzerland," Schweizerische Zeitschrift für Volkswirtschaft und Statistik, Nos. 1-2 (Bern, 1964), p. 190.

13. Sonntags Journal, No. 14 (April 3-4, 1971).

14. See Guy Baer, "Concentration as a Subject of Controversy—the Need for Concentration in the Economy and for Appropriate Limits," Neue Zürcher Zeitung, No. 133 (March 21, 1971), and No. 139 (March 24, 1971).

15. Neue Zürcher Zeitung, No. 127 (March 17, 1971).

16. Gewerkschaftliche Rundschau (Bern), LXIII, 9 (September 1971), pp. 241-51.

17. Neue Zürcher Zeitung, No. 241 (May 27, 1971).

18. Neue Zürcher Zeitung, No. 220 (May 13, 1971).

19. Neue Zürcher Zeitung, No. 205 (May 5, 1971).

20. Neue Zürcher Zeitung, No. 229 (July 1, 1971).

21. Jean Fourastié, Le grand espoir du XXe siècle (Paris: Gallimard, 1963).

22. Herman Kahn and Anthony Weiner, Year Two Thousand (London: Macmillan, 1967).

CHAPTER 10

1. Lewis Mumford, The City in History, Its Origins, Its Transformations and Its Prospects (London: Secker and Warburg, 1961).

2. Michel Praderie, Ni ouvriers, ni paysans: les tertiaires (Paris: Editions du Seuil, 1968), pp. 56-57.

3. Michel Bassand, "Quelques aspects de l'urbanisation et de ses conséquences politiques—le cas de la Suisse" (Geneva: Centre de Recherches Sociologiques, University of Geneva, 1966), p. 4. (Mimeo.)

4. Bassand, "Aspects."

5. Bassand, "Aspects." See also E. Arriaga, "A New Approach to the Measurement of Urbanization," Economic Development and Cultural Change (Chicago), XVIII, 2 (January, 1970), pp. 206-18.

6. Statistisches Jahrbuch der Schweiz, 1967, p. 12.

7. See, for example, Jean-Pierre Hoby, "Analyse der Schweizer Kantone mit Hilfe struktureller Variablen unter besonderer Berucksichtigung der Entwicklung beim Fehlen von Urbanisierung," paper presented to the annual meeting of the Swiss Sociological Society, Zurich, November 1968. (Mimeo.)

8. Ibid.

9. This line of argument has been confirmed, for example, by the publication of a newspaper article written in the canton of Valais and entitled "Mountain Agriculture Frustrated in Valais." Referring to mountain farmers, the article states that interest in help and support is declining, because such action is felt to sap people's sense of pride. Neue Zürcher Zeitung, No. 26 (January 17, 1970).

10. A comprehensive expert report commissioned by the Federal Economic Department has been issued on the subject of the promotion of mountain areas: H. Flückiger, Gesamtwirtschaftliches Entwicklungskonzept für das Berggebiet (Berne: Delegate for the Study of Economic Trends, July 1970). On the basis of this report the Delegate for the Study of Economic Trends made proposals for a comprehensive economic promotion policy for mountain areas that were approved by the Federal Council in May 1971. Provisions for the improvement of growth conditions in mountain areas and the promotion of individual farms include careful planning at the regional (and not cantonal) level, having regard to the wide variation in development circumstances in the different mountain regions; the development of suitable localities to become regional centers; the construction of efficient means of communication; the creation of advanced training facilities; compensation in respect of communal facilities supplied by mountain farmers in the form of contributions related to the area affected; easier access to sources of credit for small and medium farms; greater financial equalization within and between cantons; fiscal harmonization; and direct or indirect provision of investment loans on favorable terms for the residual financing of infrastructure projects.

CHAPTER 11

1. Louis Wirth, "Urbanism as a Way of Life," American Journal of Sociology, (1938), pp. 1-14; J. D. N. Versluys, "Urban and Rural Differences—Mutual Influences," European Seminar on Urban Development Policy and Planning, Warsaw, SOA/ESWP/1962/1 September 19-27, 1962 (Geneva: UN, 1962), pp. 146-53.

2. Georges Friedmann, Où va le travail humain? (Paris: Gallimard, 1950).

3. Pierre Clément and Paul Vieille, L'exode rural: historique, causes et conditions, sélectivé, perspectives, with introduction by Claude Gruson, Ministry of Finance and Economic Affairs (Paris: Imprimerie Nationale, April 1960); "Zusammenfassung des Grunen Berichtes" (mimeo.; Bonn, 1962); ILO, Why Labor Leaves the Land (Geneva, 1960); and Guy Pourcher, "The Settlement of Paris, Regional Origin, Social Composition, Attitudes and Motivations," Revue Population (Paris), No. 3 (1963), pp. 545-564.

4. Alain Girard, La réussite sociale en France, ses caractères, ses lois, ses effects, with introduction by Alfred Sauvy (Paris: National Institute for Demographic Studies, PUF, 1961).

5. Robert C. Wood, "The Contribution of Political Science to the Study of Urbanism," in Wentworth H. Eldredge, ed., Taming Megalopolis, Vol. I: What It Is and What It Could Be, (New York: Anchor Books, 1967), pp. 192-220.

6. UN, European Seminar on Urban Development Policy and Planning, September 19-27, 1962 SOA/ESNP/1962 (Geneva, 1962).

7. UN, Research Institute for Social Development, Workshop on the Sociology of Regional Development, Geneva, November 11-13, 1968. Reference should also be made to the present trends in such countries as France and Italy.

8. W. Christhaller, Die zentralen Orte in Süddentschland: Eine ökonomisch-geographische Untersuchung über die Gesetzmässigkeit der Verbreitung und Entwicklung der Siedlungen mit stadtischen Funktionen, (Jena: Gustav Fischer Verlag, 1933); Brian J. L. Perry and Allen Pred, Central Place Studies, a Bibliography of Theory and Applications, Including a Supplement through 1964 (Philadelphia: Regional Science Research Institute, 1965); and Robert E. Dickinson, The City Region in Western Europe (London: Routledge and Kegan, 1967).

9. C. A. Perry, "The Neighborhood Unit," Regional Plan of New York and Its Environs, No. 7 (1929), pp. 22-140.

10. E. R. Roper-Power, "The Social Structure of an English County Town," Sociological Review, No. 29 (1937); B. McClenahan, The Changing Urban Neighborhood (Los Angeles: University of Southern California, 1929); "The Communality: the Urban Substitute for the Traditional Community," Sociology and Social Research, No. 30 (1945), pp. 264-74; R. R. Isaacs, "The Neighborhood Theory: An Analysis of Its Adequacy," Journal of the American Institute of Planners, No. 14 (1948), pp. 15-23; R. Dewey, "The Neighborhood, Urban Ecology and City Planners," American Sociological Review, No. 15 (1950), pp. 502-7; and H. S. Churchill, "An Open Letter to Mr. Isaacs," Journal of the American Institute of Planners, No. 14 (1948), pp. 40-43.

11. R. E. Pahl, ed., Readings in Urban Sociology (London: Pergamon Press, 1968).

12. Janusz A. Ziolkowski, Methodological Problems in the Sociology of Regional Development, UNRISD/69/C.2 (Geneva: University of Poznan, Poland, and UN Research Institute for Social Development, January 1969).

13. Peter Hall, "Myths and Realities in Urban Sociology," New Society, (London), January 9, 1969, p. 60.

14. See, for example, Philip M. Hauser, Handbook for Social Research in Urban Areas (Paris: UNESCO, 1965); P. H. Chombart de Lauwe, ed., Famille et habitation, Vol. I: Sciences humaines et conceptions de l'habitation; Vol. II: Un essai d'observation expérimentale (Paris: CNRS, 1959-60); and William Michelson, "Urban Sociology as an Aid to Urban Physical Development: Some research Strategies," Journal of the American Institute of Planners, (Washington, D.C.), March 1968, pp. 105-8.

15. Lucius Burckhardt, Der Architekt in der Gesellschaft von morgen, Werk (November 1965); and Walter Förderer, Bauen, ein Prozess (Teufen: Arthur Niggli AG, 1968).

16. Informations Sociales (Paris), Nos. 7-8 (1966), pp. 19-31.

17. Michelson, "Urban Sociology."

18. See, for example, Alain Touraine, La société post-industrielle (Paris: Editions Denoël, 1969).

CHAPTER 12

1. Roger Girod "Geography of the Swiss System," in E. Allardt and Y. Littunen, eds., Cleavages, Ideologies and Party Systems, Contributions to Comparative Political Sociology (Helsinki, Transactions of the Westermark Society, 1964), pp. 132-61.

2. Michel Bassand, "Quelques aspects de l'urbanisation et de ses conséquences politiques—le cas de la Suisse" (Geneva: Centre de Recherches Sociologiques, University of Geneva, 1966). (Mimeo.)

3. Ibid.

4. Maurice Erard, "A Sociological Outline of Social Classes in Switzerland," Cahiers internationaux de sociologie (Paris), XXXIX (July-December 1965), pp. 15, 27. Concerning voting in referenda and elections, see also the subsequent work by Roger Girod, in collaboration with Charles Ricq, Géographie de l'abstentionnisme à Genève—Analyses et documents (Geneva: Centre de sociologie de l'Université de Genève, 1969).

5. See Jean Meynaud, Les organisations professionnelles en Suisse (Lausanne: Payot, 1963); C. J. Hughes, The Parliament of Switzerland (London: Cassel, 1962).

6. Lucius Burckhardt, Max Frisch, and Markus Kutter, Achtung die Schweiz (Basel: Verlag F. Handschin, 1955).

CHAPTER 13

   1. Walter M. Diggelmann, "Opposition Is not the Genuine Alternative," Stimmen zur Schweiz, reprint from National-Zeitung
(Basel), 1968, p. 28.

   2. Neue Zürcher Zeitung, No. 207 (May 6, 1971).

   3. Union Bank of Switzerland, Schweizerische Wirtschaftsentwicklung 1939-1964 (Zurich: UBS Economic Studies Department,
1964), p. 19.

   4. Victor Schiwoff, Konjunkturpolitik der Monopole (Zurich:
Labor Party of Switzerland, n.d.), p. 38.

   5. Neue Zürcher Zeitung, No. 29 (January 19, 1971).

ARMIN GRETLER is at present secretary of the Swiss Coordination Center for Research in Education in Aarau, Switzerland.
He is also completing his Ph.D. dissertation on educational planning
at the University of Geneva, where he graduated in sociology. After
a year of postgraduate work in Italy Mr. Gretler joined the International Labor Office in Geneva, where he served as research assistant and research officer in the Human Resources Department in
1963-68. He subsequently worked for the Institut für Orts-, Regional-
und Landesplanung at the Eidgenössische Technische Hochschule in
Zurich and as consultant to the Division of Adult Education of UNESCO
in Paris. Before taking up his present assignment, Mr. Gretler was
a member of a temporary research team set up by the Groupe Romand
pour l'Etude des Techniques d'Instruction.

Mr. Gretler is co-author of "La Suisse au-devant de l'éducation
permanente"; his publications also include a comparative study on
training of middle-level cadres edited by UNESCO.

PIERRE-EMERIC MANDL, Swiss sociologist and economist,
joined the UN in 1967 and at present is UNICEF Regional Planning
Officer for West and Central Africa. His most recent activities at
UNICEF concern the coordination of multinational research on the
needs of children, women, and youth in new planning methods in economic and social development. For several years as research officer
in Brussels at the Section Loisirs et Culture of the Centre National
de Sociologie du Travail, he was in charge of the methodology of
evaluation in the field of cultural development by mass communications.
Later on the UN Research Institute for Social Development in Geneva
entrusted him with the theoretical study and the pilot research on an
international project on the preparation of the child for modernization.

Dr. Mandl has been a consultant to various organizations (the
UN, UNESCO, the Swiss Broadcasting Corporation, ORL-Institute in
Zurich) on regional planning, education, communications, and social
forecasting. He is the author of several articles and of a book on the
child and modernization (University of Brussels).